DRAKE'S BRUTAL WRITING ADVICE

Drake's Brutal Writing Advice

Point of View, What's the Point?

Or, if you prefer...

Better Writing Through Stronger Narrative

DRAKE U

WWW.DRAKEU.COM

THIS BOOK IS PUBLISHED BY
Drake U
and imprint of
Imagined Interprises, Inc.

Proof Editors - Marion G. Harmon, Buzz Clore, Stephan McLeroy, Melissa Carden, Greg Laurich, Dylan Birtolo, and Lorraine Stalians
Cover Title Art by C.E.Rocco

Published in the United States by
Imagined Interprises, Inc.
www.ImaginedInterprises.com
6955 N. Durango Dr. Suite. 1115-391
Las Vegas, NV 89149

ISBN: 978-1-936525-73-7 (Paperback Edition)
First Edition: July 2017

Library of Congress Cataloging-in-Publication Data
Available upon Request

This book is dedicated to me. It made me realize I knew more about this topic than I assumed. It also showed me I knew way less than I needed to know.

I hope it is as kind to you.

DRAKE

TABLE OF CONTENTS

"Writing is a demanding profession, and a selfish one. And because it is selfish and demanding, because it is compulsive and exacting, I didn't embrace it, I succumbed to it."
                                        – Rod Serling 1924 – 1975
                                                    (*The Twilight Zone*)

Introduction

Hello and welcome, brave adventurer. I'm your not so humble and rarely gracious host, Maxwell Alexander Drake. Please, call me Drake.

If you're returning to the *Drake's Brutal Writing Advice* series for another dose of pain and misery, welcome back! It's always nice to meet a fellow masochist.

If this is your first trek through a *Drake's Brutal Writing Advice* book, well… misery loves company, as they say.

If you're new, let me start with some background about me so you know a bit about who is abusing you.

While I wrote my first novel some thirty-five years ago at the tender young age of twelve, I've been professionally writing for about ten years now. I've written for both large companies and small—I've done everything from being the Lead Fiction Writer for a massive video game from Sony titled *EverQuest Next*, all the way down to self-publishing some of my own work. I've worked as a novelist, graphic novelist, movie and stage playwright, and tie-in writer for the video and table-top game markets.

I've also taught creative writing for over seven years at fan conventions, book festivals, writers' conferences, as well as locally for the Library District in Las Vegas.

Many who've taken my creative writing seminars have dubbed me "the dream killer." While I appreciate this nomenclature, it's a bit unjust. In my mind, I've simply taken a very pragmatic approach to the career of writing. By extension, I teach writing in the same manner. While many of the comments I make when teaching may be things some people don't want to hear, they're things all aspiring writers need to hear.

And it's in this style I shall teach you the strange and often misunderstood topic that is *Point of View*.

Through the pages of this tome we're going to discuss Point of View in detail. I'll talk about the history of writing Prose, why it works the way it works, examples of ways to use it successfully, as well as unsuccessfully, etc. By the end, you'll hopefully have the knowledge you need to utilize this amazingly important aspect of writing in your own work.

A word of caution before we begin. If you have thin skin, or find obnoxious people such as myself offensive, you may want to put this book down. "Brutal" is in the title, after all, so don't look for me to be kind.

If you have thick skin, feel you can take a joke, or are simply intent on ignoring my warning because you've already purchased the book and are determined to find some value in it, here are a few warnings you should keep in mind.

Let me start by discussing the tone in which I'm writing my *Drake's Brutal Writing Advice* series.

As you read, you may notice that I'm not using any of my own Point of View rule suggestions. In this, you'd be correct. In fact, if you're an academic with an English degree or an editor of any worth, my writing thus far should've already cost you your sanity. (All praise to my lord and master Cthulhu, for there is no Order without Chaos.)

Seriously. I'm *almost* writing this in First Person Past Tense, as in, I'm referring to the proverbial "I". But this is also a conversation with the proverbial "you", so it's also *almost* written in a Second Person sort of way.

It's less creative writing and more conversation, since this is the way we speak verbally to each other. And that's what I want this book to feel like—a conversation between you and me.

When teaching, I state all the time that you can't write Speculative Fiction the way you speak. Creative writing is a unique form of information dissemination. It's the art of immersing the reader into a story, its world and the events taking place within it, by using only written words.

This book, however, isn't fiction. It's a how-to guide. Or more appropriately, it's a collection of deranged ramblings on my thoughts and opinions concerning *Point of View*. My goal while penning this tome, outside of driving stuffy, tie-wearing, overly-educated curmudgeons insane, is to present my views in a very informal manner. Call it my attempt to make the drudgery of learning grammar more bearable. And make no mistake about it, we *will* be discussing grammar in this book.

Boring… Dreary… Grammar… (Insert my best malevolent, villainous laugh here and imagine me drumming my fingertips together while my hate-filled eyes bore into yours.) Bwahahahaha!!!

However, I don't want you to feel like you're reading a book, especially a boring book about grammar. Instead, I hope to make this feel more as if you and I have sat down for a cup of coffee (or whatever your beverage of choice is) to discuss my views and opinions on the topic of *Point of View*. Just you and me, kicking around the concepts of writing.

Additionally, I enjoy using anecdotal stories to illustrate my thoughts on the theories and mindsets of writing. I am a storyteller, after all. You'll find many of these interludes throughout the following pages, and I hope you'll humor me with these transgressions. I've always used stories as a way of teaching, and the tales I've included should help you on your journey.

I recommend you don't skip or gloss over any of these. Don't become impatient and skip ahead to something you think is more important, assuming what I'm discussing is beneath you, or worse, feeling I have no point to my ramblings at all. Each section contains concepts, theories, and nuggets of wisdom that'll grow you as a writer. All these concepts will be needed in later sections to make new concepts and theories understandable.

By staying the course, this book will continue to build upon itself in the hopes of you becoming a *Point of View* master.

Good Luck, my friend. And Godspeed.

DRAKE

DISCLAIMER

(I know I just said you shouldn't skip anything in this book. However, if you've read my Disclaimer in one of my other *Drake's Brutal Writing Advice* books, you should ignore that piece of advice and skip this section. The following disclaimer is pretty much the same in each book of this series. If you've not read my disclaimer before, I suggest you read it. It *might* contain the key to becoming the most successful author of all time. It *might* not. Either way, I'll know if you don't read it.)

If you've ever taken one of my live creative writing classes, you know I start them with a disclaimer. If you'll indulge me, I'd like to continue that trend here.

My first and most important disclaimer is that the book you're about to read is nothing more than my opinions. I'm not, in any way, shape, or form, trying to dictate how you should write. That would be an exercise in futility.

I'm of the firm belief that what separates writers from each other is our Voices. Voices that are unique to each of us due to the fact that an **Author's Voice** is created by a lifetime of experiences. Everything an author writes comes from their own *personal well of experiences*. Every man, woman, child, monster, villain, animal, hero, etc., you create for your story comes from you. Who you are is different from who I am. Even twins raised in the same household have differences by the time they become adults. The fact that you and I are probably strangers only exasperates the chasm between how our respective origins have uniquely shaped our minds, imaginations, and moral values.

It's the reason why the same base stories can be so different depending on the writer.

As I'm a person who loves telling stories, I can't think of a better way to begin this book than with a story.

About a decade ago there were three "asteroid destroying the Earth" movies that came out nearly on top of each other. They were all the exact same story – there was a huge chunk of rock hurtling toward Earth at an incredible speed. When this rock hits, all life on our fragile planet will end. As the "villain" is an inanimate "thing", the plot of all three stories was **Character Driven**. Each was about how a group of fictitious characters who find themselves in this fictitious situation handle things. To break it down further, these are stories that attempt to teach a "what it means to be human" moral lesson (**Major Theme**) through a tragic or life-threatening event.

While each of these "asteroid destroying the Earth" stories were identical at their cores, the three movies couldn't have been more different. Why? Because each of the writers had different life experiences, and so they took the stories in different directions. More interesting to me is the fact that one of those movies was amazing, a second was meh, and a third was not very enjoyable at all.

Again, I want to stress that all three were the exact same story at their core. In other words, they all had the same base Major Theme.

Why this discrepancy then? To paraphrase the great Yoda - Created equal writers are not.

Which leads me to my first, "To be Brutal:" statement: As much as it hurts to hear, some writers are better than others. To extrapolate: No matter what your mother says, there will *always* be writers who are better than you.

It's a fact of humanity. We can't all be Michael Jordans.

Sure, all of us can learn grammar, practice the craft, and improve our skills. Unfortunately, as with all aspects of human life, there will be those who are better than others. Trust me; I get it. It's a hard pill to swallow, even for me. But I guarantee, it won't be the last one I'll be shoving down your throat.

It does, however, bring me back full circle to my opening disclaimer – these are my opinions. It's perfectly acceptable for you to disagree with anything I say. I mean, your mommy says you're the best writer in the whole wide world, and who am I to disagree?

Still, this is the perfect segue to my next disclaimer – there's *always* an alternate way of looking at things.

My hope is that, as you read through this book, you'll take one of three different paths with each statement I make.

The first path you could take is, you'll read what I've written and think to yourself, "Wow! This guy's brilliant. Why has no one ever said it that way before?" This isn't just a true statement—obviously, I'm frickin' dazzling—but the above is fantastic for a different reason as well. It means you've had yourself an epiphany, learned something you can use, and have grown as a writer. Bonus: It means someone finally appreciates my genius. Please, call my mother and let her know. She'll be thrilled to have finally been proven wrong about me.

The second path could be, you'll read what I've written and think to yourself, "Wow! This guy's a moron. How could anyone assume things work that way?" Unfortunately for me, this statement is also very true – I ain't the brightest tool in the elevator. However, it's still a fantastic one. It means you've had yourself a *different* type of epiphany, learned something you *don't* want to use, and have grown as a writer. Bonus: You may now get together with my mother and compare notes about my inadequacies.

The third path, and my personal favorite, is for you to take what you read within the following pages and think to yourself, "Wow! This guy's ideas are kind of cool. But you know what would be better? If I took his ideas and changed them a bit, molding them to fit my writing style." This is the most fantasticest method of all. Mostly because, well, I am kind of a cool guy. But no less important, it means you're using your mature brain to make your own deductions instead of blindly following me. You've had yourself the *best* type of epiphany. Based on something I said, you came to your *own conclusion*, learning something that's *uniquely yours*, and have grown as a writer. Bonus: You can now leave my mother out of our discussion, thank you very much. I'm not even sure why you keep bringing her up. It's weird, and I'd like for you to stop now.

Which leads me directly to my third disclaimer point—what I call the Big Question: "What does this do for my story?"

When learning the craft of writing, be selfish! Don't follow anyone. I've already stated that what separates us as writers is our unique Author Voice. If you try and write like someone else, you'll do so at your own peril.

Case in point: Let's say you and Stephen King are wonderful friends. (Exciting, right?) Well, let's say that one day Stephen King invites you to sit down with him over coffee and tell him your story idea. Stephen King says he'll give you his thoughts and opinions on how he would make your story the next New York Times Best Seller! Stephen King graciously listens to your idea, instructing you step-by-step how Stephen King would write your story. With notes in hand and a thrilling rush in your heart, you race home and write your story exactly the way Stephen King told you to write it.

The problem is, once you finally pen the words "The End", your story will probably suck.

Why? Duh! You're *not* Stephen King. You haven't lived Stephen King's life. You haven't experienced the things Stephen King has experienced. What works for Stephen King, works well for Stephen King. However, it doesn't guarantee any of Stephen King's Author Voice will translate into your Author Voice.

All writers are on their own.

Sure, you should get comments from as many people as you can. Seek out feedback for your writing. Get critiqued and edited until your eyes bleed. However, it's *your* name on the product. It's you, not anyone else, who's going to make the decisions on what the work contains. You're going to make those decisions based on your own unique life experiences.

In the end, what you're striving for is to be the one writing the good "meteorite destroying the Earth" movie and not the poor schlub who wrote the crappy one. Everything within your project falls squarely upon your shoulders and your shoulders alone. Make sure you believe in what you're doing.

Finally—Don't get offended, this is all a figment of your imagination.

All seriousness aside, I make things up for a living. Let that sink in for a moment before you continue reading. I'd recommend you *never* take me too seriously. Some might even go so far as to state that I'm insane, and therefore I can't be held legally liable for any statements I make.

Truth be told, I have no issues if you're offended by my words. Creative writing is about *drama*. And drama is about *conflict*. And conflict is about *opposing sides*. Chances are, I'm gonna say something in this book that'll offend you. And that's wonderful. Debate is good for the soul.

However, if you do find yourself on the opposite side of something I say, and discover that it makes you angry, please understand, I'm not attacking you. I'm simply showing you we're on different sides of a topic. Neither of us are necessarily correct, nor are either of us necessarily wrong.

I mean, I'm definitely right. But that doesn't mean you're definitely wrong. ☺ (←Smiley face. When you see this it means I'm joking, so you can't get mad. That's a rule.)

GENESIS
THE BEGINNING

In the beginning, the Storyteller created a Story. This Story was formless and void of structure. Darkness filled the hearts of all those misfortunate enough to hear it. But the spirit of the Storyteller was unperturbed by their negative comments, because the Storyteller knew that one day they would be a famous, New York Times Bestselling Author.

On the first day, the Storyteller said, "Let there be my first Story." Much to the chagrin of his friends and family, the Storyteller proceeded to recite this first story to any who would listen.

I Drake. Me walks down trail, hunted berries to stop rumblings of Tummy God. Sabretooth jumping at Drake, growl louder than Tummy God. Me really scared.

The Story was not very good, and deep down the Storyteller knew it. Mostly because, since nobody was willing to pay for such a terrible Story (even though it was available through the massive Amazonian Ethereal Marketplace), the Storyteller's money was drying up fast. Still, the Storyteller went to bed satiated by the dream that one day all this effort would pay off.

On the second day, the Storyteller said, "Let there be a more structured Story." And the Storyteller called this "First Person" narrative.

"Hello, kind sir," I said to the uninterested shopkeeper standing before me. "My name is Drake. This morning I woke up to find myself quite hungry. So, I got dressed and came here to purchase myself some food. Unfortunately, I'm a bit shy on cash—starving artist, and all that." I laughed at my

> own joke, but the shopkeeper didn't join me. Based on the ugly hag-of-a-wife looming behind him, I figured the man had little joy in his life. Clearing my throat, I got to my point. "If you will indulge me, I'll gladly pay you Tuesday for a hamburger today."

And while the shopkeeper did not give the starving Storyteller a hamburger, the Storyteller saw that this "First Person" narrative was good, and went to sleep creatively satisfied by what he'd accomplished.

On the third day, the Storyteller said, "Let there be a Story in which I'm not the main character, but where I still know all the facts." And the Storyteller called this "Third Person Omniscient" narrative.

> Drake, a brilliant, though broke writer, woke up to find his stomach attempting to eat itself. Knowing the mean old shopkeeper would never give him a hamburger, even though Drake's mother had promised to loan him some money on Tuesday, Drake decided to sneak in the back door of the restaurant and take one for himself. "Surely the law won't punish me for stealing a hamburger to avoid starving to death!" he said to his empty, one-room apartment.

And while this new Story was less immersive than "First Person" narrative, the Storyteller saw this new narrative structure was good, and set off to steal himself a meal.

On the fourth day, the Storyteller said, "Let there be a more immersive Story, closer to what "First Person" can achieve, in which I'm not the main character, but still know all the facts." So the Storyteller started breaking some of the rules created for both "First Person" and "Third Person Omniscient" narratives, mixing them willy-nilly whenever it felt right. The Storyteller called this "Third Person Free Indirect Discourse" narrative, because, why not name grammatical things in a more complicated way than needed?

Drake woke up, dreading yet one more day without food. *I'm so tired of being hungry,* he thought. But what could he do? Yesterday he had tried to steal himself a hamburger to avoid starvation, and the police shot at him for his trouble. "Well," Drake said to the mangy, three-legged cat loitering in the alleyway outside his window. "Perhaps I should stop chasing this stupid dream of being a professional storyteller, and get a real job like my mother keeps nagging me about."

The cat, its only concern being to fill its own grumbling stomach, started back impassively.

And while "Third Person Free Indirect Discourse" was more immersive than "Third Person Omniscient," the Storyteller also found that these types of Stories were sometimes even more clunky than their nomenclature. Since there were no defined ways of breaking the previously created rules of narrative, sometimes the Storyteller would fail, and the reader would be thrown completely out of the Story—like if the story happened to slip inside the mind of a mangy, three-legged cat, for example. Not that the Storyteller would ever do such a terrible thing. Oh, heavens no! Regardless of these setbacks, the Storyteller was excited by this new "Third Person Free Indirect Discourse" narrative, and despite its issues, deemed it good anyway. Even so, the Storyteller went to bed hungry.

On the fifth day, the Storyteller said, "Let there be a structured Story that is just as immersive as 'First Person', not as clunky as 'Third Person Free Indirect Discourse', and in which I'm neither the main character, nor omnipresent with god-like knowledge of the story, since 'Third Person Omniscient' narrative tends to overburden most stories and bore most readers." The Storyteller called this "Third Person Limited" narrative.

The hunger gnawed at Drake like a rabid Sabretooth, relentlessly attacking him every moment he was awake. *I can't take this anymore!* Depression licked his soul as he ran his fingers over the stainless-steel pistol resting before him.

Unbidden, tears began streaming down his cheeks. Not for himself, he knew he had wasted his life chasing such a stupid dream. *New York Times Bestseller? What was I thinking? Easier to win the lottery!*

No. Drake wept for the only thing that truly loved him, his three-legged cat, Limpy. Sure, Drake's pain would end with the simple squeeze of a trigger, but who would take care of her?

Drake looked over at the small tabby sleeping in the corner. "Hopefully, you can survive long enough for somebody to notice the smell." A sigh slipped from his lips as he placed the barrel against his temple.

He heard the ding of a new email arriving in his inbox a millisecond before his world disappeared with a loud bang.

Perturbed at being woken by a loud bang, Limpy glanced at the square box of light sitting on the table across from her. While she could not read the human script, the symbols lined up in a neat row forming a pattern. "Thank you for your novel submission. We love your well-executed narrative and would like to speak with you about purchasing the rights to publish your novel."

Limpy had no idea what the symbols meant, nor did she care. She did know she was hungry, and so decided to get herself a snack. The bright red goo covering the table next to the annoying human she kept around seemed like a good place to start. It was handy that there was so much of the goo, as it would tide her over for a while. She was planning on taking the next two days off to rest.

What? Were you expecting a happy ending? Foolish reader, I write tragedies.

But why start off with this riff on Genesis? To drive home the fact that to understand Point of View, you must understand that Story telling has changed over time. In fact, it's always in a constant state of flux. Ever evolving. Ever changing. It's still changing to this very day. And as with all innovations, once made, you can never go back.

Case in point: I get asked to look at and evaluate unpublished Fantasy manuscripts by aspiring writers all the time. One common scenario that happens is this: I'll read the work and inform the writer that it won't sell in today's market. This normally enrages the writer who then yells at me that his manuscript is written exactly like *The Belgariad*, or *The Sword of Shannara*, or *The Lord of the Rings* ("All multi-million copy selling books," the aspiring writer points out to me, as if I've never heard of these titles, and how dare I say their carbon-copy of those books isn't good!)

Well, first off, I never said it wasn't good. I said it wouldn't sell in today's market. Why? Because, while those books were masterpieces thirty, forty, or even seventy years ago respectively, we don't write that way anymore. Well, not the big sellers, anyway. Unfortunately, aspiring writers still write that way all the frickin' time. A brief troll of the self-publishing market will net you a plethora of horrible facsimiles of every major book ever published.

Still, if you want to sell enough copies of your stories to feed yourself and family, you must understand that the storytelling market has changed. Evolved. And so too must any writer who wants to break into said market.

Before we get any further into this, however, I need to take a moment to…

Define Myself as a Teacher

The first thing I want to define is *what* I'm teaching. Creative Fiction is a very broad term, with aspects a poor, uneducated country writer such as myself could never hope to fully understand.

What I'm teaching through the *Drake's Brutal Writing Advice* series specifically relates to **Speculative Fiction**. If this is the first time you've heard this term, it's pretty easy to understand. Speculative Fiction is any Fiction that falls under a **Genre Category**, such as Sci Fi, Fantasy, Murder Mystery, Romance, True Crime, Western, Steampunk, Post-Apocalyptic, Horror, etc., etc., etc., the list goes on.

Certainly, aspects of what I'll be discussing could help all types of writing, even my nemesis, *Literary Fiction*. But some of it won't. Please keep this top of mind; everything I say is directed toward improving Speculative Fiction composition.

The second thing I want to define is that I'm truly insane. At least, that's what others think. From where I'm sitting, I'm the only sane person in a world filled with all you crazies.

Still, it does put me in a pickle. You see, I feel there are grammatical terms that are used erroneously when teaching Speculative Fiction, and one of my goals throughout this book will be to fight these misnomers (an uphill battle, I assure you). I'll point them out as we get there, but I'd like to start off with a blanket statement so you'll be mentally prepared for this dichotomy.

Sure, you've heard some of the things I'm gonna be discussing. Things like First Person, Narrators, Third Person Limited, etc. But I assure you, no one looks at these topics in the same way I do. So, do us both a favor and keep an open mind as you read through this. Don't stop me with a stupid interruption of, "Wait! That's not how my third-grade teacher Mrs. Johnson taught that!" Because I'm telling ya right up front, this is going to be different.

Case in point: Let's start by redefining the term **Point of View**.

For me, this term is way too generic. It fails to do this topic justice. I promise, by the time you finish this book, you'll not only see writing Speculative Fiction in a whole new light, you'll be a better writer. But to accomplish this, using a term as generic as Point of View simply doesn't work for me.

Why? Like so many grammatical terms, it's used for far too many things. Point of View could be the perspective used, such as First Person Point of View, or Third Person Point of View. It could also mean the level of awareness the Narrator has, such as an Omniscient Point of View, or a Limited Point of View. It could also refer to a specific character, the Point of View character. I mean, we've only just started and *I'm* already confused.

To that end, I'm going to use terms that specifically mean what I want you to think about. I'll admit up front, I'm gonna make a few of these terms up. But not many. The fact is, there are a ton of grammatical terms that mean exactly what I want them to mean, but for some reason are simply not used.

I've already given you one during the Genesis chapter—Third Person Free Indirect Discourse. Chances are high you've never heard this term. And yet, 99.9% of all books written in Third Person are written in Third Person Free Indirect Discourse. The problem is, for decades now, people have been incorrectly using Third Person Limited when they mean Third Person Free Indirect Discourse. Not sure why, but I bet it has to do, at least in part, with the fact that Third Person Free Indirect Discourse is a beast of a name. Still, *in my mind*, everything I've read or taken that has taught Third Person Limited is talking about Third Person Free Indirect Discourse. Everyone I know who says they write in Third Person Limited are in fact writing in Third Person Free Indirect Discourse. Strangely enough, most who say they write in Third Person Omniscient are in fact writing in Third Person Free Indirect Discourse.

For now, don't worry about what these terms mean. Trust me, I shall beat it into your skull soon enough. My issue is; how do I teach these differences if you continue to think Third Person Free Indirect Discourse *is the same things as* Third Person Limited? I can't.

I must shatter your understanding of these, prove that you've been taught incorrectly, and then build you back up again.

And this is the exact thing that's going to cause us grief if you allow it. You're gonna want to push back. Attempt to hold on to your previous understanding. But in doing so, you'll only be hurting yourself. There's no test at the end of this, and whether you become a better writer or not does not affect my personal self-worth. You're on your own here.

My point is that I understand you think you have knowledge about this topic. And that's fine. You absolutely do. And what you know is not wrong.

However, for you to get the most out of this book, I ask that you hold your knowledge back, and reserve judgment upon my philosophies until the end. Things I'm gonna say are going to be in conflict with things you've already learned. Stay the course, don't become distracted when I contradict Mrs. Johnson's third-grade teachings. I assure you, this book will open your eyes to new and exciting ways to write stories, but only if you let it.

Circling back to the topic at hand, the redefining of Point of View. Because the term Point of View is used for so many aspects of writing, I'm not going to use it at all. Mostly, because I don't need it. But also, because it carries way too much baggage with it for my comfort. *You* have a definition in your head of what Point of View means, and I don't want to fight *your* definition for the rest of this book.

To that end, from here on out I'm going to use the term **<u>Narrative</u>** when I'm speaking about the "words" used to create a story. As in, First Person Narrative, or Third Person Narrative, etc. This replaces the term Point of View in most aspects. For more detailed subjects where Point of View is also used, I'll give you other appropriate terms to replace it as needed.

__One final note__ before you begin, one written with the advantage of hindsight being 20/20: There's way too much information in this book.

When I sat down to write this, I wanted to write a book that would be a complete collection of all my thoughts and knowledge concerning Narrative. I estimated this would take me between 30,000 and 40,000 words. I mean, we're only talking about one topic here, after all. In the end, this beast turned out to be nearly a 100,000-word monster!

I'm confident that every single person who reads this book will be a better writer from the experience. All my beta readers convinced me of that. However, none of my beta readers learned all the lessons contained between the covers of this tome.

You see, writing is a journey, and the road is long. As a writer, you are somewhere on that road. You may be at the beginning. You may have traveled some distance already.

But this book contains knowledge from the decades I've spent walking this road. Some of what I say is going to be old news to you, more of a refresher. Some of it will spark a light within you that you'll use to improve your writing skills. But there will be things I state that you simply won't be able to wrap your mind around how to implement it into your own writing. This has nothing to do with your smarts, it has to do with where you are on the road of learning the craft of writing.

Remember, One-Million Words. Years of Time and Effort.

Yes, you'll learn from this book as you read through it the first time. Have a notebook handy, because you'll want to take notes so you can remember things. I don't teach things in order. I more ramble in a general direction. Still, I believe this will not be a one-time read for you. You'll return to this book. A month from now. Six months. I don't know. But I promise you this book has more information in it than you'll be able to digest in one sitting.

I have a feeling each time you return, you'll grasp another piece of this complex puzzle, finding a place for it in your own writing.

I wish you well on your journey.

Now, let's begin the adventure of tackling the strange and misunderstood topic…

WHAT IS NARRATIVE
OR, POINT OF VIEW, WHAT *IS* THE POINT?

Understanding and utilizing Narrative effectively isn't only a difficult topic to master, it's quite possibly the most important.

That's a lie. I believe it's *the most* important aspect of writing Speculative Fiction.

Your ability to write a strong, consistent, and concise Narrative is the one thing that'll make or break your story faster than any other aspect of storytelling. Which is a shame since it's the number one thing aspiring writers screw up time and again. Worse, most aspiring writers don't even think about all the nuances of what their Narrative can do, nor how to implement it.

Why is it so important? Well, let me answer that with another little story.

At the time of this writing, I live in Las Vegas. One of the many, many attractions in this city of sin is the fact that we have a NASCAR racetrack. Now, it's only used for professional racing a few times a year. The rest of the time it just sits there, baking in the hot desert sun. Due to this, the powers that be discovered they could make a little extra money by allowing anyone to race around the track with their own personal car. No speed limit, a roadway designed for cars to go really, really fast, and a city full of idiots who already drive on the public streets as if it were the Daytona 500, so you can guess this is quite popular with Vegas locals.

Let's pretend that you live here in Las Vegas. (You probably don't.) Let's also pretend that you and I are great personal friends. (We probably aren't.) Let's take this pretending further by stating that I own a brand-new Lamborghini sports car. (I probably don't.)

Assuming all these pretend facts are factual facts, one day I say to you, "How would you like to meet me at the race track this Saturday and I'll let you drive my car for a few hours?"

Let's continue to assume that you think this is a smashing idea. The chance to take a high-performance V-12 sports car and go nuts with it pulls at your very soul. (It might not.) Still, Saturday arrives, and with a spring in your step and excitement swelling in your heart, you head to the Speedway to meet me. However, when you arrive you find that I have not brought my brand-new Lamborghini. No. Instead, I've brought my jacked up, four-wheel-drive pickup truck with the huge, knobby tires.

Your excitement flees from you as fast as children escaping a birthday party bounce house after one of the guests has vomited all over the inside. And rightfully so! You came to this racetrack with someone who owns a racecar. You expected to drive said racecar really, really fast around said racetrack. But here I am, your host, not fulfilling your expectations. Sure, the 4X4 truck may be fun to drive around the track… but it's only a shadowy facsimile of what you were hoping for.

As I'm a gracious host, I notice your distress. "Let me make this up to you," I say. "Tomorrow we'll go into the mountains, and I'll let you take my vehicle off-roading."

You look at the 4X4 with new admiration. Realizing it would be a ton of fun to drive in the right environment, you agree.

Unfortunately, when you arrive at Mount Charleston the next morning, you find that I've brought my Lamborghini.

Now, while there may be some entertainment value in watching me destroy a two-hundred and fifty-thousand-dollar automobile using it for a purpose it was not designed for, the physical act of driving off-road in said Lamborghini yourself would not be as pleasant.

And this is *exactly* what Narrative is.

Narrative is the vehicle you put your reader in to take them on the ride that is your story.

And like my farcical parable above, if you choose the wrong vehicle for your story, your readers will *not* enjoy the ride.

The horrible truth of which Narrative to use, when it comes to aspiring writers, is that aspiring writers don't even think about it. They don't *choose* anything. They simply start writing without any idea or concept that they are even *using* a Narrative type. First Person, Second Person, Third Person Omniscient, Third Person Free Indirect Discourse, Third Person Limited… these are all terms aspiring writers may have heard (probably not), but normally have no understanding of at all.

Most aspiring writers don't *choose* a Narrative type, because many don't even realize they have a *choice*! They start writing, usually in the Narrative type that was *chosen* by their favorite author. The issue is, while that Narrative type may work for that *particular* story from that *particular* author, it does not in any way guarantee it'll work for *your* particular story and *your* particular Author Voice.

And this is where the crime lies. The injustice! It's the epitome of ignorance displayed by so many wannabee writers.

"Wait," you say. "Surely, you're being melodramatic. Which Narrative type I use can't be that important or I would've been told this before now!"

Three things. One: you're not going to start interrupting me like you did with my last *Drake's Brutal Writing Advice* book, are you? Two: no, I'm not being melodramatic. The Narrative type you choose is *literally* the most important aspect of writing you must grasp, and grasp well, if you're going to become a successful writer. And Three: don't call me Shirley.

All seriousness aside, understanding all the nuances between the different Narrative types is everything.

Master Narratives, and your Prose will sing. Fail, and your chance of getting professionally published, or even finding an audience for your work if you self-publish, will drastically diminished.

Why?

Because each Narrative type has its own unique advantages and disadvantages. First Person, for example, will enhance certain types of stories. But, if you use First Person in other types of stories, you'll hurt, or even ruin the story. Just as driving a vehicle not intended for a certain purpose will ruin the driver's enjoyment.

So yes, you must make a *conscious choice* of which Narrative type you plan to use for your Story *before* you start writing it! If you don't, you may end up destroying things even before you begin.

And it's a shame how many aspiring writers don't make a Narrative type choice for their story. Seriously, I wish they'd stop. So much so, I'm willing to write a 90,000 word book on the subject.

One last anecdote here to help make my point.

I teach writing all over the world at writer's conferences, book festivals, and fan events. Inevitably, I'll run into at least one aspiring writer who tells me their story. Because, well, we're writers, and writers like to tell people their stories.

When this happens, the first thing I do is ask them, "What Narrative (Point of View) did you use to write your story in?" You'd be surprised by the number of responses I get where the writer doesn't know. It's about 20%.

Take a second to ponder that. One in every five aspiring writers who tell me about their novel, a novel that took them months, if not years to write, have no idea what Narrative they used to write their novel. Even now, I'm flabbergasted over this. How can you spend that much time and effort on something, and not even know what you used to create it?

Ghastly!

Worse is my follow-up question. If they can answer which Narrative they used (First, Third, etc.) I ask, "Why? Why did you choose that *specific* Narrative for that *specific* story?"

To this day, every single aspiring writer I've asked this question has answered with a resounding, "What?"

As in, they may know which Narrative they used to write their story in, but none of them have any idea *why* they used it. And this is a tragedy for the simple reason that if you don't know *why* you're using a specific Narrative, your chances of mucking it up are substantially increased.

Since I've already stated that each Narrative type has its own unique advantages and disadvantages, this should let you know, depending on their story, the Narrative type they didn't choose to use could be helping them, or it could be a big ole massive hindrance. The rub is, chance has decided which path they have taken, not the writer.

So let's begin, and hopefully by the end, you'll have all the information you need to confidently choose the correct Narrative type that'll best fit the story you plan to write.

The first step in picking which Narrative type will work best for your story is to understand…

It's All About the Reader

If you've taken any of my classes, listened to my podcast, read my blog, or churned through any of my *Drake's Brutal Writing Advice* books, you've heard me say, "It's all about the reader."

Why do I say this like a broken record?

Because… well… I believe with all my soul that professionally created stories are all about the reader, not the writer.

The reader is your customer. They are the person who will be paying you for your time and effort. A storyteller who writes for themselves isn't a storyteller, they're a typist.

Are you a typist, or a storyteller? In other words, are you writing your story for your own satisfaction and edification, or are you writing your story for someone else to read and enjoy? If you're the latter, all the effort I spend teaching writing is for you. If you are the former, I hope you burst into flames and die a very painful death. ☺ (Smiley face. Remember the rule! You can't get mad.)

Seriously, that may sound cruel, but please never underestimate my deep and total loathing for a quote-unquote writer who doesn't take the time to study the craft of writing. A surgeon who never studies to be a doctor isn't a surgeon, they're a serial killer. A writer who never studies the craft of writing and grammar is just as guilty of murder and in my (not so) humble opinion, should suffer the same fate. Electric Chair. Gas Chamber. Burned at the stake. Pick your poison. *Poison!* That's another good one! They should drink some poison.

But…

WHAT DOES THIS DO FOR YOU?

How this relates to you and why you need to learn all this Narrative crap is simple. The better you understand and can utilize the nuances that is Narrative, the more enjoyment the reader will get from reading your story.

The information contained in this book will help you understand the nuts and bolts to creating a story through writing strong and consistent Prose. If you master the topics we're about to discuss, your stories will shine, wrapping the reader within the worlds you create and leaving them breathless for more.

As a storyteller, I can't think of a better reason as to why I should push myself to understand the nuances of Narrative Prose.

To start our quest for becoming a stronger writer through a better understanding of Narrative, the first stop must be understanding who is going to be telling the story. So let's answer the question...

What is a Narrator?

This is a more complicated question than most realize, and should be decided at the same time you choose the Narrative type (First, Third, etc.).

One of the main purposes of Narrative is to let the reader know whose perspective they'll be "watching" the story through, as well as whom the reader is going to relate to while reading. It's choosing who the **Narrator** will be, and how that Narrator will "speak" to the reader. Do not confuse the Narrator with the Writer; they're not necessarily the same person.

Most aspiring writers think either, "Duh! My main character is my Narrator." Or worse, "Duh! I'm the Writer, so obviously, I'm the Narrator."

Unfortunately, either of these methods of thinking can spell disaster for your story.

Not that they're wrong, in and of themselves. Either *could* be the best answer for your story.

Why the dichotomy? Well, each story is going to benefit from a certain type of Narrator. On the opposite side, each story is going to be hindered, if not downright ruined, by other types of Narrators.

So yes, your Main Character *could* be your Narrator, and so could you, the writer. But there are dozens of other Narrator types. Limiting yourself to just these two means you have a greater chance of picking a Narrator that doesn't enhance the telling of your story.

Knowing this, the writer should make a conscious decision as to who their Narrator is going to be, and that choice should be based on what type of Narrator will enhance the reader's enjoyment of your story.

Let's start with a definition:

> The Narrator is the Character who is telling the story. The reader is going to experience the story through your Narrator's perspective.

As I stated above, please don't confuse the Narrator with the Writer. You (the Writer) are the one penning the words on paper, true. But that doesn't mean you're the *Character* telling the story (the Narrator). You might be. It all depends on the story, and the Narrative type you choose to tell it in.

For example, if you happen to be Billy Crystal, writing a book about the life and times of Billy Crystal as he did in *700 Sundays*, then the Writer and the Narrator are absolutely going to be one in the same. To do otherwise would hurt the story.

However, never fall into the trap of thinking the Narrator and the Writer *must* be the same.

In Robert A. Heinlein's novel *Stranger in a Strange Land*, Heinlein was definitely not the Narrator. How am I so certain? Well, first off, Heinlein wasn't born on Mars. But more to my point, Heinlein's personal opinions concerning life, politics, religion, etc. couldn't have been more different from those of the main character, Valentine Michael Smith. I'd be willing to bet that if ever those two were to meet in real life, they'd absolutely detest each other.

So how was Heinlein able to write this tale without ruining it with interjections of his oppositions? Well… Duh! Heinlein wasn't the Narrator of the story. He was simply the Writer. The person penning the words of the story doesn't have to agree with what's being penned any more than a newscaster has to agree with the motivations of the serial killer she's reporting on.

To drop another mind bomb on you, Valentine Michael Smith wasn't the Narrator of that story either. If fact, none of the characters in *Stranger in a Strange Land* were the Narrator. BOOM!

My point is, the Narrator is the heart and soul of the story. The decisions you make concerning the Narrator will affect every single aspect of your story. Yes, it's honestly that important.

So, let's take a moment to discuss…

How to Choose a Narrator?

The choice of the story's Narrator is one of the most important choices a writer will make. Choose correctly, and you drastically increase your odds of creating a story people will enjoy reading. Choose poorly and, well…

Before we begin, let me explain what I mean when I say choosing the Narrator, because you may be confused. As this book is about Narrative, and Narrative centers around the Narrator, you might think the Narrator is chosen for you. I mean, if you're writing your story in First Person, then obviously, the Character saying words like, "I" or "me" or "my" is the Narrator. Right?

Certainly.

But that's not what I want you to think about here. What I want you to contemplate right now is *which* Character in your story is going to be saying I, me, or my.

Who you (the Writer) choose as the Narrator (the Character telling the story to the reader) affects everything. The Narrator could be the main character, a secondary character, an invisible watcher who isn't part of the story at all. And the list goes on.

Unfortunately, there's no easy answer. Worse, there's no way for me to tell you which you should use. It all depends on the story you're telling, and the talent you have as a storyteller.

Still, I can give you some guidance. At least in a broad, general way. But this process of choosing a Narrator is an internal, personal quest each writer must undertake on their own.

Let's start by understanding…

WHAT TYPE OF STORYTELLER ARE YOU?

There are two types of writers: **Plotters** and **Pantsers**. I give a detail discussion of each in my book, *Dynamic Story Creation in Plain English*, but let's do a quick overview here so you can see how it relates to choosing a Narrator.

A Plotter is someone who plans things out before they start writing. Either through a detailed synopsis, a plot board, etc. These types of writers know the story from start to finish before they even pen the first word. (Full disclosure, this is how I write.)

A Pantser is a writer who either doesn't plan their story, or plans very little. Another term for these types of writers is a Discovery Writer.

These are writers who get an idea, or have a character move into their head, then sit down and write. They have no set concept of where they're heading, but assume they'll figure it out along the way.

The reason you need to know which of these two camps you fall into as a writer is because it'll affect your ability to choose a Narrator.

If you're a Plotter, then you'll spend tons of time getting to know your story, from start to finish, before you even begin writing. This is great when it comes to choosing a Narrator, because once you've figured out your story, you can take the time to look at the story and decide which type of Narrator would be best to tell that particular tale.

Yeah! And good for you! (You're the smart child, and I love you the best!)

If you are a Pantser, your road to choosing a Narrator is much more difficult, in my opinion. (Just so you know, you're the disappointment in this family.) ☺

Since Pantsers sit down and write without fully understanding the story they're writing, they're forced to choose the Narrator based off a gut feeling. Now, this may work. In fact, it works for many a professional writer. Stephen King is a loud, and often obnoxious advocate for Pantsers. This method has obviously worked out very well for him, indeed. However, you, the aspiring writer without the decades of experience Stephen King has, may find it more difficult to get lucky and choose the perfect character to be your Narrator.

Side note: I'm not calling Stephen King obnoxious. I'm calling his views on Plotting obnoxious. Pantsing works well for him. However, it doesn't work well for me, nor a plethora of other successful writers. While I love picking on Pantsers, I don't consider it an incorrect method of story creation. I do, however, feel that a writer is *either* a Pantser or a Plotter. And as I'll show you, Pantsing gives you less opportunity to think about who your Narrator will be.

To illustrate this, let's do a mental exercise.

Let's pretend we are F. Scott Fitzgerald. It's the early 1920's, and we're sitting down to write a Modernist novel set in New York. Let's pretend we're a Pantser, so we don't have all the details of our story worked out. But we do have a cool character in mind and perhaps a general idea for a climactic event.

Now, I have no idea if Fitzgerald was a Plotter or a Pantser, and I don't care. It's not important for this experiment. What *is* important is that our imagined version of Fitzgerald is a Pantser. So, outside of the above, we have no real idea what this book will be about. We have a setting and an interesting main character in mind – the Great Gatsby. For most Pantsers, that's enough.

Because of this, we may be tempted to start writing this story from Gatsby's Perspective. I mean, he's not only a cool character, one the readers will easily relate to, but he's also the character the story is about. Everything happens to him, so by that train of thought, having him Narrate the story would be natural. Right?

Well, think about how different that story would be if Gatsby was the Narrator. First off, we'd be in the head of Gatsby, thereby losing all the mystery that surrounded him and made him such a mysterious character. Second, well… Gatsby dies before the end of the book. Spoilers!

Now, remember, we're a Pantser, so we have no idea that Gatsby is going to die before we start writing. We will "discover" the fact that he needs to die as we write our story. Hindsight is 20/20, and all that. But we just started writing this story, so we have no idea how it'll end. Nor do we know this cool character we created is going to die.

(Yes, I get that *perhaps* we could've known Gatsby was going to die before we started writing. But this is my scenario. And in my scenario, we didn't know this fact.)

Still, once we get to that point in our book, that point in our "discovery writing" where we realize that Gatsby is going to die, it'll leave us in a pickle. I mean, there we are, happily writing along when all of a sudden, our main character and Narrator is dead.

Awkward!

What to do? How do we finish a tale when the character telling said tale is dead before it's finished being told?

This is where a lot of Pantsers end up ruining their story. You see, all writers, not just Pantsers, resist throwing away anything they've already written for their story. I mean, we've already written so much! And it's so brilliant! Why the hell would we ever consider ditching it?

And this is where the danger of being a Pantser seriously comes into play. We, as our imagined Fitzgerald, have written most of a novel, and we like it. Even though we know it might not be good for the story, we don't want to throw away all that hard work.

So what to do?

Well, from what I've seen, Pantsers start looking for ways to circumvent the issue. Change the thing that's causing them grief.

In this fictitious case, we might seriously contemplate not killing off Gatsby.

Can you imagine what that story would be like if Gatsby didn't die? Very different from what we have today. Worse, without Gatsby's death, I don't think the story would've worked as well. Meaning, it never would've become the classic tale we enjoy today.

Another option might be to shift into a new Narrator after Gatsby's death. This could work. We could switch to that nerdy

Nick Carraway lad for the funeral scene. But would it work as well as it did with Nick Carraway as the Narrator from the very beginning?

No. It wouldn't.

You see, in my opinion, one of the big reasons *The Great Gatsby* works for readers is that the Narrator, Nick Carraway, *is* the Everyman. And when he's sucked into the strange world of Gatsby, he's always an outsider, exactly like what most readers would be if pulled into that same situation. Meaning, it's Nick, not Gatsby, who grounds the reader in the story. Without Nick's perspective from the beginning, I feel that story would never have sold more than a few hundred copies back in the 1930s, and then disappeared into obscurity.

Alas, most Pansters don't think of the future consequences outside of, "But I don't want to throw away all I've written and rewrite everything from scratch!"

Which leads to the most common solution Pantsers use to avoid sticky situations like the above, and that is to always choose the same Narrator for every story – themselves. Unfortunately, as you'll soon learn, there are many, many drawbacks to this type of "Writer is the Narrator". Drawbacks that may not help the enjoyment of your story, or worse, ruin it completely.

Going back to our fictitious mental experiment, I feel the same about using a Writer as the Narrator for *The Great Gatsby* – it would ruin the story. I feel this for the reason stated above – the reader needs to experience the story through Nick. A third-party Narrator who isn't in the story wouldn't be sufficient enough to hook the reader. This story needed to be told in a more "limited" way, which is exactly what First Person brought to this project.

But...

WHAT DOES THIS DO FOR YOU?

Hopefully, you're beginning to realize the importance of choosing the proper Narrator. The Narrator is the one who is "speaking" to the reader, and the reader must have a connection to the Narrator. Or, perhaps the reader mustn't see the Narrator at all. (That'll make sense in a moment.) Whichever way it falls, your decision about who your Narrator shall be will make or break your story. And understanding whether you're a Plotter or a Pantser will help you think about how you're going to make that decision.

Sure, I feel Plotters have the advantage here. But I don't want you to get me wrong. I'm not against Pantsers. As a writer, you are what you are, and I love all my children equally. (Except you, Plotters, I love you the most.) I simply want you to realize that if you're a Discovery Writer, you may *discover* that you have chosen the wrong Narrator at some point while writing your story. If this happens, you'll have a decision to make. You can either rewrite the entire book from the perspective of the better Narrator, thereby creating a better story. Or you can say, "screw what's good for the story," ignore the fact that you picked the wrong Narrator, and find some workaround.

While I'll support your decision either way, if you screw what's good for the story, you'll probably write something that's not enjoyable to read.

Bottom line is, know what type of writer you are, and do your best to choose a Narrator that's the correct Narrator for the specific story you're writing.

Now, before I get into the bread and butter that is the Narrator, there's one very important aspect of a Narrator you need to understand and this is the difference between…

Limited vs. Omniscient Narrators

Believe it or not, there are two **Levels of Awareness** all Narrators can have. They'll either know everything there is to know about the story *before* they begin telling the reader about the story – **Omniscient**. Or, they won't have any knowledge about what's going to happen in the story before it happens, and will be learning things at the same time as the reader – **Limited**.

Don't confuse this with the fact that some Narrative Types are Limited (such as First Person), and some are Omniscient (such as Third Person Omniscient). This is different. That's why I've created a new grammatical term here to discuss this section – **Level of Awareness**.

When I talk about Level of Awareness, I'm specifically referring to what the Narrator knows about the story, and not the Narrative Type being used (First Person, Third Person, etc.).

I'll be going into Levels of Awareness in great detail as I delve into the different Narrative Types, so for now, let's look at Levels of Awareness from a broad, overview perspective.

In *700 Sundays*, Billy Crystal is the Main Character/Narrator and he knows everything. Not only does he know all the backstory and history that happened before the story began, he knows everything that's about to happen as well, even before it happens in the book. He also knows what happens after the book concludes—where the story goes after the final page. This means the Narrator of this story has an Omniscient Level of Awareness. Since that is a mouthful, humor me as I create another new grammatical term. Let's call Narrators who have an Omniscient Level of Awareness to the story they are telling an **Omniscient Narrator**.

Having an Omniscient Narrator works very well for *700 Sundays*. The book is about a grown man telling his life story. Obviously, he knows everything. He was there before, during, and after. All the events in the story happened in this man's past, and he's telling the reader about these events from the perspective of someone who has already been there and done that.

In other words, an Omniscient Narrator relates to Time. And by Time, I mean where the Narrator is in relation to the story.

An Omniscient Narrator lives in the "Right Now". But the story lives "Somewhere in the Past". So, as my beautiful and amazingly detailed drawing clearly shows, the reader and the Narrator are in the "Right Now", and the Narrator is telling the reader a story that happened "Somewhere in the Past".

Because the Narrator has already lived through the time period of the story, they have knowledge they didn't have while the story was actually happening.

Omniscient Narrators can be amazing for a story, because they can interject information about how the events the reader is reading *right now* shaped the future. However, while this added information can be wonderful for *some* types of stories, in other types of stories it could very easily ruin the experience for the reader.

In *Hunger Games*, Katniss Everdeen is a character in the story as well as the Narrator. At the beginning of the story, Katniss only knows her backstory – what happened to her before the story began. But she has no idea what will happen as the story unfolds. In other words, when it comes to the story she's telling, she learns the information at the same time as the reader. Her knowledge is "limited" to only what has happened before the story began, and what's happening *right now*. She's a Narrator with a Limited Level of Awareness. Let's call this a **Limited Narrator**.

Again, this relates to where the Narrator is at time-wise, in relation to the story. A Limited Narrator lives in the same time as the story.

As you can see from my amazingly realistic depiction, the Narrator and the Reader are living in the same Time as the Story — the "Right Now". Sure, they know the past. However, the future is a mystery to both reader and Narrator.

This means a Limited Narrator can never mention anything about the future, because, well, she doesn't know what the future holds.

This is an amazing experience for the reader, because it builds a strong bond between the reader and the Narrator by making the reader feel as though they're traveling through the story at the same time as the Narrator.

Limited Narrators help build tension within a story, because both the Narrator and the reader are learning things at the same time.

Let's chase a rabbit for a moment. Can you imagine how much damage would be done to *Hunger Games* if Katniss already knew what was going to happen? Do you see how having an Omniscient Narrator would negatively impact the tension of that story? Sure, it worked great for *700 Sundays*. But it would ruin *Hunger Games*. Again, it's why you need to spend Time and Effort thinking about which Level of Awareness you give your Narrator.

One word of caution before we leave this discussion. Something I've noticed of late becoming a trend is writers trying to make a Limited Narrator *even more* Limited. I mean, if it builds tension when the Narrator doesn't know what'll happen next, it only makes sense that it would build *even more* tension if the Narrator didn't know what happened in the past, right?

Usually not.

What I'm referring to here is the way-overused and normally poorly executed trope of the Amnesia-Inflicted Limited Narrator. A story in which the Narrator wakes up on page one with no memory of who she is, why she's there, nor what she'll do next.

Does it work? Sure. The issue is – it has been done to death. *The Bourne Identity, Dark City, The Maze Runner, Memento, Total Recall, Unknown,* and the list goes on and on and on. Don't get me wrong, the above stories are all wonderful. But they're the exceptions. For each of the ones listed here there are hundreds, if not thousands you've never heard of because they sucked.

Believe me, at best it's a weak gimmick to have an Amnesia-Inflicted Limited Narrator. If you're convinced that using an Amnesia-Inflicted Limited Narrator will enhance your story, I'd strongly advise taking another look at your story. You could be right. It could be awesome. But you could also be making the worst mistake you can make. Tread carefully. Just think about it before you use it. It's not only something that's no longer unique, it has become a trope that many readers will roll their eyes at. Meaning, instead of enhancing the enjoyment of your story, you may find that when a reader reads…

> I awoke with a start. I stared around the room in confusion. Where was I? I couldn't remember how I got here. In fact, I couldn't even remember my own name!

…it may be the last thing they read of your book.

Another thing to keep in mind about a Narrator's Level of Awareness is that Limited and Omniscient are mutually exclusive. You can't have both Narrator types in a single story.

Another Side Note: Anytime I say something like, "You can't do this" or "You can only have that" keep in mind I'm talking about the norm. This is creative writing. And one of my favorite things about creative writing is that any and every rule can be broken. Understand, however, breaking any rule takes skill and talent to do so without pissing off the reader. So, when I say you can't do something, and you think to yourself, "Yes I can!" good on ya. Because you can. It's up to you, however, to break those rules successfully so your reader continues to enjoy the read.

Getting back to it; Limited and Omniscient are mutually exclusive. You can't have both Narrator types in a single story.

So which to choose?

No idea. It comes down to the story you are telling, your skill and talent as a writer, and a myriad of other factors too numerous to mention.

That being said, here's the general rule I like to use when picking my Narrator's Level of Awareness:

> If the story I'm about to write is more light-hearted, or a story where I want to build a buffer between the reader and what's being read, I'll give having an Omniscient Narrator some serious thought. Omniscient Narrators tend to hinder the reader's ability to immerse themselves into the story, but that's not something I worry about if I'm writing a more humorous tale.
>
> If the story I'm about to write is a story that's more action-oriented, one in which I want to be as immersive for the reader as possible, or a story where I want to force the reader to viscerally experience what they'll be reading, I normally lean toward using a Limited Narrator.

So, keep that in mind. Omniscient Narrator's tend to be the least immersive for the reader. Stories told in this way tend to keep the reader at arm's length from what they are reading.

In other words, in Billy Crystal's *700 Sundays*, the reader never feels like they *become* Billy Crystal. And in all honesty, it would be creepy if they did.

On the other hand, a Limited Narrator tends to be more immersive for the reader. Stories told in this way tend to force the reader to viscerally experience the events the characters are experiencing.

In other words, when you read *Hunger Games*, you almost feel like you are Katniss, which makes the story more enjoyable to read.

Let's explore this just a bit more by looking at two other examples; *The Lord of the Rings*, and *The Girl with the Dragon Tattoo*.

The Lord of the Rings is told by an Omniscient Narrator. The Narrator has all the facts. But *The Lord of the Rings* is supposed to be an action story! Why use and Omniscient Narrator for an action/adventure story? I mean, I just said an Omniscient Narrator creates a buffer between the reader and what is being read. Why would you want that in an Epic Fantasy tale? Well, in my not so humble opinion, you wouldn't want to do this.

Keep in mind, it was published in 1955. A time when using a Limited Narrator was traditionally reserved to the First Person Narrative. Yeah. Creative Writing has evolved. Grown. Changed. "Limited" Third-Person didn't exist back in the 1940s. People didn't understand how to write that way. The only Limited Narrative available back then that was accepted in the publishing world was First Person, and Tolkien knew he couldn't write such an epic tale in First Person. So, he was forced to use an Omniscient Third Person.

Additionally, this was the first Epic Fantasy story ever published. What were his role models? Fairy Tales? All of those are written in Third Person Omniscient. Tolkien didn't have the choices you have.

Still, for our example, it works. The narrative of *The Lord of the Rings* keeps the reader buffered from the story. Keeps the reader less immersed.

Why is that a good thing?

In this case, I don't think it is. But using this story as my example allows me to drive home a point I stated earlier. To that end, let's take a moment to see how much damage choosing the wrong Narrative type can be. If nothing else it'll allow me to illustrate my reasons for saying, "You can't write today the way authors wrote yesterday and be successful."

I just admitted that Tolkien didn't have access to "Limited" version of Third Person back in his day, and he was more or less forced to write in Third Person Omniscient. But what about today? What about you? What about your Action/Adventure story? Today, you do have choices. And if you write like Tolkien did in his day, I believe you'll fail in today's market.

To explain this, let me first give you some "scientific" data about *The Lord of the Rings* that I've collected over the years. (Yes, "scientific" is in quotes because my data is not scientific in any way whatsoever.)

One of the things I've done as I've traveled the land teaching creative writing is to ask two questions of the audience whenever the subject came up.

> 1) How many people in this room have at least started reading *The Lord of the Rings*?
> 2) How many people who started reading *The Lord of the Rings* didn't finish it?

Keep in mind, I only ask these questions when I'm in front of a Fantasy crowd, such as when I teach at Comic Con, Gen Con, etc. So, by all rights, everyone in the room should be a fan. Tolkien defined fantasy, after all.

In answer to the first question, anywhere from 50-75% of those in attendance raise their hand. Meaning, in a room of 500 people, 300ish will admit they've at least started reading *The Lord of the Rings*.

But it's the second question that I find so fascinating, especially as it relates to story creation. The vast majority of those who raised their hands admit they never finished the book. Meaning, of the 300ish who started it, only about 50 people finished the book.

That's astounding to me. I mean, *The Lord of the Rings* is what created my genre. It's kind of a prerequisite for being a fantasy fan, right? No. The reality is, most people who start reading this saga never finish it. Personally, I've read it at least a dozen times. But most who start it can't complete the journey to the final page.

And here's my opinion on why so many people who consider themselves fantasy fans can't finish reading *The Lord of the Rings*.

Absolutely, first and foremost, we don't talk the way they did back in the 1940s when Tolkien started writing his book. Simply due to the language difference, reading it can feel "queer" at times. And most would rather be "gay" while reading a fiction story. Perhaps even enjoying the read while burning a "fagot" in the fireplace.

So yeah, words meant different things back then as opposed to now.

But outside of that, I feel it's the Omniscient Narrative that drives away most readers.

You see, when you have an Omniscient Narrator they know everything. The story becomes all encompassing. And because of this, sometimes the writer feels obligated to give all that knowledge to the reader. In the case of Fantasy, that means an entirely new world—new people, races, cultures, religions, societies, fauna, flora, physics, science (magic), history, conflicts, wars, atrocities, logic, food, and the list goes on and on and on. Believe it or not, when you shove all that detail into a novel, it can destroy the story you're telling, turning many readers off.

So, to me, the biggest reason for this book failing to hook readers is the exorbitant amount of information Tolkien shoved down the reader's throat page after page. I mean… the walking… oh, dear God, the walking…

But a close second in my list of reasons why *The Lord of the Rings* struggles to hook readers is the buffer the Omniscient Narrator creates between the reader and the story. This is an Action/ Adventure story! Immersion should be the number one thing it accomplishes. But an Omniscient Narrator doesn't allow for that. It actually hinders immersion.

So, take a language difference, add in way too much detail,

and combine it with a Narrator who hinders a reader's immersion into the story, and you have a novel that many readers find very difficult to read.

How did it become so successful then?

Duh! It was the first. It defined a genre. Oh, and it was also a really, really good story. It was not only different, but new and exciting. But it was new and exciting in 1954.

That's why your fantasy book that's written exactly like *The Lord of the Rings* is going to fail—because yours is *not* the first. Oh, and unless my calendar is *way off*, it's no longer 1954. Additionally, as I've already pointed out, writing has evolved since then. Meaning, readers are looking for a more immersive style than was available back in 1954. Or 1977 when Terry Brooks' *Sword of Shannara* was published. Or even 1993 when David Eddings' *Belgariad* was published. All great stories… for their time.

Think about it this way.

Twelve humans have walked on an alien world. Twelve. Of the billions upon billions who have been born on planet Earth, only twelve have ever walked on land that was not on Earth.

Twelve.

Knowing this, all twelve of these amazing people should not only be superstars, but their names should be known by every single man, woman, and child who live today.

But can you name all twelve people who have walked on the moon?

Yeah, neither can I.

I mean, sure, I got Neil Armstrong and Buzz Aldrin. But I can't even tell you the name of the third guy who flew with them to the moon on that first mission.

No. We humans tend to care about who's first. And that's the same with writing novels. *The Lord of the Rings* was first. Your carbon copy of it… well… isn't first.

Oh, and that third guy's name was Michael Collins, by the way. Thank you, Google!

The fact is, almost every single book written in the Third Person prior to about 1970 was more than likely written with an Omniscient

Narrator. And I feel this contributes to why so many readers today struggle with reading books written back then. Younger readers have grown up reading stories told by more immersive Narrators.

Speaking of a more immersive Narrator, let's shift to *The Girl with the Dragon Tattoo* and take a look at a completely different aspect of how a Narrator's Level of Awareness will affect your story.

In this story, there's a very horrific and graphic rape scene. Now, I know rape is a topic that makes people uncomfortable, and it should. It's one of the most despicable acts one human can do to another. Well, outside of forcing someone to see Riverdance more than once. Painful!

But we are writers. One of our jobs, if it's the will of the writer, is to make people uncomfortable. To force them to think about life in a different way than before they read our stories. So, get over it.

Since *The Girl with the Dragon Tattoo* is written using a Limited Narrator, the immersion factor for the reader is increased. Meaning, the reader is forced to experience the rape as they read it.

Why is this a good thing? I mean, since an Omniscient Level of Awareness creates a buffer between the reader and what's being read, wouldn't the writer want to protect his precious readers from such a horrifying experience?

Not in this case. No.

You see, Stieg Larsson, the writer of this book, was personally affected by rape at an early age. In addition, the country of Sweden, Larsson's home country, has always had a rape problem. As a writer, he wanted to build awareness of this issue with his fellow countrymen.

By adding such a graphic depiction of this violent act into his book, Larsson forced his readers to experience a slice of this tragedy.

Uncomfortable, sure. But that's kind of the point. And the reason using an Omniscient Narrator would have hindered this story. Or, at the very least, not allowed Larsson to bring this topic to the forefront of conversations.

It's also one of the reasons people began talking about this book in the first place, and helped create its huge success. No, before you interrupt me, I'm not telling you to add a rape scene into your story. I've never written one, and at the time of me writing this creative writing book, I have no plans on ever writing one. Again, I personally find the act deplorable.

My point is that depending on what you're trying to accomplish, your Narrator's Level of Awareness can help or hurt your story. In the case of *The Girl with the Dragon Tattoo*, it helped in many ways. It helped the immersion of the reader, and made the story more enjoyable. It helped raise awareness of a tragic issue. It helped get people talking about the book, which helped its sales.

In the case of *The Lord of the Rings*, I feel having an Omniscient Narrator hinders the enjoyment for many a reader.

Again. Time. Effort. Think about which Level of Awareness would be best for your story, and then use that to your advantage.

The final thing I want to briefly touch on before we leave this topic is that I don't want you to confuse a Narrator's Level of Awareness with writing a story in either **Past** or **Present Tense**.

I'll be going over Tenses to a nauseating level as you continue this journey. For now, understand that you can have a Limited Narrator tell a story to the reader as it's happening (Present Tense), as is the case with *Hunger Games*. However, you can also have a Limited Narrator tell the story to the reader as if it has already happened (Past Tense), as is the case with *The Girl with the Dragon Tattoo*.

Same with an Omniscient Narrator. An Omniscient Narrator can tell the story as if it's happening right now (Present Tense), as is the case with J.M. Coetzee's *Disgrace*, or as if the story has already happened (Past Tense), as is the case with *700 Sundays*.

But...

WHAT DOES THIS DO FOR YOU?

Hopefully now you can see how an Omniscient Narrator with knowledge of everything can either enhance or weaken a story. The same is true for using a Limited Narrator. Don't worry if you don't; we'll get into plenty of examples of all this "Level of Awareness" business once I delve into the different Narrative types available to you.

For now, just realize it all comes down to the writer understanding the story they're telling. Time. Effort. It's never too early to start thinking about how having either a Limited or Omniscient Narrator is going to affect the telling of *your* tale.

The crime happens when a writer does not understand what they're doing, and never realizes they have a choice in these matters. Take the time to understand how either of the Narrator's Level of Awareness will affect your story, and decide which will be the best for *your* story.

Now that I've covered the general topics, let's delve a bit deeper and look at two…

QUESTIONS TO HELP SELECT A NARRATOR

There are many types of Speculative Fiction stories; Action/ Adventure, Sci-Fi, Fantasy, True Crime, Romance, Western, etc. However, I find that no matter what type of Speculative Fiction story I'm telling, there are two very specific questions, which when answered, pretty much tell me either who my Narrator should be, or at the very least, who my Main Character should be.

These two questions are:

1) Which character is going to be the most impacted by the events of the story?
2) Which character will be the most Transformed during the story?

Speculative Fiction is for the reader, not the writer. Because of this, a reader must become invested in the story. And that means the reader must be viscerally connected to the main character or, at the very least, the Narrator.

Often, the character within the story who's most impacted by the events that transpire will be a wonderful candidate for the roll of the **Protagonist**. (Just for the sake of saying I leave no stone unturned, a Protagonist is defined as the leading Character in your story—the character that's at the center of it all.)

But the Protagonist is not always the Character Narrator.

Returning to *The Great Gatsby* example, Jay Gatsby is not the Character Narrator. There's no doubt he's the Protagonist. But that story uses what's called a **Peripheral Narrator** through a secondary character named Nick Carraway.

Earlier I said that Valentine Michael Smith was the Protagonist, but not the Narrator in *Stranger in a Strange Land*. That's because the Narrator in that book is not any of the characters within this story.

This will all make sense once I get into the different Narrator types.

For now, understand that when it comes to Speculative Fiction you must either viscerally connect the reader directly to the Protagonist, or figure out how to viscerally connect the reader to the Protagonist through an interesting Narrator. The Character most impacted by the events of the story is normally a Character the reader will relate to. If you fail to do at least one of these, you'll probably produce a story that'll fail with readers.

Concerning the second question, Transformation is key if you want a successful Speculative Fiction story.

I go into great detail about Transformation in my *Dynamic Story Creation in Plain English* book, but let me break down my theory of a Story for you in one simple to understand sentence.

Stories are about moving between two opposite concepts or states of being.

A Story starts with the character lonely, and ends with them finding true love.

A Story starts with the character a pauper, and ends with them becoming king.

A Story starts with the character hating everyone, and ends with them filled with love and generosity for his fellow citizens.

A Story starts with a serial killer a free man, able to kill at will, and ends with either his imprisonment or death.

A Story starts with the Citizens of a country giving up personal freedom for better safety, and ends with them giving up safety for personal freedom.

A Story starts with someone believing that his fellow humans are basically all right, and ends with them realizing that all humans are evil at their core.

Etc.

Etc.

Oversimplified. Maybe. But each of the above is at the hearts of such timeless stories as, *As Good As It Gets* (or any love story), *The Prince and the Pauper* (or many fantasy stories), *A Christmas Carol* (or most 19th century literary works), *The Jackal* (or every single crime/police/layer/serial killer thriller/cat cozy murder mystery ever written), *V for Vendetta* (or stories with an external theme about society), and *The Lord of the Flies* (or any story about the perils of humanity).

The reason this is so important is, if you know which character will be Transformed the most, you'll know which character will be delivering your story's **<u>Major Theme</u>**.

A story's Major Theme is the main message the story is meant to convey to the reader. I could go into Major Themes for tens of thousands of words. In fact, I did. It's called *Dynamic Story Creation in Plain English*, by Maxwell Alexander Drake. I may have mentioned it once or twice. ☺

But...

WHAT DOES THIS DO FOR YOU?

The answering of these two questions goes a long way to helping you pick your Narrator, because they help you understand what type of story you're telling.

In a story like *Hunger Games*, which is a story heavy on action, having the Protagonist also be the Narrator does a great job of forcing the reader to consume the Major Theme of the story through the Transformation of the Protagonist. From a frightened country girl to the person who shakes the very foundations of an empire—that's Transformation! As the Major Theme of that story deals with the inequality between the rich (those in control) and the poor (those being controlled), having the reader live life with the Narrator as she fights the oppression means the reader has no choice but to consume the Major Theme. It ends up being on every page they read.

The fact that it's told by a Limited Narrator enhances the story's immersiveness as well, continuing to add to the reader's enjoyment. With just those few things pointed out, do you now understand that the way *Hunger Games* was written helped in its eventual success? Sure, it's a great story. However, *how* it was written was just as instrumental in making that story successful.

"Okay, okay, okay," you say. "I get that the Narrator is going to impact the story. So what? There aren't that many types of Narrators, are there?"

Oh, my fair-weather friend, that's where you're wrong. If the writer is very clever, and very good at their craft, there could potentially be as many Narrators as there are Protagonists. As with most aspects of writing, aspiring writers simply miss understanding the power that is...

THE NARRATOR

I wasn't kidding when I stated there could potentially be as many Narrators as there are Protagonists. In fact, the sheer number of different types of Narrators that have been used in literature to date is staggering. There are way too many to go into here, but I'll talk about some of the more useful ones.

What I can do to simplify this process is to group Narrators into two different camps—Limited Narrators, and Omniscient Narrators. Yes, talking about their Level of Awareness here.

As with most aspects of writing, these can be used for nearly any type of story. But for simplicity sake, let me state it this way.

Limited Narrators will work best when using a Limited Narrative. I'll be discussing three Limited Narrative types in this book—First Person, Third Person Free Indirect Discourse, and Third Person Limited.

Omniscient Narrators will work best when using an Omniscient Narrative. I'll be discussing two Omniscient Narrative types—Third Person Omniscient and Third Person Free Indirect Discourse.

If you are clever you may have noticed that one Narrative type falls into both the Limited and Omniscient Narrative category. Again, you'll have to be patient for the answer of why this is so.

If you are *very* clever, you also may have noted I didn't even mention Second Person. Yes, I'll go over Second Person in this book (no stone left unturned, and all that). But as you'll see, it's a bit different. Besides, you probably aren't writing in Second Person, anyway.

The following isn't an exhaustive list by any means, but it should be enough to both make my point, as well as getting your creative juices flowing. And that's what I want you doing as you read through this section. Listen to what I'm saying, pay attention to how the examples I give were used to create their stories, and then extrapolate ways you might use unique Narrators in your own work.

Let's start with Limited Narrators, and look at the most common Narrator type of all…

The Protagonist as the Narrator

For me personally, I tend to write Action/Adventure Stories. Many of my stories center around a character who must take up a quest that's way beyond their capabilities, but failure of said quest normally involves the destruction of all life as we know it.

Due to this, the Major Themes of my stories tend to revolve around more life-altering topics such as Overcoming Atrocities, Battling Oppression, Facing One's Own Mortality, that sort of thing. You know, the classic Good vs. Evil type motifs.

Due to *this*, my Major Themes tend to be Internal Themes, as opposed to External Themes. Meaning, whatever my Major Theme is, it'll be answered *inside* the Protagonist, as opposed to externally by the world as a whole. (Seriously, read my *Dynamic Story Creation in Plain English* if you want to learn all about how great stories are developed.)

Still, having a life-altering Major Theme that'll be decided inside my Protagonist means that the majority of my stories are going to be written using the Protagonist as the Narrator. In addition, to enhance the immersiveness for the reader, I tend to give them a Limited Level of Awareness.

Using a Limited Narrator will increase the odds that the reader will viscerally connect with my Protagonist (since the Narrator and the Protagonist are one-in-the-same), as well as force them to consume the Major Theme of the story with little to no effort on their part (since the Major Theme is a part of every step of their journey).

Hunger Games by Suzanne Collins is a wonderful example of a Protagonist being the Narrator. In this story, the main character is not only the character who is at the center of the events of the story, she's also the character telling the story to the reader.

As we've already discussed, *Hunger Games* uses a Limited Narrator, so the reader learns what's happening at the same time as the Narrator. The future is unknown to both.

I'll get into tons of tricks and ways to utilize this amazingly powerful Narrator once I delve into First and Third Person Limited. For now, this is enough information to give you a good base understanding of what I mean when I say, "The Protagonist as the Narrator."

But the Protagonist as the Narrator isn't the only Narrator that's traditionally reserved to Limited Narratives. Let's talk a little more about the…

Peripheral Narrator

A Peripheral Narrator is a Narrator who is a character within the story, but who is *not* the Protagonist of the story. Examples of this are many. I've already mentioned *The Great Gatsby*, where the Protagonist is Jay Gatsby, but the Narrator is Nick Carraway. In *Moby Dick*, the Protagonist is Captain Ahab, but the Narrator is Ishmael. (Well, for most of it, anyway… that book breaks a lot of Narrative rules—some that work well, and others that, in my not so humble opinion, hurt the story.) Another great example of a Peripheral Narrator is Dr. Watson from the *Sherlock Holmes* stories.

But why use a Peripheral Narrator? Why not simply use the Protagonist in every story that has a Narrator with a Limited Level of Awareness?

Again, this is a complex question that's going to be specific to each story. However, let's look at these three examples.

We've already talked a little bit about *The Great Gatsby*, and discussed the one issue that story has is that Gatsby dies. And this is a good thing for the story, because for the reader to consume the Major Theme, Gatsby needs to die. (Google it, if you want to understand why I just said that.) It's kind of hard to have the person who's telling the story die before the story is finished. So, it makes sense to have the person who will be telling the story be someone who was there when the story happened, but who isn't the character who will end up six feet under. It worked in *Moby Dick*, too. Spoilers!

But the reason a Peripheral Narrator works so well for *The Great Gatsby*, in particular, is because of the type of character Gatsby was. He wasn't the most relatable character, and many readers might have found him annoying to follow as the Narrator. And if the reader never connected to the Narrator, they might not have enjoyed what they were reading, or worse, never finish reading the book. But Nick is an Everyman. Most readers are going to find a connection to him. Way more than would have connected to Gatsby. Which is why having Nick as the Narrator instead of Gatsby aided in this story's success.

Un-relatability is the biggest reason I feel Arthur Conan Doyle chose Dr. Watson as his Narrator as opposed to Sherlock Holmes. I mean, Sherlock is perfect. Worse, he solves the mystery in the first few seconds of entering the room where the dead body is. How's that for a terribly short story?

Sherlock entered the room, and while it impressed him how careful the murderer had been in concealing their identity, it was blatantly obvious to him who the culprit was. He stopped the police as they were taking away the now handcuffed butler. "It was not the butler who did this," he said. "It was Mr. Pickles, the family cat!"

He then proceeded to tell them exactly what had transpired.

Sherlock returned home, satisfied after yet another amazing adventure.

The End

No. It would be terrible if the reader was inside the mind of Sherlock. He's so far beyond the average human as to be an alien creature. Which is why the Narrator is Dr. Watson, because Watson is someone the reader can relate to.

It's also why Sherlock wastes so much time allowing Watson to fumble around in the dark trying to figure things out for himself. Watson is the reader, and a story is all about the reader. Hmm… seems I've read that statement somewhere before. ☺

For *Moby Dick,* I think the reason is similar, but different at the same time. Ahab is so single-mindedly driven, I feel he's a character who a reader would have a hard time caring about. If your reader doesn't care about the Narrator, they'll have a hard time caring about the story. So, having Ishmael be the Narrator allows both the Narrator and the reader to be on one side, looking in disbelief at the decisions ye ole Captain Ahab makes as he forces his way through the story. The reader and Ishmael can relate to the fact that they both think Captain Ahab is crazy!

Stepping away from Limited Narrators, let's now explore some of the different types of Narrators that are traditionally used in Omniscient Narratives. Since for the most part this means Third Person Omniscient and Third Person Free Indirect Discourse, we can lump them all into one big group called…

THIRD PERSON NARRATORS

For thousands of years, stories have been written in Third Person. These are your typical:

> **O**nce upon a time, some poor, uneducated fart
> set out to write the Great American Novel.

The massive bulk of all stories ever written in the history of mankind fall into this category.

Within the Third Person Narrative family, there are three main sub-species that I'll be covering in this tome: Third Person Omniscient, Third Person Free Indirect Discourse, and Third Person Limited. I'll be discussing each of these in detail, but right now I'm talking about the Narrator, and not the actual Narrative style. Or did you forget that? Well, perhaps you should be paying more attention. I'm not even sure why I'm bothering with all this if you're just going to… (sigh) Never mind.

Anyhoo, getting back to it, all I need you to understand right now is that there are different types of Third Person, and each will have a different impact on the type of Third Party Narrator you choose.

In addition, keep in mind that each of these Third Person Narrators could have either a Limited or an Omniscient Level of Awareness. I'll give you some examples of these as we progress.

While each of these have their advantages, they each have their disadvantages as well. Let's look at them separately, starting with…

The Writer as the Narrator

Many aspiring writers, and some not so aspiring ones, feel the Narrator and the writer are the same person. And this is fine. As both Third Person Omniscient and Third Person Free Indirect Discourse are… well… usually considered Omniscient Narratives. Meaning, the person narrating the story has all the facts, even before the reader gets those facts within the story. So, having the writer and the Narrator be the same person is completely acceptable.

This is by far the most common type of novel. But I don't think it's the most common because it's the best. I think it's the most common because it takes absolutely no thought on the writer's part to decide to write this way. It's the crappy default, and in my not so humble opinion, the one that has the least amount of benefit for both the story and the reader.

Before you hunt me down over my last statement, hear me out.

One huge advantage to the Writer being the Narrator is, once the writer develops their "voice", they can find pleasure in the simplistic repetition of using that same "voice" to write novel after novel. This works well for many readers, as a lot of readers find comfort in these types of writers. Authors such as Nora Roberts, John Grisham, James Patterson, and Tom Clancy have cultivated a huge number of fans who love their "voice". Those readers know what to expect each time they pick up a copy of one of these author's books.

The disadvantage to this is that the Narrator is always the same, story after story, book after book, tale after tale. This can cause the author to become lazy, and stop pushing themselves in new ways. I mean, let's be real. While I've read and enjoyed books from all the authors I listed above, I have heard more than one person say, "If you've read one of [insert one of the above author's names here] books, you've read them all."

It's also the reason I've met so many people who have told me,

"I've read a few of [insert one of the above author's names here] books, but I got bored with them after the first couple and haven't read anything by them since."

Don't get me wrong, I'm in no way attacking any of the above authors. They have each found huge success with how they write, and I personally enjoy each of them. I'm simply stating I've met readers who don't appreciate the similarities throughout their stories.

My point here is to warn you that if you plan on always being the Narrator for each book you write, you should stay vigilant, trying to avoid being repetitious within each story you pen. Or, crap, don't be vigilant. Because, let's continue to be real. The authors named above are all doing very well despite my observations here. So, what the hell do I know?

As a reminder, remember that this "Writer as the Narrator" style is *very* prevalent within the Pantser community. If this is the type of story creator you are, so be it. I feel I have sufficiently warned you, and it's now your task to take this warning and apply it to what you write.

However, if you want to push yourself with this business of the "Third Person Narrator", there are a myriad of ways you can do this and make it more interesting for the reader.

One way is to use an…

OBSERVER NARRATOR

The Observer Narrator is a storyteller who simply sticks to telling the story. This type of Narrator never injects their own opinions. They're not in the story, so how or why would they?

The Observer Narrator could be either a Limited or Omniscient Narrator, but as they never interject their own personal opinions, this matters very little. For the most part, they're going to tell the events as they happen in the story *right now*. Meaning, even if your Observer Narrator is an Omniscient Narrator, they'll rarely, if ever, tell the reader anything about the future. Still, knowing the Awareness Level of your Observer Narrator might help you wrap your mind around writing this type of Narrator.

The interesting advantage to this type of Narrator is that the author's "voice" normally becomes invisible to the reader. This can be nice, and help the reader suspend disbelief, because the reader can forget they're being told a story by someone and concentrate on the story itself.

That's the reason why this is the most common Narrator type used with Third Person Free Indirect Discourse. Now, I don't want to get into too much detail here, since there's an entire chapter waiting for you on Third Person Free Indirect Discourse, but here's a brief, and possibly very confusing overview of Third Person Free Indirect Discourse.

Third Person Free Indirect Discourse is unique among the Narrative types, as it has at least two Narrators. It has a Third Person Narrator who is not in the story, and it also has at least one Character Narrator who is inside the story. As the writer, when you're telling this tale, you Shift back and forth between the Third Person Narrator to the Character Narrator as you feel is needed.

Confusing, I know. But it'll all make sense soon.

(Oh, in case you're wondering why I keep using the full term "Third Person Free Indirect Discourse" so much, remember, I'm fighting an institution here that has used Third Person Limited incorrectly for decades. VIVA LA REVOLUCIÓN!)

Let's go back to my Heinlein's *Stranger in a Strange Land* example. Remember I said I would enlighten you as to the type of Narrator used? Well, consider yourself enlightened, for that book is written using an Observer Narrator. Meaning, the Narrator pretty much disappears as far as the reader is concerned. And this enhances the enjoyment for the reader. It not only allows the reader to focus on the events of the story without being distracted by some annoying Narrator, it also allows them to formulate their own opinions about the events they're reading. And for this particular story, those are wonderful bonuses.

However, using an Observer Narrator can be a two-edged sword. While the advantage is an invisible Narrator, this is also its disadvantage, for this type of Narrator adds nothing to the story. Meaning, you had better be a fantastic writer who is creating a fantastic story if you plan on using an Observer Narrator, because the Narrator will give your story no help. Again… the whole point here is to make them invisible.

But I think the biggest disadvantage to this type of Narrator is the natural tendency to fall into the trap of writing in a very **Telly** way, as opposed to a **Showy** way. To avoid this, stick to writing only what's going on, but don't fall into the trap of telling more than is needed for the reader to "see" the story. To make this type of Narrative shine, you must truly embrace what it means to Show the story through your narrative. And this is a tricky and complex topic all on its own, and one that I could write an entire book about. In fact, the current plan is to do just that with my next *Drake's Brutal Writing Advice* book. For now, understand that the Observer Narrator must be written by a very strong writer with a wonderful Author Voice.

The last big disadvantage of an Observer Narrator I want to discuss is why you can't allow the Observer Narrator to be noticed by the reader. You see, to pull off the Observer Narrator, the Writer needs to disappear. You must work hard to ensure the Observer Narrator never comes into the limelight. For if the Observer Narrator ever comes to light, you're guilty of **Author Intrusion**. And it's very easy to Author Intrude using an Observer Narrator.

I'll give you a detailed description of Author Intrusion when I discuss Third Person Limited. For now, think about it like this. Since this Narrative style is all about making the Narrator invisible to the story, if the reader ever notices the Narrator, you are Author Intruding.

Drake sighed in disbelief. He hadn't realized how difficult creating a book on the intricacies of Narrative would be. I know that later in his life he would look back on this project with pride. But for now, it was a struggle to come up with good examples that would illustrate his points.

The line, "I know that later in his life…" is an Author Intrusion. An Observer Narrator is not supposed to be seen. With the interjection of this piece of information, the reader can plainly see that there is a Narrator telling this tale.

Now, this could be fixed in one of two ways, depending on whether your Narrator has a Limited or Omniscient Level of Awareness. If you're using a Limited Level of Awareness, you might do something like this:

Drake sighed in disbelief. He hadn't realized how difficult creating a book on the intricacies of Narrative would be. <u>He hoped that later in his life</u> he'd be able to look back on this project with pride. But for now, it was a struggle to come up with good examples that would illustrate his points.

It's a simple change, but one that keeps the Narrative more in the now (Limited), as well as the Narrator invisible to the reader.

If you're using an Omniscient Level of Awareness, then you can tell the reader the future. But you still want to keep your Observer Narrator invisible to the reader. So, you might try something like:

Drake sighed in disbelief. He hadn't realized how difficult creating a book on the intricacies of Narrative would be. <u>Later in his life</u>, he would look back on this project with pride. But for now, it was a struggle to come up with good examples that would illustrate his points.

This lets the reader know how the event will shape the future (Omniscient), but still keeps the Observer Narrator invisible to the reader.

Again, these are very minor adjustments. But that's writing. Understanding how the most minor nuance can dramatically impact the reader's enjoyment is sort of your job.

Shifting gears, if you want your Third Person Narrator to impact the story to a greater extent, you might enjoy using a…

Commentator Narrator

This type of Third Person Narrator is a Character who is telling the story, but is absolutely not a Character within the story. The Commentator Narrator could be you, the writer, or you could create a persona for this Third Person Narrator. Either way, somehow, this Commentator Narrator has learned about this story, all its facts and figures, and is now telling all this wonderful information to the reader, while at the same time interjecting their own thoughts and opinions, even though they were not involved in the story directly.

Drake smiled. *Today is going great*, he thought. He had nailed his interview, and while I personally don't understand his desire, he had been offered his dream job as a Dogfood Taste Tester. He was now on his way home to his loving wife. Little did he know, she was having an affair with the door-to-door spatula salesman who had been stalking his neighborhood for the past month.

Both Stephen King and Charles Dickens are wonderful examples of having a Commentator Narrator.

But be warned, using a Commentator Narrator can be very jarring, and even when done perfectly, can still pull a reader out of the immersion of the story. It's the reason this type of Narrator can turn readers off. While Stephen King is arguably one of the most prolific novelists of our generation, there are many who refuse to read him specifically because he uses a Commentator Narrator in most of his works.

For me, if this type of Narrator is going to be used, there must be a very strong, story-based reason behind it. And no, that reason can't be, "Because I'm gonna write just like Stephen King so I can be the next Stephen King because my mommy says I'm better than Stephen King." (Please read the previous line in an incredibly winy, four-year-old voice for maximum effect.) Oh, and in case you're one of the delusional ones—you're not going to be the next Stephen King because there's only one Stephen King.

But let's take this Commentator Narrator further. There are two main schools of thought with this type of Narrator. One is for you, the writer, to be this Commentator Narrator. This is the style Stephen King favors. Even though the writer isn't involved directly in the story, they have somehow gained the knowledge of what happened, and have decided to write it down for others to read.

Let me tell you a little story about an insane man who went by the name Drake.

The other option is to create a fictitious third-party character who somehow gained the knowledge of this story, and is now writing it down for others to read. Keep in mind, this third-party character isn't the writer, so the writer can spend some time making this third-party character feel unique. It also means you might be able to inject this third-party character deeper into the story itself by making a more personal connection between this third-party character and the Protagonist.

And while I felt this man who insisted I call him Drake was insane, I agreed to listen to his strange tale.

Both have their advantages, and each puts a different twist on the tale you're telling.

If it's going to be you as the Commentator Narrator, you must have an incredibly strong Author Voice to pull it off. The advantage to this is that as you develop your Author Voice, it becomes consistent, and you can use it book after book to entertain your readers. Again, Stephen King.

And while Stephen King uses this Commentator Narrator type for his horror stories, for me, this type of Narrator is best suited for a story that's more light-hearted, or even a Comedy. And this is just a personal opinion, but when the story has a more humorous Tone, the interjections of a Commentator Narrator feel to me as if they are less distracting for the reader. Less jarring. Both Terry Pratchett and Douglas Adams were masters of this, and their Commentator Narrators' voices added volumes to their works.

However, for me and how I write, I don't feel this Narrative style helps more serious stories. In fact, I think it cheapens a more serious story by breaking the reality of what the story is trying to create. Again, personal opinion here.

Like any time when the Writer is the Narrator, the down side to using a Commentator Narrator who is also the writer is that all your books could start to sound the same. While I'm personally a huge fan of both Pratchett and Adams, having read all their books multiple times, I know many a reader who have said, "Yeah. I read a couple of their books. But after a few, they all seemed like the same book to me. So, I haven't read any since."

Personally, I like to make up a new character for each of the stories where I plan on using a Commentator Narrator. That way, I can customize the Character who is the Narrator to better match the story. This also allows me to keep things feeling fresh. (Full disclosure, I rarely use a Commentator Narrator. In fact, I rarely use the Third Person Narrator at all. I prefer my Protagonist to be my Narrators. Not because I'm stuck in a rut with how I write, but because they enhance the stories I tend to write. Remember, it's about learning this stuff so you can make an informed choice as to who your Narrator will be.)

Another twist to this whole Third Person Narrator business is to create an...

Interviewer Narrator

This type of Narrator allows for the Narrator to ask questions of the characters, delving deeper into their reasons for doing what they did, or finding out more about how they felt about the things they went through. These types of Narrators will normally have a Limited Level of Awareness, learning the events of the story at the same time as the reader. This enhances the immersion for the reader, for the story creates the illusion that the reader is there with the Interviewer Narrator as their questions are asked. If set up well, the reader might even feel like they've *become* the Interviewer.

In my opinion, the best example of this is Anne Rice's *Interview with a Vampire*. I mean, that book literally opens with a character who is inside the story interviewing a… well… interviewing a vampire. But this allowed Anne Rice to use this Interviewer Narrator throughout the story, helping to keep the reader immersed both in the story the vampire was telling, and reminded the reader that they were also in a room interviewing that same vampire. Very brilliant and amazingly well done.

However, this Interviewer Narrator has been used for ages.

C.S. Lewis used a unique variation of this style in the *Voyage of the Dawn Treader*.

> It brought both a smell and a sound, a musical sound. Edmund and Eustace would never talk about it afterwards. Lucy could only say, "It would break your heart." "Why," said I, "was it so sad?" "Sad! No," said Lucy.

Interestingly, Lewis' Interviewer Narrator had an Omniscient Level of Awareness, as opposed to Rice's Interviewer Narrator who had a Limited Level of Awareness. To me, this made reading the *Voyage of the Dawn Treader* more jarring than what I experienced with *Interview with a Vampire*.

I mean, in *Interview with a Vampire* I was there with the

Interviewer Narrator, and both of us were learning the story at the same time. So, when the Interview Narrator interjected a comment, opinion, or asked a follow up question, it felt as if I was the one doing this.

To peel back the curtain a bit, this is exactly why I do my silly, "Stop Interrupting me!" skits in this book series. Those interruptions, while I blame you for them, are actually me trying to anticipate a question you may actually have. I want you to feel like you and I are together, and one way I do this is by "pretending" you're interrupting me.

Now, stop interrupting me, so we can get this done!

The reason I felt the Omniscient Commentator Narrator in the *Voyage of the Dawn Treader* was more jarring was I never felt like I was there with them when they were interviewing the characters of the story. How could I? This Interviewer Narrator had already interviewed everyone *before* he told me about this story.

Again, Omniscient Narrators are telling you a story that happened sometime in their past. (Flip back and look at my amazingly accurate and incredibly detailed drawings of how Time and the Narrator are related if you need a reminder of what this looks like.)

But to really push the Third Person Narrator into the story, you can always use a…

Narrator Who *Was* a Character

This is when the Narrator telling the story *was* a Character within said story. And before you ask, *was* is the word I meant to use here, not is.

This is a very common Narrative style. I've mentioned *700 Sundays* many times now, but it's still a great example of a "Narrator who *was* a Character" in the story. Billy Crystal is the Narrator who is narrating the life of a younger version of himself.

Now, don't confuse this type of Narrator with the "Protagonist as the Narrator", nor with a "Peripheral Narrator". They seem very similar, sure. But they are different.

Why? It's a slight shift, but one that creates a very interesting thing you can play with during your story.

With "Protagonist/Peripheral Narrators", the Narrator is in the story as it's happening. And that's what you get to play with, a Character who *is there during* the events.

With this Narrator, in a way, you get two versions of the same Narrator. You get the Character in the story, as well as an older, wiser version of that Character who is telling the tale.

To better explain myself, think of it like this. To pull off this Narrator type, just remember the Character in the story is a Past Version of the Narrator. Meaning, even though they're also a character within the story, that character is a younger version of who they are as the Narrator. Here's an example of how this can affect a story.

> Of course, Drake knew now this was all nonsense, and today if someone said this to him he'd give that person a swift kick in the ass. But back then, well, back then he was a good deal less experienced. Drake honestly believed that he would love the job of a Dogfood Taste Tester.

You'll note that in a way, there are two people in this paragraph. One, the Character of Drake, and two, the Narrator who knows more than Drake.

Now, I wrote this example in Third Person, because, well…, I called this section Third Person Narrators. But honestly, this type of Narrator is more often used in First Person. Here it is again:

> Of course, I know now this was all nonsense, and today if someone said this to me I'd give that person a swift kick in the ass. But back then, well, back then I was a good deal less experienced. I honestly believed that I would love the job of a Dogfood Taste Tester.

Still, you can see there are two versions of the same person in this paragraph. There is the "I" in the story, and there is an older, wiser "I" who is telling the story.

However you write it, the point is to show that the Narrator has grown and changed since. Sure, they are the same person, but in name only. Just as I'm not the same person I was when I was sixteen.

It's the reason this Narrator type is almost always done with an Omniscient Level of Awareness. And that makes sense since the Narrator is telling about events they've already lived through. They know how it ends.

The wiggle-room you have as a storyteller when using this Narrator is how much does this Narrator know of the events that happened *after* the story concludes.

Are they an old man, telling of an event that happened in the early years of their lives? If so, they are truly Omniscient, and know everything, including how the world changed by the events they are describing.

Is this a tale that happened just a few years ago but the fallout from the events of the story have yet to settle? If so, then the Narrator is still living in a time of uncertainty. They know how they got here, but are still not sure this is a better place.

Or, a twist I've seen more than once, is the Narrator living in a time that's the exact moment of the climax of the story? As in, are they telling the story of these events that led up to the climax, but said climax hasn't happened yet. This allows the Narrator to be Omniscient for most of the story, and then Shift to a Limited Narrator for the climax. If done well, this can enhance the tension of the climax. Still, as with all things, if you fail to pull this off, it will ruin your story. So, tread carefully if this is a gimmick you wish to use.

Depending on how you play this "Narrator who was a Character", you can create some very interesting things within your story.

Another interesting twist on this type of "Narrator was a Character" is to have them be a…

Narrator Who Is a Secret Character

This type of Third Party Narrator is the Narrator who is telling the reader the story, but they're also one of the characters the reader will be following within the story. The twist is, the Narrator never admits that they are one of the Characters.

Normally this "Narrator who is a Secret Character" has an Omniscient Level of Awareness. Meaning, they've already lived the events of the story as they happened, and are now putting that story down on paper for the reader. But they're doing it in such a way as to hide the fact that they were one of the characters within said story. *A Series of Unfortunate Events* is a wonderful example of this. Because of this Narrator's use in this story, a weird Tension is created in the fact that the reader *knows* the only way this Narrator could possibly know the story they're telling is if that Narrator had been there. But the reader just can't figure out who this Narrator was. It's one of the charms of *A Series of Unfortunate Events*.

When you give this Narrator a Limited Level of Awareness, you create a different type of experience for the reader, because doing so completely hides the fact that the Narrator was a character in the story. This means that when the Narrator reveals they were one of the characters, the reader gets a pleasant surprise. This was done in *300*.

The Narrator for *300* was one of Leonidas' soldiers, but for much of the story, it felt as if it were being told by a Narrator who was *not* in the story, and one who only had a Limited Level of Awareness – meaning the Narrator who was telling the tale only knew what was happening "Right Now." The beautiful twist came at the end when the reader discovered that the Narrator was in fact Dilios, the soldier who lost an eye during the fighting and was sent back with the wounded. It was only then, in the last few pages, that the story Shifted to reveal that there had been a Secret Character Narrator who was telling this story to the reader. This also lent to his ability to give such a moving speech about the sacrifice of those who died for their people.

Yes, once you learn all the different ways a Third Person Narrator can affect a story, you'll be able to start experimenting with new ways to use them in your own stories. Exciting, right?

Be warned. While this type of Narrator should be Omniscient, meaning they have all the facts and can interject their own thoughts and opinions, doing so can easily break the magic of what this Narrator type can bring to your story.

For me, I find that on the few occasions I've written in an Omniscient Narrative, I've had way more pleasure in creating a...

STORYTELLER NARRATOR

A Storyteller Narrator is a Character I can create who is not me, the writer. They are also not a Character within the story. They are someone who has somehow learned about the events of this story, and have sat down to tell the reader all about it.

Why would I do this? For several reasons.

The first, and for me the best reason, would be to allow myself to avoid the trap of repetition within my own Author Voice. You see, all writers, whether they realize it or not, develop a *style* to their writing. From the way they construct their sentences and paragraphs, to the words they choose, to what things they bring attention to, each writer is unique in how we craft a story. This is our Author Voice, and it's created by your own unique personal life experiences.

When I force myself to create a unique Third Person Narrator who is a Character all their own, it means I force myself to create a unique Author Voice for that Character in the same way I'd create a unique voice for any Character within the story. I must give them their own personality, one that's different from my own.

This pushes me as a writer, which is always a good thing.

Another wonderful bonus is that it also means I'm not limited to my own personal opinions about the story being told. In other words, I personally may be against the actions of the Protagonist or what the message of the story is. However, me being against whatever this idea might be, could ruin the story by breaking the Major Theme. Having a Storyteller Narrator means I can give that Narrator an opinion that's different from my own. I.E., this Storyteller Narrator could *agree* with whatever this idea is. It might be semantics, but you would be surprised at how this subtle mental difference enhances the writing of the story.

Case in point: *Lord of the Flies*. Now, this novel was *not* written this way. I'm using it here to make my point because of its Major Theme. You see, the Major Theme that is asked during *Lord of the Flies* is, "Are all humans evil at their core?"

Believe it or not, even though I tend to write gory, graphic, dark, tragic stories, I'm an optimist at heart. I truly believe that we humans, as a whole, are good. Sure, there are some despicable people who live amongst us. And while they get all the attention, I feel they are very much in the minority. Most of us are wonderful people. Stupid at times, sure. But wonderful, nonetheless.

So, had I been the one to pen *Lord of the Flies*, my answer to the Major Theme question would be, "All humans are *not* evil at their core."

But that's not what that story proved. It proved that, "All humans *are* evil at their core."

So, if I was penning that tome, and I wanted the story to show that all humans are evil at their core, I'd be in a pickle. That answer goes against my personal belief. However, I could create a Storyteller Narrator who feels that all humans are evil at their core. Then I could sit back and let that pessimistic bastard tell the tale. Due to the fact that this Storyteller Narrator agrees with the story, they'd do a much better job telling that story than I ever could.

It's a way of separating my personal opinions from the story. And believe me, this is not easy. However, if you do a good job of creating this Storyteller Narrator Character, it does make your task easier.

But...

WHAT DOES THIS DO FOR YOU?

Hopefully you're starting to realize how important choosing the correct Narrator will be for your story. More importantly, I hope you can see that there are more varieties of Narrators than, "I'm the writer, so obviously, I'm the Narrator."

And honestly, at this point, if you have to ask what all this does for you, then I'm not sure you're cut out to be a writer. Perhaps you should take up another impossible dream? Like, I don't know, it obviously takes no talent to be a YouTube sensation. Why don't you give that a try?

All seriousness aside, hopefully throughout this section your imagination has been tickled. Things I said should have triggered the muse inside you to say things like, "Oh! It would be cool if I...."

I hope this has caused you to realize how important it is to take the time to think about who will be telling your story. That I've opened your eyes to how many avenues of possibilities you have for creativity. Ways to enhance the telling of your tale. Things that will make for a more interesting and entertaining read.

One thing you may be asking yourself is, "How does Drake know about all these different types of Narrators?" Well, I'm disappointed you would ask such a silly question. Still, I believe wholeheartedly there are no silly questions, only silly answers.

This is one issue I've run into time and time again with aspiring writers. To answer your question, "I read. A lot." It infuriates me how many wannabe writers I meet every year who inform me they don't read. Shocking. Disgusting. How the hell do you think you can be successful in a craft that you don't practice yourself?

Seriously? I really want an answer to this. I've asked this of nearly every aspiring writer who tells me they don't read, and to date, none of them have an answer outside of a blank, brainless stare.

Look, it all boils down to reading. You need to read. A lot. Read every single day. Read good books. Read bad books. Read.

But don't read as a reader. Read as a writer. Read to dissect. Read to discover what works, what doesn't. Why things are the way they are, etc.

I know this stuff about all these Narrator types because I've dissected the books I've used as examples, plus many, many more. They were my instructors, my teachers, and my guides. Through some of them, I learned what I felt worked. I was then able to incorporate those things into my own craft. Through others, I learned what I felt didn't work. This allowed me to steer clear of mistakes I might otherwise have made.

I read Speculative Fiction to learn how to write Speculative Fiction better.

And for those of you out there who live behind the farcical lie of, "I don't read because I don't want it to influence my writing." Trust me. No one is a good enough writer that a little influence would be a bad thing. Being influenced by other writers is always a good thing. Best case you learn a new way of doing something cool. Worst case, you read something terrible and realize why you shouldn't do things that way.

And that's how I've learned what I've learned. It's why I can take a topic like "What is a Narrator," which most writers can barely fill a blog post discussing, and instead write 13,977 words about it and still not feel I covered it completely.

I read every single day as a writer. And if you're going to push yourself in this craft, I suggest you do the same.

Alright, I'll step off my soapbox now and step into the heart of the subject that is this volume of *Drake's Brutal Writing Advice*. It's time for us to discuss the three different…

Narrative Types

Now that I've forced you to spend some of your brain cells on who your Narrator shall be, and you've hopefully started to wrap your mind around how important the Narrator is to the story, it's time to get into the meat that is Narrative from a grammatical standpoint. And I'm talking about First, Second, and Third Person here.

Which Narrative type you choose matters because it sets many of the "rules" you'll be forced to follow while you write your story. It dictates what **Pronouns** you'll be using, what **Verb Forms** are available to you. It also sets the distance between the reader and the story, how deeply the reader will be able to see inside the Narrator's mind—basically, the Narrative you choose to write in will determine how immersive your story will be for the reader.

In my opinion, there's no greater way to ensure your reader enjoys your Speculative Fiction story outside of perfecting your grasp and implementation of Narrative. Sure, you must create a compelling story with interesting characters and lots of drama. But much of that is talent. And you either have talent, or you don't. Sorry, I can't help you there.

Creating a Dynamic Story takes more than talent, however, it takes skill. And that's something you learn through Time and Effort.

Assuming you have the talent, your grasp of Narrative in particular is the be-all end-all device that will either help the reader enjoy your story, or turn them off after the first few pages.

There are three main types of Narratives, and I'm certain you've heard them all—First Person, Second Person, and Third Person. As I've also mentioned, I'm going to be discussing three versions of Third Person—Third Person Omniscient, Third Person Limited, and Third Person Free Indirect Discourse.

It should come as no shock to you that all three of these Narrative types are way more complicated than people assume.

Before I get into these, I need to discuss a topic that affects them all. For while there are many different Narrative types to choose from, each also has a…

Narrative Tense

Whether you know it or not, every piece of prose (be it a short story, novella, or novel) is written in a **Narrative Tense**. Narrative Tense means "when" the story feels like it's taking place in relation to the reader.

In English grammar, there are only two Narrative Tenses stories can be written in – **Present Narrative Tense**, and **Past Narrative Tense**. No, before you interrupt me with one of your silly questions, there's no such thing as a Future Narrative Tense story. Yes, I get that there are Future Tense versions of verbs, but while a verb's tense creates Narrative Tense, it's not *THE* Narrative Tense.

Narrative Tense is an incredibly complicated and boring topic. But you need to understand; the number one mistake all writers make is not being able to hold their Narrative Tense. Number One! Imagine me holding up a finger to stress that this is the number one issue writers have. Perhaps it's my middle finger, perhaps not. I'll leave that up to your imagination.

The reason is simple. Holding your Narrative Tense means learning grammar—in particular, learning all about Verb Forms. Of which there are at least a dozen… and all of them are boring as crap… because learning grammar is boring as crap… something I wouldn't wish upon my worst enemy… but *you're* the one who wanted to become a writer… even though your mother begged you not to chase this ridiculous dream… because she wanted you to do something more realistic with your life… like sell shoes or something… but since you broke her heart by pursuing this writing business anyway, learn grammar you must… even if it's so boring it'll make your eyes bleed.

But all those boring grammatical details aren't needed for me to get my points across. Booyah! Procrastination wins again!

WARNING! The following are the thoughts of a deranged madman. My name is Mrs. Johnson and I was Drake's third-grade teacher. I totally disagree with what he's about to say concerning Narrative Tense! If he were still in my class, I'd give him detention for the rest of the school year.

Okay, yes. I don't look at Narrative Tense the way others do. I find it too limiting. Too narrowminded. What I'm about to describe could very well put you off. It's definitely not what they teach in school. All I ask is that you hear me out. It may open your eyes to a cool new tool you can use to enhance your writing. Or... Mrs. Johnson could be correct, and what I'm about to say is all drivel.

I've already talked about one grammatical term I made up, the Narrator's Level of Awareness. But let's recap here so I can tie that theory into this one.

An Omniscient Narrator knows what happened in the story before, during, and after.

A Limited Narrator only knows what happened before the story began, and what has happened up the page the reader is currently reading.

The reason I made up the term "Narrator's Level of Awareness" is that I see this as something that's not attached to Narrative Tense.

However, most do see it as attached.

Most feel that anything written in Present Tense is being told by a Narrator who is Limited to only knowing what is going on *Right Now*. And anything written in Past Tense is being told by a Narrator who has already been there and done that, so they know everything.

I disagree with this. More so, I feel this way of thinking limits a writer's ability to tell a compelling story.

Understanding that I'm going against conventional wisdom here, let's begin.

Stories can be told in two *Tenses*—**Past Tense**, and **Present Tense**.

From their names, you can guess that they're talking about

time. However, I see this Time as it relates to the *reader* reading the story and not the Narrator of said story.

Perhaps this is semantics, and perhaps I'm slicing hairs here, but to me looking at it this way makes it easier for me to understand.

To me, if the reader is reading a story that feels like it's happing *Right Now*, then this story is being told in Present Tense.

If the reader is reading a story that feels like it happened sometime in the past, then this story is being told in Past Tense.

However, I still feel that the Narrator is free to be either Limited or Omniscient in either Tense.

Why do I separate this from a Narrator's Level of Awareness? Because I feel that when it comes to Narrative Tense (Past or Present), you can mix and match a Narrator's Level of Awareness with both types of Narrative Tenses. Depending on how you do this, it will affect the story you're telling in different ways. You can have:

A LIMITED NARRATOR TELLING THE STORY IN PRESENT TENSE.

Drake begins typing his next example. He has no idea what he will write. He isn't smart enough to think things through. So, he places his fingers upon his keyboard and trusts that they will figure it out.

For the reader, this feels like the events are happening as you read the words, in the *Right Now*. This is Present Tense.

However, if you pay attention to the Narrator, Drake, you can also tell that he has no idea what will happen next. He is a Limited Narrator.

Both line up, and this makes this feel very natural. Again, this is the way most people teach Present Tense.

However, let's look at the same thing, but in Past Tense.

A Limited Narrator telling the story in Past Tense.

Drake began typing his next example. He had no idea what he would write. He wasn't smart enough to think things through. So, he placed his fingers upon his keyboard and trusted that they would figure it out.

For the reader, this feels like the events have already happened sometime in the past. This is Past Tense.

However, as with the above, it's obvious that the Narrator, Drake, has no idea what will happen next. And you can write an entire Past Tense story in this manner, where the Narrator has no idea what will happen next. Even though it's written in Past Tense, so logic should dictate that the Narrator does know.

The beautiful thing is, you can stick to this Limited Narrator throughout a Past Tense story, and the reader will feel like they are learning things at the same time as the Narrator.

But conventional wisdom teaches that with Past Tense (especially Third Person Past Tense, as I wrote here) means the Narrator must be Omniscient. But as you can see from the above, or anything that I've ever had published, this is not the case.

Again, to me, this is all about the reader. The reader may feel like this happened in the past, but they also feel like they are learning what will happen at the same time as the Narrator. This is because the Narrator has a Limited Level of Awareness.

Let's take this a step further with some more examples.

AN OMNISCIENT NARRATOR TELLING THE STORY IN PAST TENSE.

Drake began typing his next example. He had no idea what he would write, which is something that would haunt him once this book was published, because the example he would come up with would be terrible. Still, what could he do? He wasn't smart enough to think things through. So, he placed his fingers upon his keyboard and trusted that they would figure it out.

Here we see what many feel is traditional when telling a Past Tense story. We have an Omniscient Narrator, someone who has been there and done that, and they are telling the story in a way that makes the reader feel the events have already happened.

This absolutely works perfectly. There is nothing wrong with this whatsoever. Well… except you lose the ability to make the reader feel like they are learning things at the same time as the Narrator. Not a bad thing, depending on the story you are telling.

However, can it work the other way? Let's find out.

AN OMNISCIENT NARRATOR TELLING THE STORY IN PRESENT TENSE.

Drake begins typing his next example. He has no idea what he will write, which is something that will haunt him once this book is published, because the example he'll come up with will be terrible. Still, what can he do? He isn't smart enough to think things through. So, he places his fingers upon his keyboard and trusts that they will figure it out.

Does it work. Yes and no. This one is tough because when you write in Present Tense, it does build a reality that things are happening *Right Now*. When the above Narrator interjects their future knowledge about how this book will affect Drake in the future, things get a bit wonky.

So for me, I believe Past Tense can be told by either a Limited or Omniscient Narrator seamlessly. But for Present Tense, I do believe it's harder to use an Omniscient Narrator, and doing so might ruin the story for the reader.

But I'm not here trying to prove to you which is better. I am simply here trying to show you it can be done.

And this is the reason I created the term Narrator's Level of Awareness, and separated it from Narrative Tense, making both independent from each other. For me, it helps me look at the story's Tense separately from how much the Narrator knows.

Now, if I'm being completely honest here, the main reason I think this way is due to the types of stories I create. Since I tend to write a lot of complex, dark, tragic epic fantasy stories, I like to write in Third Person Limited. I'm a firm believer that Third Person Limited should only be written in Past Tense. However, both my reader and my Narrators learn the story at the same time. Meaning, even though it's written in Past Tense, my Narrators are all Limited in their Awareness Level.

Traditional teaching frowns upon this idea, and many are stuck in the rut thinking Past Tense means the Narrator must already know what will happen next.

For completeness, here are the four examples again, but this time written in First Person.

A Limited Narrator telling the story in Present Tense.

I begin typing my next example. I have no idea what I will write. I am not smart enough to think things through. So, I place my fingers upon my keyboard and trust that they will figure it out.

A Limited Narrator telling the story in Past Tense.

I began typing my next example. I had no idea what I would write. I wasn't smart enough to think things through. So, I placed my fingers upon my keyboard and trusted that they would figure it out.

An Omniscient Narrator telling the story in Past Tense.

I began typing my next example. I had no idea what I would write, which is something that would haunt me once this book was published, because the example I would come up with would be terrible. Still, what could I do? I wasn't smart enough to think things through. So, I placed my fingers upon my keyboard and trusted that they would figure it out.

An Omniscient Narrator telling the story in Present Tense.

I begin typing my next example. I have no idea what I will write, which is something that will haunt me once this book is published, because the example I'll come up with will be terrible. Still, what can I do? I am not smart enough to think things through. So, I place my fingers upon my keyboard and trusts that they will figure it out.

I hope you can see the same is true for both First and Third Person—you can definitely mix and match them. But just as before, the one that becomes awkward is an Omniscient Narrator written in Present Tense. Present Tense just doesn't play well with an Omniscient Narrator.

Very minor differences indeed. And to really understand those differences, you need to learn all about Verb Forms. Since I'm not going over those in detail, I want you to wrap your mind around *the why*, and not *the how*.

Narrative Tenses go a long way to helping the Narrator tell the story. As you can probably guess, using a Past Tense Narrative can help an Omniscient Narrator. After all, he's looking *back* at what happened as he tells you about it. He has the advantage of perspective. In the same way, using a Present Tense Narrative can help a Limited Narrator. Since it's happening *Right Now*, it's natural that the Narrator doesn't know the future. But as you saw, they can be mixed and matched.

It comes down to understanding what type of Narrator you're using, what type of story your Narrator will be telling, and how using either Past or Present Tense to deliver that story will help create immersion or enjoyment for the reader.

And that's where the magic happens.

It's how I can write in Past Tense, but remain true to Narrators who have a Limited Level of Awareness.

But that's enough of that for now. Keep in mind as I move through the different types of Narratives, when I say Past Tense, I mean the story is being told in a way the *reader* feels it's already happened. And when I say Present Tense, I mean the story that makes the *reader* feel like it's happening Right Now.

To that end, let's dip a toe in the dark and foreboding waters of...

VERB FORMS

I said I wasn't gonna go into detail about Verb Forms, and I'm definitely holding to that. Verb Forms are incredibly complex, and it would literally double the size of this already huge book to explain them all.

Still, I want to touch on them briefly.

A story's Narrative Tense is dictated by which Verb Forms you use. In other words, when it comes to holding which Narrative Tense you're writing in, it all comes down to choosing the correct Verb Form for each verb you're using in a sentence.

While Verb Forms can feel complicated—there are a lot of them, after all—they're not as bad as you might assume. Mostly because, provided you've grown up in an English-speaking country, you've been "hearing" the rules of Verb Forms your entire life.

Now don't get me wrong here, I'm not saying that because you can speak English you can write. I've always taken the *opposite* stance on that.

What I'm saying is that when using Verb Forms, the biggest bonus to an English-speaking native is that when the wrong Verb Form is used, it will *sound* wrong. This, in and of itself, does not mean it is wrong. However, it's a great place to start.

Unfortunately, the issue comes into play with the fact that most writers never *hear* their writing. When they're rereading their own stuff, editing, they're doing so silently. There's a *HUGE* issue with this!!! You read way too fast in your head. The average person reads 250 to 350 words per minute. When you're reading this fast, you're not actually reading every word. You're skimming, skipping words and letting your brain fill in the gaps. How the hell do you think you can "edit" your work by skimming it?

You can't.

When I'm reading anything I've written, I do so out loud. *Always*. Every word. I also do all my character voices in character. And I'm a horrid actor. So all my character voices sound terrible. But I do it anyway. Because it makes me a better writer.

Time. Effort.

Case in point: This book. I've reread the book you're reading right now about half a dozen times as I've been writing it, and each time I reread it, I did so out loud.

Seriously. Read your stuff out loud. It'll slow you down to about 80 to 100 words a minute, which will allow you to actually read every single word. Bonus, you'll be able to *hear* each sentence. This will help you tremendously when it comes to recognizing whether or not you've used the correct Verb Form. To really understand Verb Forms, you need to understand how each is created, and how they affect the verbs in a sentence. I'm not going into all this detail here, but there is a ton of sites out there that do.

Shifting back to Narrative Tense, let's look at my definitions:

> If the story makes the reader feel that it's happening at the same time the reader is reading it, in other words, it feels to the reader like the story is happening *Right Now*, then the story is being told in **Present Tense**.

> If the story makes the reader feel that it's happening sometime in the past, then the story is being told in **Past Tense**.

Keep in mind, this has nothing to do with the Narrator's Level of Awareness. As I showed earlier, you can write any Narrator type; First, Second, or Third, in any Narrative Tense; Past or Present, using either a Limited or Omniscient Narrator.

Now, I know I harped on the fact that First Person should be written in Past Tense, Second Person in Present Tense, and all the Third Persons written in Past Tense. However, throughout the remainder of this discussion, I'll try and treat them all equally, and keep my prejudice biases in check.

I assure, it won't be easy for me. *Some people* feel I'm an opinionated jerk when it comes to Narratives. Not sure where they got that idea from.

Let's begin this little adventure of ours one step closer to completion by looking at the *Right Now* and talk about…

Present Tense

The prevalence of Present Tense in fiction is a new phenomenon. If you read books published before 1960, you'll be hard pressed to find many written in Present Tense. Unfortunately for readers like me who despise reading a story in Present Tense, that's no longer the case.

In fact, in 1987 the trend had become so obvious to scholars that Robie Macauly and George Lanning wrote about the trend of using Present Tense in fiction. In that paper they said: "It is the most frequent cliché of technique in new fiction." Unfortunately, it has only gotten worse thanks to the success of books like *Hunger Games* and *Divergent*.

To that end, let's look at a few advantages and disadvantages of Present Tense so that hopefully you can use this knowledge to make an informed choice about not using this obnoxious Tense. Er… so you can make an informed choice and decide if this Tense will ruin your story. Er… if this Tense will ruin or help your story.

Happy?

Let's start by looking at some of the advantages writing in Present Tense gives to a story.

1) The biggest advantage is that Present Tense has an immediacy feel to it over Past Tense. Meaning, the reader is experiencing the story at the same time as the Narrator. There's a sense of togetherness in this for the reader, for they feel they aren't being told of past events, but experiencing them with the Narrator. It's the reason you should use a Limited Narrator when writing in Present Tense. If done well, this can enhance not only the reader's feelings over the changes the Narrator goes through, but the story's climax as well.

First Person Present Tense

I open the basement door. Two glowing red eyes glare back at me. A scream attempts to rip from my throat, but I'm frozen in place. The monster lunges, razor-sharp claws materialize from the darkness.

SECOND PERSON PRESENT TENSE

You open the basement door. Two glowing red eyes glare back at you. A scream attempts to rip from your throat, but you're frozen in place. The monster lunges, razor-sharp claws materialize from the darkness.

THIRD PERSON PRESENT TENSE

Drake opens the basement door. Two glowing red eyes glare back at him. A scream attempts to rip from his throat, but he's frozen in place. The monster lunges, razor-sharp claws materialize from the darkness.

As you can see, in each Narrative type the events are in your face and in the now. Always a good thing when you're writing horror. But depending on the genre, this in your face-ness may give your reader an awkward feeling and the desire to stop reading.

2) Another great advantage of using Present Tense is to enhance the mindset of a Character Narrator who lives only in the moment. As in, if the Narrator only lives for the Right Now, then that Narrator doesn't care what happened in the past, nor what's going to happen in the future. By writing this Narrator's story in Present Tense, you force the reader to experience life in the same way – the here and now.

Joyce Cary wrote *Mister Johnson* in Present Tense, and he gave this as his reason. "As Johnson swims gaily on the surface of life, so I wanted the reader to swim, as all of us swim, with more or less courage and skill, for our lives."

In other words, Joyce Cary *CHOSE* to write in Present Tense because he *DECIDED* it would enhance his story. He didn't simply start writing willy-nilly.

When we were discussing First Person I showed you the one story of mine that was written in Present Tense—the crazy one published for Sony's *EverQuest Next*. I wrote it this way for much the same reason as Cary. First, it's a short story, only about 3,000 words, so I'm not forcing my readers to suffer long. But the real reason I chose to write it in Present Tense was due to the fact that the Narrator was that weird little monster creature that I describe as being like a six-year-old child hooked on crack. He doesn't think about what happened to him two seconds ago, and has no care of what will happen to him two seconds from now. In other words, I *CHOSE* to write that story in Present Tense because I *DECIDED* it would enhance the story I was writing.

3) Writing in Present Tense can add weight to events in a story that happened in the past.

Sometimes in a Present Tense story you're going to need to tell events using Past Tense, as those events happened before the events of your story.

For an example, look back at the first example in this section. There's a line that reader:

> A scream attempts to rip from my throat, but
> I'm frozen in place.

The scream is attempting to rip *Right Now*. However, I was frozen in place *before* that. Hence why I used Frozen, which is the *Past* version of Freeze.

When writing in Present Tense, there will be times you will be forced to do this type of "Tense Shifting".

However, if you're writing a story that for some reason you want to stress the importance of these past events and how they shaped the life of your Narrator, it may be advantageous to write your story in Present Tense to emphasize the importance of those past events and show how they affect the here and now. Now, I can't for the life of me think of any story that would benefit from this. But I'm a very specific type of writer who writes very specific types of stories. So, I list them here because I can see that it would be interesting for the reader. The issue with this advantage is, it also creates a huge disadvantage (see #3 in the disadvantages below).

4) If you understand Verb Forms, writing in Present Tense can

be the easiest Tense to hold. As I'll show you in a moment, holding to Present Tense means mastering only a limited amount of Verb Forms. Two, for the most part. But no more than five.

But being easier to maintain does not mean it'll enhance your story. Yes, I listed this as an advantage, but it's only an advantage for the writer. It does nothing in adding to the enjoyment of the reader.

Worse, since Present Tense is *not* how we talk, you'll have a longer learning curve for this to become the "easiest Tense to hold". Trust me, because of the foreign nature of Present Tense, you'll struggle for a long time learning to master this Tense.

All the above sounds wonderful, right? I'm certain you found reasons that validated why you're going to snub me and write your story in Present Tense. Hold on to your britches, partner. Circle the wagons and take a gander at some of the disadvantages writing in Present Tense will straddle you with.

1) I've already talked about what I feel is the biggest disadvantage of Present Tense—that as many as 30% of readers I've spoken to about this Tense do not like reading stories written in Present Tense.

Again, to be fair, these are readers of my genre—Fantasy. Other genre readers, such as those of YA Romance, are way more accepting of Present Tense. Depending on what genre you plan to write, this disadvantage may not be as terrible for you as it is for me. Still, it's worth contemplating before you dive head-long into the Present Tense swimming pool.

In the end, this is something that you, the writer, must weigh and measure on your own. If you feel Present Tense will benefit you, wonderful. Use it.

2) Writing in Present Tense also means you're severely limited in how you can manipulate **Time** throughout the story.

Present Tense normally forces your story to be told in a very rigid, chronological fashion. You must start with the first events, and move logically to the next chronological event, etc., until your story's conclusion. If you skip around in the timeline of the story, you break the primary reason for using Present Tense – events happening in the *Right Now*.

This is a huge limiting factor on how complex your Plot can be. Think about your story, and make sure you're using a Tense that'll enhance the telling of your particular story.

3) To me, this inability to manipulate Time creates the biggest issue with writing in Present Tense, which is the fact that it becomes more difficult to create dynamic characters.

Why? Because Present Tense prose doesn't have access to Verb Forms with the techniques that allow a writer to manipulate **Order** and **Duration**. Remember, one of the advantages of Present Tense is it's easier to hold due to you being limited to just a few Verb Forms. Well, that limitation means you no longer have access to using English grammar in all its glory.

Sure, you can still create dynamic characters in Present Tense, it's just harder—I.E., more work for the writer. It also requires a skill level most aspiring writers lack.

Basically, with the limitations that Present Tense puts on the writer's ability to use different Verb Forms, it becomes harder to convey the Narrator's **Subjective Experience of Time**, which hinders your ability to create **Depth** and **Realism**. It also hinders your ability to **Complicate the Character**. In other words, the more the reader knows about a character's past, the more they can relate to their present. Without this dynamic ability to convey the complexity of how the past has shaped our characters, our characters can become relatively simplistic and generic.

"But wait," you say. "I can still use Past Tense in a Present Tense story! You even gave me an example!"

Sure, you can use Past Tense Verb Forms within a Present Tense story. But doing so leads to the second half of this huge disadvantage.

4) Backstory/Flash Backs/Past Events all become problems quickly in Present Tense because they can feel forced and unnatural, throwing a reader out of the story.

They also ruin the reason for using Present Tense in the first place. Every time you shift into Past Tense during a Present Tense story, you pull the reader out of the *Right Now*. Basically, if your story is going to need backstory information to be immersive for the reader, using Present Tense wasn't the right choice to begin with. Why not simply write in Past Tense and avoid this issue?

As always, it comes down to thinking about what type of story you're telling.

Time. Effort.

5) Present Tense severely hampers a writer's ability to use foreshadowing to increase suspense for the reader.

Because the Narrator is living in the *Right Now*, there's no real vehicle to give the reader the extra information that'll foreshadow events that may or may not happen in the future. For a simple action adventure story like *Hunger Games* or *Divergent*, this is not an issue. The suspense of "what will happen next" is enough to hold the reader's interest. But if you're writing a story that's not so simple, this can very easily become an issue that ruins a reader's potential enjoyment of what your story could have been had you written it in Past Tense.

6) The final big issue I see with writers who write in Present Tense is the tendency to include scenes that describe mundane actions, such as walking from one place to the next.

We talked about a version of this during our First Person discussion when I warned about "Falling too deeply into your Narrator".

This is the same, but different.

For whatever reason, be it the inexperience of the writer, or the way Present Tense baits the writer to convey every aspect of a character's life to keep the story "in the Right Now", stories written in Present Tense tend to have a ton of "Shoe Leather" scenes. In other words, scenes that do nothing to drive the plot.

Shoe Leather is a movie editing term that describes a superfluous shot where actors are walking somewhere, usually into or leaving a scene. For film, this is not horrible. Most Shoe Leather scenes take a fraction of a second of screen time, and audiences don't notice them much unless they drag on too long. (I won't comment on *Lord of the Rings* here. I won't!)

In prose, however, these types of "Shoe Leather" scenes put a huge strain on a reader's desire to continue reading. (Still not going to mention *Lord of the Rings*.)

Think about it like this: Shoe Leather scenes are scenes that fall between one scene that matters, and the next scene that matters.

Due to the nature of Present Tense wanting you to keep the story in the "Right Now", many aspiring writers include these boring and unneeded connecting scenes.

Case in point:

> Chapter One: Drake is sent a letter informing him that he has been hired to lecture at a university in Zimbabwe.
> Chapter Two: Drake goes shopping for new clothes for his trip.
> Chapter Three: Drake travels to Zimbabwe. During this trip he meets Sally, who will become his romantic interest for the story.

Chapter One has something that's important to the story—the Narrator gets something that starts the adventure. Chapter Three also has something that's important to the story—the Narrator's love interest is introduced. However, do the readers really need to go with Drake as he shops for new clothes?

Sure, we could have something happen during this shopping trip that affects the Plot of the story. But that's not what I'm talking about here. What I'm talking about is when a writer writes our fictitious Chapter Two in a manner that's nothing more than Drake shopping for new clothes! Nothing happens that affects the story outside of the fact that Drake needed new clothing.

And it's these types of worthless scenes I see in book after book that's written in Present Tense. Scenes where the character does nothing more than change clothes, eat a meal, watch some T.V., etc., but does nothing that's story related or moves the Plot.

These scenes are written because Present Tense straps the writer with telling the story in a very rigid chronological manner, making the writer feel they are missing something if they don't write every single mundane moment of our "in the Right Now" character's life.

Trust me, these scenes can and should be cut.

So yes, Present Tense can help a story, despite what old curmudgeons like myself say. But it can also ruin a story just the same.

Let's leave the *Right Now*, and head back into the *Before Now* by looking at...

PAST TENSE

As is my norm, I have the desire to start this Past Tense discussion with a history lesson. However, since I've already told you the oldest written piece of fiction ever found was the *Epic of Gilgamesh*, some 4,100 years ago, I'll instead do this:

> Drake stepped onto the stage, pulled the mic from its stand, and glared at the audience. "The *Epic of Gilgamesh* was written in Past Tense." He dropped the mic and walked away.

Yeah. Past Tense has been around a long time. More importantly, there are no scholars complaining that it's a "frequent cliché of technique".

As a Speculative Fiction writer, you must understand why Past Tense is your friend. Sure, Past Tense has both advantages and disadvantages, just like all aspects of Creative Writing. And I shall dive into them in a moment. However, before we get to that, I feel obligated to dispel the biggest myth that has been circulating the Internet over the past decade about why Present Tense is better than Past Tense.

Now, this is something I've harped on a few times already, but I want to put the nail in this coffin once and for all.

> Just because Present Tense has an immediacy feel to it, doesn't mean that Past Tense *can't* have an immediacy feel to it.

Yes, I've already shown you how Present Tense makes the reader feel like things are happening in the Right Now. But Past Tense can absolutely do the same thing.

Here's an excerpt from the epic fantasy saga I'm currently writing:

Without pause, Clytus slipped north into a narrow alleyway. As soon as the buildings blocked the men from his sight, he ran. Left, right, straight—he let chance and whim decide his course through the squalid side streets. All he cared was keeping to a westerly direction, knowing the safety of his villa was now his only hope.

After more than ten seasons traversing this city, Clytus could almost navigate it by instinct alone. That finely-tuned intuition kicked in as a flanged mace materialized from around a corner aimed at his face.

Throwing out a hand, he pushed off the building next to him, redirecting his momentum. The weapon whistled through the air, smacking the wall with enough force to splinter its unpainted wooden slats.

Pivoting, Clytus rotated to face his attacker. As he moved, his sword slipped free of its sheath with a whisper of metal on leather. A steel saber forged by the Essence during the War of Power, Dorochi stood a pace long. In addition to a finely etched guard and pommel, it held an edge so keen it had never needed sharpening. He had rarely found its equal.

Three men dressed in sailor's garb spread out from the alley, each holding a fléchette crossbow. The fourth, a burly man wielding the mace, hovered behind, a wicked grin painted across his thin lips. Grim-faced men all, their eyes left no doubt of their intent as they moved to cover all exits. The distinct sounds of someone failing to quietly stalk up behind informed Clytus he was surrounded.

Five to one, no less...

How did that feel? Just like you were watching the events as they happened, right? As if those events were happening in the Right Now?

I'll give your answer for you. "Yes, Drake! That's exactly what it felt like to me!"

Of course, it did.

Yet, that's written in Past Tense.

Again, this goes back to why I separate Tense from a Narrator's Level of Awareness. I refute the definition that Tense dictates whether the reader will feel like things are happening in the Right Now.

I believe that the Narrator's Level of Awareness *combined* with Tense creates this feeling for the reader.

In the above, even though it was written in Past Tense, it doesn't feel like the outcome of the events are decided. It feels more fluid, chaotic, that anything could happen next. This is because, as you read it you feel like the events are happening Right Now. Is Clytus going to escape these men? Or will they capture, wound, or even kill him?

And don't give me that bull crap about, "But since the story is in Past Tense, there's no way Clytus can die."

I think this is the stupidest argument concerning Present and Past Tense because to me, it's the exact opposite.

It amazes me how many people believe that writing in Present Tense will make the reader feel the Narrator might die, and writing in Past Tense will make the reader 100% sure the reader will survive.

To me, that's the difference between First and Third Person, and has nothing to do with the Tense.

In First Person, the Narrator can't die or the story will never finish.

In Second Person, the Narrator can't die because in a weird way, they are the reader.

In Third Person Omniscient, the Narrator can't die because they're not even in the story.

In Third Person Free Indirect Discourse, since there's a third-party Narrator telling the story who isn't in the story, and therefore can't die, you absolutely can kill off any Narrating Character you want willy-nilly. That third-party Narrator will continue to tell the tale.

In Third Person Limited, Character Narrators are islands, and the reader is consuming the story as a whole. So, killing off a Character Narrator simply ends that one Character Narrator's Plot Arc. As they say in theater, "The show must go on." The story will continue to be told by the other Character Narrators.

Meaning, since I'm one of those bastard writers who kills off my Character Narrators, as a reader of my work, you never know when I'm gonna do it again. Bwahahahahaha!

Now, that previous example is written in Third Person Limited, which only works if you write it with a Limited Narrator. So, this "Right Now" feeling is kept consistent throughout the entire story.

If I was to Shift into a third-party Narrator (and write this instead in Third Person Free Indirect Discourse), or simply hold to the third-party Narrator that is Third Person Omniscient, I'd break this "Right Now" feeling every time. Yet one more reason I hold myself to the strict structure that creates Third Person Limited.

Still, my point is made. If done correctly, both Present Tense and Past Tense can have the feeling of immediacy.

Without further ado, let's take a gander at some other advantages and disadvantages of writing your story in Past Tense.

1) For me, the biggest advantage of Past Tense *by far* is the fact that all Verb Forms are available to me. And because of this, I own Time's ass! I can move so seamlessly forward and backward through Time it'll make your head spin.

Let's return to the example I just used. Did you even notice that I shifted from the "Right Now" of this Past Tense story and into a point in time even further into the past?

Probably not. That's the beauty of Past Tense. Here it is again, so we can discuss it:

> Pivoting, Clytus rotated to face his attacker.
> As he moved, his sword slipped free of its sheath
> with a whisper of metal on leather. A steel saber
> forged by the Essence during the War of Power,

> Dorochi stood a pace long. In addition to a finely
> etched guard and pommel, it held an edge so keen
> it had never needed sharpening. He had rarely
> found its equal.

The first two lines are in the "Right Now" of this Past Tense story. However, the third sentence slips back 1,500 years into the past without even breaking stride.

> A steel saber forged by the Essence during the
> War of Power,

And then we snap back into the "Right Now" of this Past Tense story, only to BAM!

> it held an edge so keen it had never needed
> sharpening.

…slip back into the distant past once more.

Try *that* in Present Tense and your reader will be thrown so far out of the story they'll be there when the *Epic of Gilgamesh* is being chiseled on those clay tablets!

If that isn't power, I don't know what is. But that's the beauty of Past Tense. Since all Verb Forms are available to you, and the story is already holding a Past Tense Narrative, shifting in Time can be done without the reader even noticing it happening.

2) This control over Time that Past Tense has lends itself well with helping deliver a more complex story, and deeper, more interesting characters.

Now, this doesn't overcome the shortcomings that are inherent to certain Narrative types. In other words, Past Tense won't overcome the deficiencies of First Person when it comes to story complexity. However, I guarantee you, a Present Tense First Person story is *WAY MORE* limited than a Past Tense First Person story. So even with First Person, Past Tense will open a few doors that aren't available had you written your story in Present Tense.

However, Past Tense prose organically allows for the techniques to manipulate **Order** and **Duration** of events, as well as lets the writer show the Narrator's **Subjective Experience of Time**, enhancing that character's **Depth** and **Realism**.

All that's just a fancy way of saying Past Tense enhances a complex story and helps create relatable characters. But it's the truth.

Combine these bonuses to what Third Person already brings to the table, and you should understand why I was so adamant about Third Person being written in Past Tense.

Go a step further and give your story the Limited Character Narrators available with Free Indirect Discourse and you can see why this Past Tense Narrative makes stories like *Silence of the Lambs* so exciting to read.

Take this to the extreme, ditch that third-party Narrator and hold to the strict rules of Past Tense Third Person Limited, and you should see why this creates the most immersive Narrative available in Speculative Fiction today.

3) Another huge advantage is in the fact that writing in Past Tense is traditional.

This may sound like a stupid reason, but remember how I feel about my job. I write *for my readers*. And since most readers are very comfortable reading Past Tense, I know it'll take less time for them to fall into my story.

The faster someone falls into my story, the more likely they are to read the entire thing.

The only way for someone to read a second book of mine is to have finished reading the first.

See where this is going? I write in Past Tense because it helps me continue to write as a career.

Remember, I've talked to thousands of readers like myself, readers who refuse to read a book based solely on the fact that it's written in Present Tense. Never have I bumped into a reader who refused to read a book solely based off the fact that it was written in Past Tense.

This is a serious issue to me, because like with an actor, an author is only as good as their last book.

Unfortunately, like all things creative writing, Past Tense is not without its faults. Let's look at a few.

1) I would say a huge issue with Past Tense is the topic we're discussing here—Verb Forms. While being able to use all of them is amazingly liberating, it also means there's way more opportunities for a writer to screw them up.

As I've already stated, the number one thing aspiring writers mess up is not being able to hold their Narrative Tense. In Past Tense, you're going to use at least eight Verb Forms. You may end up using a dozen different ones to tell your story.

Lots of opportunities for a misstep.

2) But the biggest issue Past Tense has by far is in the fact that so many people fall into the trap of Telling, instead of Showing.

Past Tense is a sneaky beast. One that can destroy your story if you're not ever vigilant. And this all has to do with mindset.

When writing in Present Tense, the mindset of the writer is locked into the Right Now. Meaning, due to the structure of what you're writing, Present Tense will help you stay focused on the fact that you need to keep the reader grounded in the Right Now.

However, as Past Tense always has the feel of something that has already happened, the writer can get lazy, lulled into a false sense of complacency. And this will cause you to drift in your writing, Telling your story to the reader instead of Showing it to them.

It's why I stressed that you must write Third Person Limited exactly as you would First Person. It's the only way to make that style shine for the reader—you must keep it feeling as if it's in the Right Now.

And this will take you years to master.

Without further ado, let's stop dillydallying and dig into the heart of Narratives. As they are in numerical order, and I'm a lazy cuss, let's go through each starting with...

FIRST PERSON NARRATIVE

First Person Narrative has been around since the dawn of time, and this makes perfect sense. Every single human being on this planet capable of speech has told a story using First Person Narrative from the time they were about three years of age.

> I was sitting over there and Drake came and took my candy. And then he stuck his tongue out at me! That's why I bit his finger off.

In a First Person Narrative story, the Narrator is not only the Character telling the story, they're also the Character participating in the events of the story. These are stories that are told in a very personal way, as with one friend telling another, or as is done in a journal/diary, or even as a running commentary of thoughts.

The reader is not watching this story unfold in the same way they would if this was on a movie screen. On a movie screen the viewer (reader) can see all the characters, including the Narrator.

In First Person, the reader is watching this story unfold *literally* through the eyes of the Narrator. I call this the **Imaginary Camera**, and with First Person, it's as if the Narrator's eyes are the Imaginary Camera. Because of this, the reader sees, hears, feels, and understands everything through the Narrator's perceptions.

To tell the story, the Narrator uses first person Pronouns such as I, me, my, etc. In addition, the Narration (all the words that surround the dialogue) are extensions of the Narrator. This is the reason you shouldn't use **Inner Monologue** with First Person (dialogue that's said inside a Narrator's mind), because technically *all* the Narrative is Inner Monologue.

The reality with First Person is that when done correctly, this Narrative can do some amazing things that none of the others can. The biggest bonus is that First Person Narrative is very *Personal* to the Narrator. So, adding Inner Monologue feels redundant.

I look around the corner, but can't see the monster. Is it still there? Where did it come from? I have no idea. *But I'm not sticking around here to find out!* I thought to myself.

As you can see, all the Narration feels like Inner Monologue. And that is the beauty of First Person. There is absolutely no need to specify Inner Monologue.

Oh, and since I'm here, let me jump up on my soapbox for a moment. For the love of all that's holy, please stop writing the words, "thought/think *to myself*" or "thought/think *to himself/ herself*"! Anyone who thinks is *ALWAYS* doing it to *themselves*!!! The only alternative is to say the words out loud, and then it's no longer Inner Monologue. Stop! Just… stop!

Now, getting off my soapbox, let me take a moment to explain what I mean by keeping things **Personal to the Narrator**. Or, more accurately, what I *don't* mean.

You might think that because First Person Narrative is so personal to the Narrator it must be the most immersive Narrative for the reader. But you'd be wrong. That distinction belongs to Third Person Limited. I'll explain about Third Person Limited when I get there. As for First Person, it's a close second when it comes to immersion because the reader is always reading about "I" as in… the Narrator. It's never "you", the reader. And this fact alone drives a tiny mental wedge between the reader and the story.

Case in point:

Dylan sat next to me with a groan, looking like last night had been a rough one for him. I figured what happened to me could cheer him up, so I didn't even wait for him to say anything before I launched into my story.

"Dude! You will *not* believe the night I had last night. It was awesome! So, like, I was at this bar, right? And that's when *she* came in. Thin. Red-headed. Legs that went all the way to the ground. She was definitely good looking enough to be model, but it turns out... she's a pharmaceutical rep."

Dylan's mouth dropped open.

I smiled. "Yeah, better than model gorgeous. Pharmaceutical rep gorgeous."

Dylan's eyes got big, and his frown turned upside-down. We'd always daydreamed about one of us hooking up with a pharm rep so the other could be introduced to her friends. But seriously, how were two schmoes like us ever gonna get the chance to meet a woman like that? Better odds of meeting a unicorn!

"Somehow, I ended up next to her and we began talking. I was so intimidated by her, it never even crossed my mind to hit on her. We just talked. Really talked. At the end, she gave me her card." I held up the small business card, giving him enough time to read the front before I flipped it around. "With her personal phone number handwritten on the back!"

Sure, the reader is there with the Narrator and Dylan. The reader is also inside the Narrator's head. But still, the reader never *becomes* the Narrator.

Why? In my opinion, it has to do with the fact that we've also been consuming First Person narrative stories since we were about three. We've been preprogrammed to consume these stories about *someone else*. Sure, it's both a natural way of telling and receiving a story. But it's always a story that's happening to *someone else*—the Narrator. Due to this, there's a natural buffer between the reader and what's being read. Worse, that buffer is strengthened every single time the Narrator uses a pronoun that refers to themselves—I, me, my, etc.

Meaning, if the reason you chose to write in First Person was because you felt it was the most immersive for the reader, you've chosen poorly. Still, it's a *very* close second, so no harm no foul. Bonus, there are a ton of amazing reasons to write using First Person Narrative.

But before I get into them, let's look at how First Person utilizes what I discussed in the Narrator chapters, shall we? That's a rhetorical question, by the way. Even if your answer is "no", there's nothing you can do to change the fact that I'm going to do it anyway. So, let's start with who can be the...

NARRATORS IN FIRST PERSON

When it comes to First Person Narrative, your choice of a Narrator is wider than most think. Again, I can't stress enough how depressing it is knowing most aspiring writers don't even realize they have a choice in their Narrator.

Especially when it comes to First Person, most aspiring writers default to just one type of Narrator, "My hero is my Narrator". So depressing.

Because a choice you have. In fact, one could call the sheer volume of Narrators available to First Person Narrative a veritable smorgasbord.

Obviously, and the most common, is to use the Protagonist as the Narrator. *Hunger Games*. The reason this is so common is it's a wonderful way to viscerally connect the reader to the Protagonist. It means the reader is *literally* inside the Protagonist's mind, giving them unfettered access to what the Protagonist is thinking, their reasons and motivations for doing what they do, and everything about how they feel concerning the world around them.

But the choices are not limited to just the Protagonist. I've already talked about *The Great Gatsby*. Yes, it's written in First Person, but the Narrator isn't the Protagonist. Instead, that story uses a Peripheral Narrator—a Secondary Character who was there to witness the events of the story but who wasn't the Protagonist. And I've also talked about why this worked so well for that particular story.

The third most common is for the writer to take on the role of Narrator. But let's be honest here, most of the time that makes the writer the Protagonist, so this is the same as the above.

But the list doesn't stop there, my friend. Oh, no! In fact, every single Narrator type I listed as a Third-Party Narrator could be adjusted to be a First Person Narrator.

Your First Person story could be told by a unique third-party character who is *not* a character within the story itself—the elusive Storyteller Narrator. Yes, think about a First Person Past Tense story written by an Omniscient Narrator who wasn't in the story! You could conceal your Narrator as a Secret Character within the story. A Commentator, an Interviewer, etc. (If you've forgotten what all these are, or any of the others I have already gone through, flip back to the Narrator section and reread it.)

And while the choices of a Narrator for a First Person Narrative are vast, I can only gloss over these different types of Narrators at this point. Why? Mostly because there are so many I could never list them all in one book. But also because, for me to recommend which of these will to work for you and which will ruin your story, I would need to understand your unique story. Which I don't. Nor do I want to. That's all you, bub.

Be creative! Think about the story you want to tell, and then imagine what the differences would be for the reader by that story being told by the different types of Narrators that exist.

The defaults are wonderful, it's the reason they are so prevalent. However, you if you're clever enough, you may just figure out a way to make your story really shine.

The same can also be said about your…

First Person Narrator's Level of Awareness

As I've already stated, a First Person Narrator can have either an Omniscient or a Limited Level of Awareness. And again, this all depends on the type of story you're telling.

For the sake of laziness, I'll reiterate my previous examples. *700 Sundays* was told by an Omniscient First Person Narrator using Past Tense, while *Hunger Games* was told by a Limited First Person Narrator using Present Tense. Each of these Levels of Awareness went a long way to helping their respective stories become successful.

The fact of the matter is, First Person is a Limited Narrative Style, not due to how much knowledge the Narrator has about the story, but because the *Imaginary Camera* the reader is using to *see* the story is *inside* the Narrator's head. This *Limits* what the reader can *see*.

Due to this, having a Narrator with a Limited Level of Awareness is downright natural in First Person. Bonus, if you're writing any type of Speculative Fiction—Sci-fi, Fantasy, Mystery, Romance, True Crime, Western, etc.—odds are, having a First Person Narrator with a Limited Level of Awareness is probably the right thing for your story.

And if you're clever, you should be able to guess that having a Limited Narrator means you can use either Past or Present Tense to equal effect.

But you'll never know if you don't consider all these options, weighing them against the story you want to tell.

It's always about the *why*.

Think about your story. Then, go through the mental exercise of what that story would be like if told by a Limited Narrator—where both the reader and the Narrator only know up to the word the reader is currently reading, and no further. Then, consider how the story would be affected if you had an Omniscient Narrator who could give the reader information about how the events that are happening in the here and now of the story affected the future.

Remember my general rule of thumb:

Limited Narrators tend to help a more serious or action oriented story.

Omniscient Narrators tend to help a more light-hearted or humorous story.

Then do the same mental exercise with both Past and Present Tense. Time. Effort. In the end, you should get a Narrator who is perfect for the story you want to tell.

With the Narrator out of the way, let's dig into where the Narrator and reader are *Time Wise*, in relation to the story being told. This means looking at…

First Person Narrative Tense

As with all Narratives, First Person can be told using both Narrative Tenses—Past and Present. However, as with all the Narratives, there are both advantages and disadvantages to using either.

Now, I get there's a trend that has taken place over the past decade where it's becoming more and more common to write First Person in Present Tense. And I understand it. I really do. But I doubt you do.

Once again, allow me to pull out my proverbial soapbox, and rant about why I don't feel First Person Present Tense should be used as much as it is.

Most have come to the conclusion that writing First Person in Present Tense must add to the tension. As in, since it's being written as if it's happening *Right Now*, obviously this would make for more exciting read, right?

Not that I believe, no. This type of tension is *not* created by which Tense the story is written in, but by the Level of Awareness of the Narrator. The fact that the story is happening Right Now, or in the past is irrelevant to the tension the reader feels.

If you look back at the examples I used in the Tense section, you'll notice that the tension of each is built when the Narrator has a Limited Level of Awareness, regardless of the Tense used. Actually, don't look back. Those examples weren't designed to show how Tenses affect tension. Instead, let's look at a more relevant example to this topic, and then talk about a few things.

To begin, let's look at something written in First Person Present Tense.

> I love Dylan so much! How did I get so lucky as to find a man like him? Sure, he's physically gorgeous, all tan-skinned and muscular. But he's tender, caring, and a great listener as well. He really is the

complete package. Even my mother likes him, and she's never approved of any man I've ever dated.

Is this what happiness feels like? Before now, I couldn't have said. But here I am, standing in front of my dorm room door, and I can't wipe the stupid grin off my face. I know my roommate, Tim, is inside—I can hear him bustling about. He's been giving me fits about how I've rushed into this new relationship.

Is he right? Am I being silly? We've only dated for a few months.

No. I'm not. Dylan is perfect. He's the one.

I let the stupid smile sit where it is and fish my keys from my pocket.

Unlocking the door, I step inside and freeze.

Tim's bed is a pile of blankets and naked bodies. Two sets of eyes stare at me. I stare back.

One set of eyes belongs to Tim. The other, Dylan.

My heart snaps in half. How could he? He said I was the man of his dreams.

Dylan stands up, pulling a sheet around his nude body. "Drake, I—"

I hold up a hand. "Don't. Just… don't."

I return to the hall, gently closing the door as a numbness falls over me.

This is Present Tense, so it reads like it's happening Right Now. But is that where the tension comes from? No. The tension comes from the fact that the Narrator, Drake, is not expecting Dylan to be rubbing uglys with his roommate Tim. Drake is a Limited Narrator.

Now, one could argue that this is the nature of First Person Preset Tense. Sure, I showed you earlier that First Person Present Tense works best with a Limited Narrator. But that's not what we're discussing here. What I want you to discover is, is there any difference in the tension built between First Person Present, and First Person Past Tenses?

Let's look at the same piece as above, but in Past Tense and see if one feels stronger than the other.

I loved Dylan so much! How did I get so lucky as to find a man like him? Sure, he was physically gorgeous, all tan-skinned and muscular. But he was tender, caring, and a great listener as well. He really was the complete package. Even my mother liked him, and she had never approved of any man I'd ever dated.

Was this what happiness felt like? Before then, I couldn't have said. But there I was, standing in front of my dorm room door, and I couldn't wipe the stupid grin off my face. I knew my roommate, Tim, was inside—I could hear him bustling about. He'd been giving me fits about how I'd rushed into this new relationship.

Was he right? Was I being silly? We'd only dated for a few months.

No. I wasn't. Dylan was perfect. He was the one.

I let the stupid smile sit where it was and fished my keys from my pocket.

Unlocking the door, I stepped inside and froze.

Tim's bed was a pile of blankets and naked bodies. Two sets of eyes stared at me. I stared back.

One set of eyes belonged to Tim. The other, Dylan.

My heart snapped in half. How could he? He said I was the man of his dreams.

Dylan stood up, pulling a sheet around his nude body. "Drake, I—"

I held up a hand. "Don't. Just... don't."

I returned to the hall, gently closing the door as a numbness fell over me.

When it comes to the tension built, as you can see, there's very little difference between First Person Present and First Person Past Tense. In my opinion, neither builds more tension than the other.

The reason the tension in this scene exists is that the Narrator (Drake) has a Limited Level of Awareness. He has no idea Dylan is cheating on him, and only learns this detail when the reader does.

DRAMA!

The fact that either is written in Past or Present Tense does not help nor hurt this tension.

Worse, while the trend over the past decade has made First Person Present Tense more popular to writers and publishers, thanks to the success of books like *Hunger Games*, it's not necessarily the most popular with readers.

Personally, I hate it. And I'm not alone.

As I've traveled this world, another question I find myself asking when I'm in front of a large crowd talking about Narrative is, "Who in this room does not like reading First Person Present Tense?" You'd be surprised. It's always about 30%. 30% of all readers don't like reading First Person Present Tense. Why?

Well, for me, it's not a natural way to consume a story.

It all falls back to how I feel about a writer not breaking the reality they create. You see, when someone (a Narrator) tells me a First Person story, in my mind's eye that Narrator is standing right in front of me as they tell me their story. I'm the reader, and the Narrator is standing with me telling me their tale.

For First Person *Past Tense*, this is a natural exchange of information. The Narrator stands before me and tells me about things the Narrator saw or did in the past somewhere else. My mind can wrap itself around that. You're here with me telling me a story that happened to you somewhere in the past. Got it!

Bonus: as I have hopefully proven, you can still tell that story with a Limited Narrator, giving the reader the added tension of not knowing the future.

Switch that around to *Present Tense*, however, and you force me, the reader, into an uncomfortable situation. Because you're now the Narrator, standing before me *Right Now*, telling me about events you are doing and seeing *Right Now*, but somewhere else *Right Now*.

How can you be standing before me telling me about what you're doing simultaneously somewhere else? It makes my brain hurt!

Do you see why this would feel odd to some readers? Yeah, about 30% of them. Now, understand, I speak mainly in front of Sci-Fi/Fantasy fans. And First Person Present Tense isn't all that common in my genre… yet. Romance and YA are the predominant perpetrators of this perversion, to be sure. Still, it's creeping into other genres like an unchecked cancer.

Perhaps no amount of loathing on my part will break that fact. Or will it? Think of it like this:

Let's start with readers. I just told you that about 30% of all Sci-Fi/Fantasy readers don't like reading a book written in First Person Present Tense. I mean, if it wasn't for the fact that I teach this stuff, I never would've suffered through *Hunger Games* as a reader. Not that the story was bad—it was wonderful. Great plot, interesting world, realistic characters. It truly deserves to be a best seller. But I never would've read it as a reader due of the Tense it's written in. Unless compelled, I refuse to read a book written in First Person Present Tense. And about 30% of readers feel the same.

Is it smart for an aspiring author to write a book where up to 30% of their potential fanbase will refuse to read their book simply based on its Narrative Tense? It's incredibly hard to get readers. Can you, a new writer with limited fans, afford to alienate a swath of potential readers?

And for what? A Narrative Tense that, as I've shown you, might not even add any tension to the story?

Switching to the industry, they're the real deciders, right? I mean, you want to sell your book, and if the industry is publishing more and more First Person Present Tense stories, it's only logical for you to write in that Narrative Tense, correct? A way to increase your odds of getting published?

No.

You may think that because of the genre you're targeting, you *must* use First Person Present Tense, because that's what all the best-selling books of that genre use. And this might lead you to believe that the industry isn't going to purchase any books written in First Person Past Tense. But I assure you, you're wrong. And here's why.

The industry only cares about a few things. The number one thing is: is the story compelling? That pretty much trumps everything else. I mean, do you think *Fifty Shades of Gray* was published because of its grammatical value? Ha… hardly.

The reality is, how the book is written from a grammatical standpoint is a very distant second behind, "Is the story compelling?" You'd be surprised at what this industry defines as "well written." For the most part it means, "Does the writer know how to hold their Narrative while telling a compelling story?" And that's about it. If you can, at the very least, hold a cohesive Narrative, the industry will probably be satisfied, provided your story is compelling. Why? Two reasons. One, because the vast majority of the buying public are not grammar Nazis like me. Most readers can overlook poor writing provided the characters are interesting and the story is compelling. And two, the industry knows that. It's not the publishing industries job to publish perfectly written, grammatically correct books. It's their job to publish books readers are entertained by.

In addition, provided the Narrative is solid and tells a compelling story, pretty much everything else can be fixed in the editing stage. However, fixing Narrative issues or taking a story that's not entertaining and making it entertaining, are major overhauls, normally requiring a full rewrite. And that's something the industry is usually not willing to waste their time on. They have too many choices available.

The real reason the trend of First Person Present Tense has become so popular is because of the warning I started this book off with—aspiring writers don't realize they have a choice when it comes to Narrative. They write in the Narrative they read. And since everyone writing YA teen drama stories have read *Hunger Games*, they end up writing their YA teen drama in First Person

Present Tense without even considering why. More of this type of story is being written, meaning more is being shopped to the industry, resulting in more being purchased. Not for the reason of, "This story works best in this Narrative" but more in the "Since my favorite story is written in the Narrative, I'm gonna write my story in that same Narrative".

My hope and dream for you is that after reading this book, you won't be *that* type of writer.

Make your own decisions on how you'll write your book, and base those decisions on what you feel would be the best for your story.

When it comes to First Person *Present Tense*, there are some serious issues. Issues that are the reason I've only had one short story ever published that was written in First Person Present Tense. Why did I write it that way? Because it was the best Narrative Tense for *that* story!

All other First Person projects published of mine have used Past Tense.

To that end, let's look at the reasons I feel First Person Present Tense should be avoided in most stories.

I've already spoken about how it turns a percentage of readers off. But I do feel this is a very compelling reason in and of itself and bears repeating. Readers are hard to get. I never want to alienate a large percentage of them for something as silly as the Narrative Tense I chose.

I've also talked about the fact that I don't feel it adds to the tension of the story. Past or Present Tense, when done properly, are equal when it comes to building tension.

But let's look at some other negatives to First Person Present Tense.

To me, outside of those listed above, the number one reason to avoid writing a story in First Person Present Tense is how difficult it is to *maintain*.

Since it's not a natural way to tell a story, and since we've been telling First Person *Past Tense* stories since we were three, aspiring writers struggle to maintain Present Tense. It's ridiculous how frickin' easy it is to slip into Past Tense when you're writing Present Tense. Because of this, writing in First Person Present Tense has a much longer learning curve than the more natural First Person Past Tense. It also means more time spent in the editing stage trying to fix all those **Tense Shifts**.

Writing is hard. Why would you want to add to its difficulty by writing in a Tense that's difficult to maintain?

Another issue I have is more of a myth than a real issue. And that's when I hear, "Oh, I write in First Person Present Tense because I want my readers to always be concerned that the Narrator may die."

Really?

Really!?!

Do you know how hard it is to kill off a First Person Narrator and not lose the loyalty of your reader? There's a reason books of this ilk are so rare. Killing a First Person Narrator is damn near impossible to do in a way that's satisfying to a story. Because of this, there's not one single reader out there who ever concerns themselves over the fact that a First Person Narrator may die. I mean, the Narrator is telling the tale. If they die, how is the tale ever going to be finished?

No. When a reader is reading First Person, and the Narrator gets themselves into a deadly situation, not one reader is ever thinking, "I wonder if this Narrator is going to die?" Instead, they're thinking, "Oh, I wonder how this Narrator will get out of this situation."

Both are a type of tension, but they're a very different type of tension indeed. If you want a reader biting their nails over the possibility that your Narrator may die, stay away from First Person. Third Person is where you need to look for that type of tension.

And before you interrupt me again, yes, I get that a way to do this just popped into your head. Unfortunately, what you're thinking is *terrible*. Believe me, it'll cause your readers to hate you, swearing to *never* read anything you write again.

Instead, I'll hold my hand up and say, "Don't. Just… don't."

Still dying to interrupt me? Fine. The idea that popped into your head is one of the worst, most trite methods for attempting to continue a story after killing off a First Person Narrator, because switching to a new Narrator doesn't work.

Why?

It breaks the reality you've worked so hard to create for the story. You created a reality where there was this First Person Narrator telling the reader a tale. You have spent tons of time and effort making sure the reader is viscerally connected to this Narrator. Then you kill off this Narrator, and now there's a *new* Narrator who has stepped in to finish the tale? Where the hell did this new Narrator come from? How did they even know I was listening to this tale? And why are they now talking to me? I don't care about them. I cared about the other guy, you know, the one killed. Why should I try and get invested in this one? Whose to say you won't just kill him also?

No. Switching to a new Narrator will leave the reader in an awkward situation, one in which they no longer have a connection to the Narrator. Not good.

It can be done. And has been done. But it's incredibly difficult to pull off. If you're an aspiring writer, it's a good rule of thumb to leave the master-level stuff for when you've actually, you know, become a master of your craft.

One-million words, time and effort, all that.

Another myth about First Person Present Tense I hate is when I hear someone say, "Well, I wanted the reader and the Narrator to learn things at the same time, so that's why I used First Person Present Tense."

I would give you half-credit for that answer if I hadn't already explained to you that the Tense the story is being told in has nothing to do with the Narrator's Level of Awareness. There's absolutely no doubt that having a Limited Narrator in Speculative Fiction is awesome for building tension. But since I've already shown you that you can have a Limited Narrator in either Past or Present Tense, I won't.

Instead, I award you no points for your answer, and may God have mercy on your soul.

In conclusion, when it comes to the Narrative Tense you choose to write your First Person in, as with all aspects of story creation, think things through. For all that's holy, don't blindly follow me. Sure, I obviously have strong opinions *against* First Person Present Tense. Then again, I also have a story published in First Person Present Tense. So, I guess that makes me a hypocrite.

What you need to do is *think about it*. Weigh your options, because options are what you have. Write some test chapters using both Narrative Tenses with both Levels of Awareness. Get your writers group to read both. Discuss which works better and why.

Do your homework! Time. Effort.

Full disclosure, that story I wrote in First Person Present Tense was not originally written in that Narrative. I first wrote it in Third Person Limited Past Tense but didn't feel that Narrative worked for the story. Then I rewrote it in First Person Past Tense, but again found it a bit lacking. And finally, I re-rewrote it in First Person Present Tense, which I liked the best and felt did the story the most justice.

If you're still determined to write in First Person Present Tense, my biggest piece of advice would be to study the crap out of *Hunger Games*. Suzanne Collins couldn't have done a better job at holding her Present Tense Narrative. Truly, it's one of the best examples of First Person Present Tense you can study.

While I may have been very negative in regards to using Present Tense while in First Person, it does have its advantages as well. Unfortunately for you, you'll have to wait till the end of the book when I discuss Present Tense in detail as it relates to all Narrative types. Or… hell… don't wait and just skip on down there now. It's just a book after all, and we aren't actually sitting together talking.

Now that I have the basics out of the way, let's get personal with this very personal Narrative by looking at some…

ADVANTAGES AND DISADVANTAGES OF FIRST PERSON

Each Narrative comes with its own unique list of advantages and disadvantages. You, the writer, need to consider everything, weighing them against the story you plan to write, and decide for yourself if the advantages outweigh the disadvantages. And you need to do this with every story you create individually, because each story is unique.

To do otherwise, would be downright silly.

Let's dig into the reason why First Person is both an awesome Narrative, and one that could literally destroy the story you want to tell.

I've already touched upon this, but First Person is the…

MOST NATURAL WAY TO TELL A STORY

And by this, I'm talking First Person Past Tense.

But it's the truth.

You've been telling stories in First Person your entire life. Unless you're the Rock back when he was a professional wrestler, every time you've opened your mouth and told someone about something you've done or seen, you've done so using First Person… past tense.

This is great news for the aspiring writer, as it means your learning curve is pretty shallow. Write the way you would normally talk, for the most part, right? Not really. It's way more complicated than that, as you'll soon see. But that's the basics of it, yes.

The reality is, because First Person is the most natural way to tell a story, this is both a blessing and a curse for the aspiring writer.

It's true that of all the Narratives, First Person absolutely *feels* the simplest and most natural.

But that's also its danger. Because of how it *feels*, many aspiring writers never take the time to learn how to use it effectively. Something I guarantee, you won't have an issue with once you finish this book.

It also causes another issue, though admittedly, one that's not such a concern in today's publishing industry.

Because First Person is the default way of telling a story, in the past, the publishing industry considered it a red flag. Basically, whenever they were presented with a story written in First Person, they would question whether the writer *chose* this particular Narrative, or defaulted to it. As most new writers defaulted to it, it was a sign of an immature writer.

Since in today's publishing world, the vast majority of aspiring writers are untrained, this issue has become more of a moot point. Well, in reality, it's simply being ignored. Now the publishing industry considers *all* new writers as immature, untrained, and unskilled writers. For the most part, they're correct. Which is a shame for those of us who have spent years studying the craft of grammar, or who attended college and got their MFA degree in creative writing.

But this is the world we live in, so deal with it.

Now, I'm not saying don't get that degree. You MUST get this knowledge from somewhere, and college is a wonderful place to gain the skills you'll need. I'm simply saying that in today's publishing world, the vast majority of people trying to break in are people who never considered writing as a career in the earlier part of their lives. They went to college (or didn't) but for other purposes. They then dove into life; marriage, kids, house, career, etc., and only after all this did they think to themselves, "Hey! I can speak English. I should be a New York Times Best Selling Author!"

These are the aspiring writers who never realize they have a choice in all the things we've already discussed because they have no knowledge to base those choices upon.

Getting back to First Person, the naturality of it lends itself well to the fact that writing in First Person means it's…

EASY TO STAY IN THE NARRATOR'S HEAD

Keep in mind, First Person is a **Limited Perspective** Narrative. As with most things, this could be either a bonus or a drawback. Now, please don't confuse this term with a Limited Narrator, as that is the Narrator's Level of Awareness. This is completely different.

The *Perspective* has to do with where the **Imaginary Camera** sits that's used to show the reader what's being seen. For First Person, it's *incredibly* easy to understand.

The Imaginary Camera *is* the Narrator's eyeballs.

That's it. Seriously.

The exercise I make my students do is this: take your thumb and pointer fingers and make a pair of glasses out of them. Hold those up to your eyes. Whatever you can see through your finger-glasses, you can write. If you can't see it, you can't write it.

Easy peasy pumpkin squeezy.

What this means is that if your camera leaves the room (the Narrator's eyeballs), then whatever happens in that room after they've gone is unknown to both Narrator and the reader. Period.

Why is this a bonus? As the writer, to hold your First Person Narrative, you simply need to ensure you never write anything outside of what your Narrator is personally going through.

This means you can only describe what the Narrator sees, experiences, and thinks. It's that simple. All the Narration must come directly out of the mind and body of your Narrator.

Because of this, it becomes very easy to build consistency within your Narrative. For anytime you write anything that's outside of the Narrator's mind or body, you know you've broken your First Person Narrative.

Once you've learn to stay within the limitations of this narrative, you've learned how to hold First Person.

Why is this a negative? Because First Person is a Limited Perspective Narrative. Meaning, when your camera leaves the room (the Narrator's eyeballs), then whatever happens in that room after they're gone is unknown to both the Narrator and the reader. Period.

This could put you into a sticky situation if the telling of your tale requires the reader to know what happens in that room after the Narrator has left.

What to do? What to do?

To overcome this limitation, a lot of aspiring writers use one of two very horrid solutions that destroy the integrity of First Person.

They either use the extremely trite and cliché:

> After leaving the room, I huddled next to the open window to hear what was being said about me. And this is what I heard...

Don't do this.

The second way used to fix this, and the absolute worse way, is to create a scene (or Head Hop) into a different character who is still in the room, using this new character as the Narrator for a moment—long enough to give the reader whatever information the writer deems so vitally important they needed to break the reality of their story.

This is an unforgivable solution, for so many reasons. Reasons I'll get into when I discuss using multiple First Person Narrators later. For now, I'll say, "Don't. Just... don't."

So, what do I recommend you do when you find there is information you want to give to the reader, but the scene you feel you can give this information is one in which your Narrator is not in? Simple. Be creative. That's kind of the reason a writer exists. Stories don't write themselves. Figure out a clever way that'll allow your Narrator, and by extension, your reader, to learn the information that was given when the Narrator was not around.

Yeah, it's hard. It's part of being a writer.

Speaking of **Head Hopping,** First Person is meant for stories with *one Narrator*. You should never leave the head of your Narrator when using First Person narration.

Ever.

Yes, right now you're hopping mad, with spittle flying from your lips as you curse my very name. Fine. But I get the last laugh because I'm going to make you wait to learn the reasons I feel First Person should be held to one Narrator. That topic doesn't fit in the flow of my thoughts just yet.

For now, just buy into the fact that the power of First Person lies in its ability to build a bond between the reader and the Narrator. Slipping into a second First Person Narrator during the story breaks the bond you've worked so hard to create. Again, "Don't. Just… don't."

If your story is going to require multiple Narrators, that's the domain of Third Person. But I'm not ready to talk Third Person yet, so let's continue to see why having a Limited Perspective Narrator helps First Person so much by discussing how it…

CONVEYS THE NARRATOR'S FEELINGS AND EMOTIONS

Because the reader is forever inside the Narrator's head, it means the reader should be able to understand and experience the feelings and emotions of the Narrator. Everything. And this is wonderful, because the reader should *literally* be wallowing in *why* the Narrator feels the way they do about things. Here's an excerpt from something I'm currently writing (yes, some of my actual writing, and not just some horrid example I puked up on the fly):

> It was chilly, even though it was August, and the street was deserted, even though it was about three in the afternoon. Across the road from me sat Café Jax—an ancient rust-colored brick building with a stained red and white stripped awning and an eerie wooden statue sitting beside its front door. What the hell was that thing even supposed to be? An Indian? An old white man? A child molester? I really had no idea.
>
> Still, the windows promised "Old Fashioned Shakes & Malts" as well as "Awesome Burgers &

Fries", and since I hadn't eaten a thing since early that morning, they had my full attention.

Out of habit more than need, I looked both ways down the empty street before crossing to the café.

Inside, red-leather-topped stools sat in a neat row before a counter filled with all the knickknacks one needs when eating burgers and shakes. Matching booths lined the walls under the windows, with free-standing tables filling the space between. It had that homey, nineteen-fifties retro look, though I doubted it was retro at all. More like, this was what the place looked like when it was built in the nineteen-fifties, and it hadn't changed by a hair since.

Lucky for me, the windows hadn't lied—the food was pretty good. Though the cute boy who served me was better. About my age, he had tussled brown hair, matching warm brown eyes, and that strong thin body reserved to young men on the cusp of manhood. Perhaps a year or two too young for me, but I was only looking for some eye candy.

As shy as he was cute, it was all I could do to get him to talk. Not that I'm Ms. Outgoing or anything. But it'd been a long trip, and I was hungry for both food and a little conversation from someone born within the same decade as me.

"You lived here long?" I asked when he brought out my food.

In case you didn't pick up on it, this is written in First Person Past Tense, with a Limited Narrator. Meaning, the reader and the Narrator both learn things at the same time.

Notice in this example, much of narrative has some emotional value attached to it so that the reader can understand why the Narrator feels the way she does. *She* is the one experiencing the world of the story, so everything that's given to the reader is given from *her* perspective.

It's chilly. But she feels it shouldn't be, because it's August. So, either it's unseasonably cold, or she's in a place that's unfamiliar to her. (Hint, it's the latter. Sorry, you missed several pages before this excerpt. She is newly arrived in a land that's unfamiliar to her.) The street is deserted, something she also finds odd. There's a weird statue she can't identify, and it creeps her out. It may not creep others out, but that's not her concern. She's the Narrator, so she only tells it from her perspective. And the statue creeps *her* out.

I could go on, and you should. Go through the above and look at the Narration. See how everything described is filtered through the Narrator's perception. How I tried to make sure the reader could feel what the Narrator was feeling. You missed all the setup, but all you need to know is that the Narrator is a nineteen-year-old girl who was invited to a mysterious college far from home. She's just arrived at the small town where this college is located. If you look closely at how the descriptions of the world are written, you'll start to get a good sense of who this Narrator is and how she feels about the things she interacts with.

That's the power of First Person. Every single piece of Narration should be filtered through the perception of the Narrator. Not the writer! *I'm* not a nineteen-year-old girl. I just happen to be the schmuck penning the words of *her* story. *She* is the Narrator. The world of the story is filtered through *her* perception, not mine.

This ability to convey the feelings and emotions of the Narrator is also the reason why First Person is so great at…

CREATING A STRONG BOND WITH THE NARRATOR

Which is wonderful! And exactly what we want in Speculative Fiction—to immerse the reader into the story the Narrator is telling.

Because the reader is always inside the Narrator's head, and understands their emotions and feelings, it's natural for the reader to develop feelings of their own for the Narrator.

If your reader never cares about the Narrator, they'll never care about the story. The only exception to this could be with a Narrator who isn't the Protagonist. But, even there, not caring about the Narrator makes it harder to get the reader to buy into the story.

In keeping all the Narration filtered through the perception of the Narrator, you force the reader to see the world as the Narrator does. If you do your job as the writer, and create a living breathing character (Narrator) for the reader to relate to, then the reader will fall into that role and become even more immersed in the story.

Looking back to my example, the reader should see the Narrator's age coming through with how she describes the world around her. The reader should also be able to empathize with her loneliness, and understand her desire to strike up a conversation with the young waiter.

If I continue to build this bond, the reader will continue to care more and more about the Narrator. And if the reader continues to care about the Narrator, they'll totally buy into the Narrator's plight, and hope this Narrator overcomes whatever the conflict of the story turns out to be.

It really is that simple.

And speaking of simple, doing the above consistently through the story will also…

BUILD EMPATHY IN THE READER FOR THE CHARACTER

Seriously, without even adding anything beyond doing a good job of writing a First Person story through the filter of your Narrator's perception, you are *not only* making it easy to stay consistent and hold your Narrative, as well as ensuring you *are* conveying your Narrator's feelings and emotions, *AND building* a strong familiarity bond between the reader and the Narrator, you *are also* building the reader's empathy for *why* your Narrator does what they do.

Why is that important?

Well, instead of answering that, let me ask you a question. After this book is finished, I'm gonna pour gasoline on a person while they sleep and set them on fire.

What I want to know is, will you help me?

I know, I know… murder is *baaaaad*. Right. I get that. And burning someone alive is probably a horrible way to murder someone. So what? I'm going to do it anyway. And I want to know, are you going to help me, or not?

Hopefully your answer is that you would not help me. If you would, please, don't let me know. In fact, I hope you and I never meet.

The reason your answer should be "no" (outside the fact that murder is wrong) is there's no empathy between you and my desire to burn someone alive.

However, take a story like *The Burning Bed*. In that story, we meet the Narrator, a kind and caring woman who married a total asshat—a man who beats her on a regular basis. As the story progresses, his abuse of her intensifies to an unbearable level. Lucky us, we get to experience all that abuse along with this poor Narrator. We, the reader, live through every painful detail.

Because of this, we, the reader, grow attached to this woman. We… *care* about her. And this builds our empathy for her and her situation.

Meaning, while the average person should be repulsed at the thought of murdering someone by burning them alive, once the reader has lived through what this Narrator has lived through, that repulsion disappears, being replaced by empathy. In fact, by the end of this story you're hoping she'll do just what she does. In more fact, by the end, you realize you have a can of gas in your garage that you'd be willing to bring over and donate to the cause. You'd *help* this woman murder another human being by burning said human being alive!

You should be ashamed of yourself.

Building this level of empathy between your reader and your Narrator should be the number one concern of the writer. It's vital to the story's success. And First Person, when done properly, does that almost automatically because the reader is always inside the Narrator's head. Always seeing the world through the filter of the Narrator's perception. Always being force fed how the Narrator feels about the world around them.

It is a powerful tool wrapped inside the burrito of how we've been telling stories since we were children.

Nice. (First Person, that is. Not my last analogy… that was terrible. Burrito… what was I thinking?)

Speaking of powerful tools, one of the things having a Limited Narrative inside First Person gives you is the ability to have an…

UNRELIABLE NARRATOR

An Unreliable Narrator is a Narrator who *thinks* they are telling the truth, but in reality, they could be very, very wrong. Why is this so wonderful? One word—*DRAMA!*

Remember my very brief love affair with that heartbreaker, *Dylan*? In that example, the Protagonist, Drake, was also the Narrator with a Limited Level of Awareness. But Drake was also an Unreliable Narrator. (Surprise, I know!)

The beauty in an Unreliable Narrator is that readers tend to believe what the Narrator tells them. So, if your Narrator paints a certain type of picture, the reader will normally go along with it. That way, when you get to the **Turn** in the scene, the reader will be as shocked by this new information as the Narrator. *Drama!*

In my example, when Drake walks in on Tim and Dylan, that's the Turn in that scene. Every scene should have a Turn. [Plug *Dynamic Story Creation in Plain English* here] ☺

And before you get all, "But I saw that coming!" Of course you did. It was an incredibly short example, one I made up on the fly that's a pretend snippet of a story with no actual setup whatsoever. It was a simple example to help make my point, not a great example of covertly covering the reality of a situation. If I was actually writing that as a story, I'd spend a bit more time, perhaps even a few chapters, making sure the reader was totally hooked by how awesome Dylan was. He would be the perfect boyfriend for Drake, catering to his every need. Never would I even hint that Dylan was a backstabbing traitor. That way the **Reveal** of the affair would be more shocking to the reader. *Drama!*

But that's the beauty that having an Unreliable Narrator brings to a story—the ability to lie to the reader. If done well, you'll be able to spring things on your reader they never see coming. Just remember there are *rules* to Turns, and if you cheat, readers will feel cheated and stop reading your stuff.

Meaning, for this to work you can only have an Unreliable Narrator if your Narrator has a Limited Level of Awareness. If done well, it not only enhances the drama, it does so without breaking the reality you create for your story.

Why only a Limited Narrator? It comes down to immersion for the reader.

You see, one of the things you need to be ever vigilant about as a story creator is to never break your own created reality. And this doesn't simply hold true with the physics of the world you create, but with your Narrative, as well.

With a Limited Narrator, you create a reality where the reader and the Narrator are leaning things at the same time. So, when the Narrator "lies" to your reader, the reader is cool with it, because they know it's not really a lie. The Narrator didn't know either, so they're held harmless. The reader and the Narrator have become cohorts in crime as they traverse the story.

Due to this, looking back at my example, the reader can't get mad at Drake for not telling them that Dylan was a piece of crap, because (at least in the reader's mind) the reader and Drake both learned that detail at the same time. Another bonus, it continues to strengthen the empathy bond between the reader and Drake since they both just went through the tragic event together. (Starting to see how effectively utilizing First Person can work to make your story shine?)

On the flip side, if you use an Omniscient Narrator, then you create a reality where the Narrator has all the facts. This means the reader can totally trust everything the Narrator says. If you break that, by doing something similar to my example above, you hurt the reality you've built for the story, and pull the reader out of the reality you've created.

Meaning, if the above example was being told by an Omniscient Narrator (Drake) who knows the future (something the reader is fully aware of), that would change how the reader sees the Narrator (Drake). It would mean Drake's word would be gospel to the reader. If, in that example, the Narrator (Drake) then lies to the reader, the reader would get pissed at Drake, thinking things like, "Why didn't you tell me Dylan was a snot? This already happened to you, dammit! You should've warned me!"

The last thing we want to do is drive any type of wedge between our reader and our Narrator.

And this should go without saying, though I've never been a man who could keep my mouth shut. An Unreliable Narrator can be done using Past or Present Tense.

The beautiful thing is, when you start to understand First Person, you start to realize how easy it is, and how important it is, to stay…

CONSISTENT WITH STYLE AND TONE

Let's face it, since First Person is being told from inside your Narrator's head, once you learn your **Narrator's Voice**, you've pretty much mastered how to keep things consistent in regards to Style and Tone.

I've discussed that all First Person Narration is an extension of the Narrator, so there's no need to use Inner Monologue with First Person.

But let's take this a step further and look at how that helps us remain consistent with our Style and Tone, and what this does for the reader.

The reader can learn much about the Narrator without ever being told one thing about them, just by developing your Narrator's Voice.

Let's take a look at a small excerpt from one of the craziest things I've ever had published. It was a piece I wrote for Sony's *EverQuest Next*, and it's the only piece I've ever had published that's written in First Person Present Tense. I'm not going to lie, this might be a tough thing for you to read. But I think it'll be a great example for us to talk about Tone and Style, so please, read it.

Here's the first two pages of this short story:

"I is smart and I is brave."

Not like the others. Look at them gathered 'round me. Crammed into this cabin. All my people who lives in this mining camp. They is all listening to me. Waiting to hear what I says next. Waiting to hear what the big snake with wings did tell me. They is stupid. Scared. I hates them. I hates them all.

But I loves them too. They is my people.

And they loves me. Cause I was chosen. Chosen over all others. Chosen cause I stayed. When the others ran. Hid. I stayed. I was not scared. I is brave.

I glare at those closest. "When the big snake with wings came out of the dark dark, I stayed while you ran. I stayed and I listened. I listened to the big snake with wings. He was hard to understand cause he no talked good. He hissed. But I stayed and I understood."

My people gasp. They is still afraid. Not brave like me. They ran when the big snake with wings came to us in the mine. Came to us in the dark dark. But I stayed. They is all gathered round me now. They listens to me. I feels good. I likes it that they all look at me. I feels like I is now the big snake with wings.

"He spoke to me in his whisper voice. 'Brave one. The dragonsss are calling their children home.' The big snake with wings says."

He called me brave. I likes that.

"'The dragonsss call upon you.' The big snake with wings got real close. I saw the red death in his eyes. His breath smelled of flesh. I wasn't scared. He leaned in close and asked, 'What are you called, brave one?'"

"He wanted to know my name. I wasn't scared.

'Glave,' I tells him. 'I is Glave,'"

The others whisper my name. It makes me feel good. I likes hearing them say it. I listens as everyone in the cabin whispers my name. All the others. The entire camp, crammed into this one room. They says my name again.

"The big snake with wings looked at me for a long time. 'Glave.' He says my name as if tasting it. 'That isss a ssstrong name.' Then the big snake with wings rose up tall. He asked me, 'Are you ssstrong, Glave? Can you be a leader?'

He liked my name. I likes that.

"'I is strong,' I says. 'And I is brave.' I liked the big snake with wings. You all ran. But I liked him."

I said it was crazy.

Now, before you start yammering on about how many of my own rules I broke in this, yes, I know. Every one was broken on purpose, I assure you. And all of them were broken because they enhanced the story for the "targeted" reader. Meaning, this was written for a *very specific* project, for a *very specific* type of reader—players of the Sony *EverQuest* franchise. I can't stress enough how important it is for a writer to understand their targeted reader. Still, the above may have made your eyes bleed, but that's not why I used it. Well… ☺

No. I gave you this example because I want to talk about Style and Tone. And there's no denying that this piece has a very distinct Style and Tone.

Ignoring all the grammatical issues with the above, without me ever describing anything about the Narrator, just the fact that I stayed consistent with my Tone and Style gives the reader a ton of information about who this Narrator person is.

You can tell the Narrator doesn't have a good grasp of language, that this character is probably uneducated, possibly even a slave, that before this event happened, they probably had a low opinion of themselves, that they are probably not human, and probably not a very large creature.

Funny thing is, none of those details are ever mentioned in the above example.

Through nothing more than the consistent Tone and Style I created for this little guy, I gave tons of information to the reader without spelling these things out. This does a lot for a story. It means the reader is getting details organically, without me info dumping all over them.

Sure, I could've started this story more traditionally. I could've described the mining camp, the guards, what these little creatures look like, how intelligent they are, etc. But why? None of those details enhance the story I'm telling. In fact, those details would overburden it with unnecessary data.

By creating the Tone and Style I did for this Narrator's Voice, I used that Tone and Style to convey lots of things to the reader without wasting words.

"But it's hard to read!" you whine.

Gaa! You and your interruptions.

Stop being a baby. Yes, it's a bit hard to read. And I did spend some brain cells on that, attempting to mitigate the negative effects of how it was written. One major factor that helped me decide to do it this way was the fact that this story is only 3,051 words from start to finish. Meaning, readers of this piece don't have to suffer long. But I went further than that. I scrutinized every word, especially those used incorrectly, with the eye of trying to lessen the pain of reading this.

This is a sidetrack, and I'll keep it brief, but if you're writing Sci-Fi or Fantasy, a great point to always keep top of mind is your **Fantasy Speak**. Fantasy Speak is the industry term for all your made-up words. It also includes when you "write" incorrect speech, such as "I is smart." While this stuff is easy to listen to, it can be very annoying to read. So, whenever you use it, spend at least four-times longer scrutinizing it as you would any other word. Really test it out, and ask anyone who reads your work direct questions about it, and how it affected their read. It's not enough to use unique words, they must not make your reader's eyes bleed. If they do, it hurts the story instead of enhancing it.

We now return to our regularly scheduled topic.

Your Narrator's Voice is vital and can convey tons of information to your reader. Spend time developing it in all Narrative styles, but especially within First Person. The Style and Tone you choose can greatly enhance not only the reader's enjoyment, but their understanding of who the Narrator is.

Okay. I just threw a bunch of stuff at you. Let's take a break and give your mind a chance to wrap itself around all these theories by…

PUTTING THIS ALL TOGETHER

The beautiful thing about well executed First Person Narrative is that once you learn it, it is a simplistic Narrative to hold. Because you're always inside your Narrator's head, provided you remember to never leave your Narrator's head, you'll never have to worry with POV Shifting or breaking your Narrative. Always being inside your Narrator's head also makes it very easy for you to convey the Narrator's Feelings and Emotions. Conveying these to the reader builds a strong bond between the Narrator and the reader, which kind of automatically builds empathy in the reader for *why* the Narrator does what they do. And because of all that, if you have a Narrator with a Limited Level of Awareness, you'll have ample opportunity to take advantage of what having an Unreliable Narrator can bring to the story.

Wrap all this inside a consistent Style and Tone for your Narrator's Voice, and you have everything you need to deliver your story to a reader in a wonderfully immersive manner. All you need to add is your talent and skill as a storyteller, and you stand a good chance of writing a story worth reading.

All of this lays an amazingly strong foundation to build your story upon. Hopefully that ties all of the above together so you can better see how they all relate to each other. But there are a few other advantages First Person has that you should keep in mind, starting with…

First Person Narration Can Be Less Formal

This may not sound like an advantage, but I assure you, it is. Because the Narrating "Character" is telling the story and not you, the Narration must be both an extension and a reflection of that Narrator.

This means you can keep the Narration at whatever level your Narrator is at. If they are intelligent, keep it intelligent. If they are simple minded, keep it simple. If they are a child, keep it at a child level. If they are an angry person, keep it angry.

You get my point.

Keep in mind, it's your Narrator telling the story, not *you*! That means keeping all the Narration consistent with your Narrator's Voice. Their Tone and Style.

Look back at my previous example and you can see how I stayed consistent with that Narrator's Tone and Style. Sure, the short, repetitive sentences may have been something that some readers found annoying to read. But it gave that little guy a *feel* to how he thought and spoke. It showed the reader how that little guy saw the world around him. The short, choppy sentences, the repetitive way his mind ran in circles, it all gave a nervousness to the read, making the reader understand more of this Narrator than I ever could have written in the story itself.

Here's another example from another one of my short stories:

> Once all was in readiness, Mr. Erpressung gathered the staff together in the main hallway to address us. "You all know what part you play in this, and what your duties are for this evening's…" He laughed, though it held little mirth. "…entertainment. Is everything in order?"
>
> I opened my mouth to respond but the bitch of a cook spoke over me. "Ja, Herr Erpressung." I glared at the obese woman, wondering which was thicker, her German accent or her fat ass.

Just through the Style and Tone of this Narrator's Voice the reader can see that he's intelligent. But they also glean a few other key pieces of information such as he's an angry, hateful individual.

My point here is to notice that since this Narrator is intelligent, the Narration is more formal, especially when compared to my previous example.

Let's look at one last example from one more of my shorts.

"I remember the night they came and took my father." I looked down into my grandson's eyes, excitement battling fear in his brown irises. I hated telling this story to him. The story of my past. My life. The story of our race. Of our fight to survive. But this story had to be told to the next generation, lest history repeat itself.

"Soldiers came banging on our front door." The last rays of sunlight were filtering through the window. Dusk was approaching. "It was about this time when they knocked. My family and I had just finished dinner. My mother and younger sister were busy clearing the table, washing the dishes. My father, grandfather, and I were sitting around the fire, much like you and I are now." I glanced around the room, and it struck me how similar this house looked to the home in which I grew up. Not surprising, considering how important tradition is to our race.

The living room where we sat was small, but comfortable—with a warm and welcoming fire blazed in the hearth. This living area spilled into an open dining room, which in turn flowed into the small but useable kitchen. My son's wife and their daughter were both busy in there, cleaning up after the final meal of the day. My son and his oldest boy were out back, playing some sport or another.

This piece sits between the two examples we've looked at here. The old grandfather who is the Narrator in this is not stupid, but I wouldn't call him overly educated, either. He's definitely not angry. More melancholy, as he tells his grandson the tale of his past. And I show this in how he sees the world around him.

That's the point of First Person—telling a story through the Perception of your Narrator. So, create your Narrator's Voice with care, and then work to not only keep it consistent, but to use it as a method of delivering unwritten information to your reader.

The last advantage I'd like to discuss is a double-edged blade, and that is the fact that First Person is wonderful at…

HIDING INFORMATION DUMPS

I've used the term **Information Dumps** a few times now without defining it. Let me correct that.

An Information Dump is an industry term meaning, "A long paragraph or series of paragraphs that give the reader tedious or dull information through the voice of a Narrator."

The issue is, there's no way to tell a story without "giving the reader tedious or dull information". I mean, you must describe the room the Narrator is in. It's the only way the reader can "see" where they are. And describing a room is, by default, "tedious and dull".

Whether an info-dump is bad or not will depend on the writer's skill. During times when you must give the reader tedious or dull information, you must work hard to give them this information in a way which doesn't feel tedious or dull to the reader.

One of the biggest advantages with First Person is that all the Narration is an extension of the Narrator. Because of this, everything feels more like it's dialogue than Narration. (Again, the reason why using Inner Monologue within First Person is redundant.)

This is wonderful for hiding the fact that there are things you must write in order for the reader to "see" the world around your Narrator.

Let's take a look at the opening of yet one more of my shorts so I can discuss this.

> Carnage lay everywhere I looked.
> The main structure, a pile of rubble that used to be an office building, had caved in after its front wall had been blown away. The buildings on either side had partially collapsed as well, leaving a pile of bodies, or pieces thereof, entwined in broken glass, shattered bricks, twisted steel, and destroyed furniture. The smell of burning flesh, so near the aroma of frying pork, hit my nose. I gagged.
> It was an image I may never forget.
> I admit, I instantly gave up on the people in the wreckage. My mind couldn't comprehend anyone surviving... *that!*
> Instead, I turned my attention away from the main blast area and started scanning the surrounding urban landscape.
> It didn't look much better.
> Shop windows lay shattered down the debris-strewn street. Cars sat at the curbs, dented and smashed—a few still burning. Small sections of other buildings had been demolished in what seemed like random patterns.
> The dead and dying lay everywhere. I had entered a war zone.

All the above is information given so the reader can "see" what the Narrator is seeing. It's all information that's given through the filter that's the Perception of the Narrator. But none of that changes the fact that it's a lot of information without any action or dialogue.

Is it wrong?

In my opinion, in this case, no. But in other people's opinions, it might be. Remember, Speculative Fiction is... subjective.

Information Dumps, like so many other aspects of writing, are subjective as well. However, they're something I try and stay hyper-vigilant against, giving enough information to "paint the scene", but not so much as it overburdens the story.

Because of the nature of First Person Narrative, the writer has the ability to give information in a way that feels personal to the Narrator. This makes that information feel like a natural extension of the story. It should, for all the reasons I've already discussed. And this is a huge advantage. Everything is personal to the Narrator, so therefore it's easily consumed by the reader.

Awesome!

Look at the above. Yes, all I do is describe a destroyed section of a city. However, I do so in a way that's personal to the Narrator. This connects the reader to the Narrator, while at the same time making all that information feel less telly and more showy.

It's also one of First Person's biggest disadvantages.

Due to the fact First Person is so good at hiding Information Dumps, untrained writers never look for them, so they tend to be everywhere. This bogs down the story, piling on words the reader is forced to slog through. A very bad thing, indeed because it can make the story so tedious to read, the reader abandons the story.

This can easily become an issue for even seasoned writers who can fall into the trap of not staying vigilant against Information Dumps.

My point is, when you're using First Person, every time you're describing anything, scrutinize it. Take the time to see if you could say the same thing using less words, or better, can you cut entire sentences and still ensure the readers "sees" what you need them to see.

The rule of thumb is, so long as your descriptions are personal to the Narrator, allowing the reader to see the world through the filter that is the Perception of the Narrator, you should be okay.

But you have to learn to balance that with realizing when you have too much information in any given paragraph/scene/chapter.

And since I'm on the subject of Disadvantages, let's shift away from the good, and look at several of First Person's biggest offenders starting with…

FIRST PERSON IS A LIMITED NARRATIVE

I mentioned why this is an advantage when I first began discussing First Person, but I want to *reeeeally* stress why it's a huge disadvantage as well.

Remember my finger-glasses exercise? About looking through a set of finger-glasses, and only being able to write what you can see? That's a wonderful way of keeping in mind how to implement this Narrative. Seriously, everything that's written in First Person must come only from your Narrator's head.

While this is the single reason for all those wonderful advantages I listed about why First Person is so awesome at connecting your reader to your Narrator, it's also the single reason why First Person cannot be used for all stories. If it's used in the wrong type of story, it'll totally ruin what you're telling.

Now, understand, I'm talking big-picture here. In other words, all those advantages I discussed are advantages for your *Narrator*. When it comes to your *story*, you must be very cautious when choosing First Person.

Why?

Because First Person shines with very simplistic stories. First Person hinders complex stories.

"That can't be true," you interject. "*Hunger Games* was written in First Person!"

Yes. Yes, it was. But where you're missing the point is in the fact that you can't get a more simplistic story than *Hunger Games*.

Story Complexity has nothing to do with the setting, or even the characters. Sure, *Hunger Games* was set in a complex world, with complex politics, etc.

Story Complexity has to do with the *structure* of the story. And from a story structure standpoint, it doesn't get more simplistic than *Hunger Games*. It's a story written from a single character's point of view, about events that happen to the character in a very linear way. It starts (we meet the Narrator and get her backstory and information about the world she lives in), it moves forward (she sacrifices herself for her younger sister and is forced to enter a game where she must fight for her life), and it ends (with her not only surviving but challenging the very thing that forced her into this whole mess to begin with). Everything happens to the Narrator directly, and there's no need for the reader to be anywhere else other than inside the Narrator's head.

It doesn't get any easier than that from a story structure standpoint. And this is the reason *Hunger Games* works so well being told using First Person.

You'd be surprised at how many great stories that *feel* complex are just as simplistic. For these types of stories, First Person is a wonder fit.

However, if your story is more than that, then First Person will probably be a hindrance to you.

If you have a story that needs to be told by multiple Narrators, or have events that need to be shown to the reader that take place in multiple locations, or perhaps even multiple time periods, if you want to use sub-plots, or even foreshadowing, then First Person is not your Huckleberry. While it can be done, remember what I said about breaking the reality of the story you create. Every time you change to a new First Person Narrator, or some variation of the same, you break the reality of your story that's created by using First Person. Doing this will drive a wedge between your reader and your story every time.

Now, that being said, I'm not saying you can't do these things in First Person. You can, you simply have to work very hard to mitigate these issues. And the fact is, you can never eliminate them completely.

So, if your story is more complex than what I described for *Hunger Games*, you should think long and hard before using First Person as your vehicle. If you try and force First Person to work with a story that is too complex for it to handle, you may find that your readers don't turn into fans.

That's the reason 90% of everything I've ever had published is written in Third Person, because my stories tend to be very complex.

And while this is the biggest issue, it's far from the only issue having a Limited Perspective Narrative creates. It also means your Narrator has…

NO IDEA WHAT
ANY OTHER CHARACTER IS THINKING

It's called a "Limited Perspective Narrative" for a reason. It's Limited to the Narrator. This is an easy thing to grasp, it really is. Imagine you're sitting in a room full of other people. Look around and see them. Do you know what any of them are thinking? Of course not. You don't have E.S.P. You're in your head, and your head alone. So, while all those other people may be treating you nice, that does not mean they like you. For all you know, they could despise you.

You're not in their heads. You don't know what they're thinking.

And that's a Limited Perspective Narrative.

There are two-and-a-half Narratives that are Limited Perspective Narratives. First Person, Third Person Limited, and half of Third Person Free Indirect Discourse.

I'll be going into both Third Person Narratives in a bit. For now, let's just stick to First Person.

As I said, First Person is a Limited Perception Narration. You can only write what your Narrator can see, know, feel, etc.

You can't write something like:

> Sally, Betty, and I were sitting at our favorite café, drinking coffee. It was a beautiful sunny day. My drink had come out perfect, but Betty didn't like hers. Though she didn't tell us, she felt there was not enough sugar in it.
>
> Sally excused herself and went to the bathroom. I watched her leave, wondering what she was up to. In the bathroom, Sally pulled out her phone and dialed her drug dealer. She hoped to talk him into murdering her husband so she could collect on his life insurance policy.
>
> Betty and I continued to talk oblivious to all of this. "How have you been?" I asked my dear friend.
> *God, I hate the way her voice grates on me,*

Betty thought before she answered me with a sweet, "Good. And you?"

When writing in First Person, the reader can only see what the Narrator sees. So, having a Secondary Character leave the room, and then describe what that Secondary Character does in a different room is ridiculous. It breaks the reality of First Person, throwing the reader out of the story.

The same is true with minds. The reader is only in the mind of your Narrator. Period. Hopefully you can see how Shifting into Betty's thoughts destroys the above story even further.

Just like real life, your reader is only inside one person's mind — your Narrator.

So, how do we "show" our readers things about secondary characters?

Simple.

Secondary characters thoughts and motivations must be shown through either their actions, or their dialogue. These are the only things our Narrator can interact with. Think about it this way, how do you know what your friends are thinking, or the type of people they are? By what they *say* and *do*. That's exactly how you must handle Secondary Characters in your story.

The reader shouldn't be in their heads, nor be able to follow them around, so there is no other way to accomplish this.

Sally, Betty, and I were sitting at our favorite café, drinking coffee. It was a beautiful sunny day. I took a sip of my drink and was pleased to find it perfect. "Mmm. So yummy!" I exclaimed.

Betty wrinkled her nose after her first sip. "Not mine. Needs more sugar."

Sally excused herself and went to the bathroom. I watched her leave, wondering what she was up to. Once she was gone, I leaned in closer to Betty so the people around us couldn't eavesdrop. "Is Sally okay? She's been acting strangely of late."

> Betty's smile turned into a frown. "God, your voice is so grating, no wonder your husband left you."
>
> Her statement hit me like a hammer. Where had that come from? I sat there in stunned silence until Sally returned.
>
> She snagged Betty's arm and pulled her to her feet. "I got in touch with—" She cut her eyes in my direction. Was that worry in their depths?
>
> "I got in touch with that *guy* for that *thing*. We have to meet him now, though."
>
> While I was still reeling from Betty's hurtful comment, I couldn't help but wonder what these two were up to. Nothing good, I was sure of that.

Or some such. You get my point. You need to keep your First Person Narrative grounded firmly inside the head of your Narrator. The reader will get to know the other characters through their actions and dialogue, as well as from how the Narrator feels about them. Which brings me to another limitation of First Person, which is…

SECONDARY CHARACTERS MUST ALIGN WITH THE NARRATOR'S PERCEPTION

This is going to be a complex topic, and one that dips into the realm of writing theory more than writing practicality, but try and follow me here.

It comes down to thinking about the ability you, yourself, have interacting with the world around you. A First Person Narrator should have the same limitations.

I just discussed that when it comes to other people around you, you never know why they're the way they are, because you're never in their heads. But we're creating a story here, meaning we're creating a reality for our readers to live inside one head.

When it comes to the Secondary Characters in our First Person story, how our Narrator feels about them needs to be consistent with how they act and speak. If not, it hurts the reality you create for the story.

Case in point:

> Professor Stevens was a total jerk. I hated that I needed his class for my degree. He was the worst kind of person. Simply the worst. Selfish. Egotistical. Rude to everyone. Not to mention, dumb as a wet mop. People like him shouldn't be allowed to teach. No one ever learned anything from him. We were all just wasting our money on this stupid class.
>
> "All right, everyone. Let's quiet down." Professor Stevens arrogantly sauntered out of his office and took his normal position at the front of the room like he was a king or something. He sat and smiled warmly at those in the front of the lecture hall, but he wasn't fooling me. I knew he didn't care about anyone but himself. "I hope everyone had a relaxing spring break."
>
> Several of the students nodded, like he cared about any of them. The self-centered prick.
>
> Pretty little blonde Sally's hand shot up and Stevens motioned for her to speak. "How was your trip to South Africa?"
>
> Stevens waved a dismissive hand. "Oh, no one wants to hear about that." He was right—the last thing I wanted was to hear him brag about his extravagant exotic vacation.
>
> I guess the rest of the class was in a stupid mood because there was a cacophony of voices asking him to tell his stupid story.
>
> He waved his hands again to quiet everyone. "Fine. It was pretty great. We ended up finishing construction on the school as well as digging wells

in two remote villages that didn't have access to fresh water." He picked up his notebook. "But you're here to learn Theoretical Physics, not hear me ramble on about charity work. After class if any of you want to stay, I'll tell you all about it."

Yeah, I bet he would! Anything to get more attention for himself.

"Oh, but before we get into things, I want to congratulate Dylan on his acceptance to N.A.S.A.'s J.P.L. Great job, Dylan!"

The rest of the drones clapped as Dylan stood. "I couldn't of done it without you, Professor."

A stupid arrogant grin came upon Stevens, and he shook his stupid head. "Nonsense. That was all you, son. And you more than earned it."

I hated this man's pompous attitude.

Hopefully you can see that Professor Stevens is not selfish, nor arrogant, nor pompous, nor anything the Narrator thinks he is. Sure, the narrative words describe him as such, but Stevens' dialogue and actions do not show that he is. Because of this, what you end up doing is alienating the one thing you don't want to alienate—the Narrator.

With the above, where the Narrator is obviously incorrect in his assumptions, this makes the reader dislike the Narrator. And once that happens, the reader will probably stop reading the story.

However, that's not to say that you can't set out to make the Narrator unlikeable or untrustworthy on purpose. If you have a solid, story-motivated reason for doing it, and you have figured out how you are going to compensate for the fact that this may turn the reader off, good on you. Time. Effort. Just don't do it *unintentionally*.

Another twist on this is to have a Narrator who doesn't understand people. Returning to the above example, you may have found it fun to read because I was showing you a disparity between the Narrator's views and the behavior of the teacher. Sure, at times I laid it on a bit thick (I was making a different point), but you may have also gotten sucked into wanting to know why this person was so wrong, or even better, you may have found yourself with the desire to not only see how they changed their minds, but hoped they got caught in a situation that taught them a lesson that forced them to see people in a better light.

The variations of this are limited only by the writer and what type of story they are telling.

Time. Effort.

And last, please don't confuse this with *lying* to the reader. A story can absolutely lie to the reader for all the reasons I've already discussed.

In other words, I could start the above story with the Narrator thinking Professor Stevens is all those terrible things, and then have them discover they were wrong, thus changing their mind.

I could also reverse that, with the Narrator thinking the Professor is a wonderful man only to find out he's in reality a terrible person.

It's understanding how your Narrator perceives each Secondary Character, and then making sure the Narrator's perceptions and the secondary character's actions line up until there is a reason for them to shift. Once the shift happens, they should fall back in sync.

Meaning, if we started the above with the Narrator hating the Professor for being terrible, then the Professor needs to do things that could be perceived as terrible. After the Narrator discovers they were wrong, the way they perceive the Professor should change to fall in line with this new perception.

A wonderful example of this would be Professor Snape from the *Harry Potter* series. If you read this series, you know what I mean. If you didn't, well… I'm not going to be the one who spoils it for you!

Just remember, while it's absolutely true that your Secondary Characters are defined by their actions and the words that come out of their mouths, they are also defined by how your Narrator Perceives them.

In First Person, not only can it be a chore to make sure all the Secondary Characters are well represented, it can also be…

Difficult to Describe your Narrator

Since with First Person, the Imaginary Camera that your reader is looking through is inside the Narrator's head, there's no way to directly describe the exterior of your Narrator. Thoughts, motivations, emotions... absolutely! We're inside their head, so that stuff's as easy as pie. But the color of their eyes, whether they have a big nose, the fact that one of their ears sticks out more than the other, those things can get a bit tricky.

And for the aspiring writer, the solution is normally terrible. Something like:

> Stumbling into the bathroom, I gaze into the mirror. How did I get so old? My hair used to be a lush, beautiful blonde. Now, after a decade of coloring, it was thin and lifeless. And is that a zit? How is it fair that a woman of thirty-eight still gets zits?
>
> Oh well, I guess that's why I spend two-hundred thirty-two dollars and twenty-eight cents plus tax every month on makeup.
>
> I gaze deeply into my lackluster brown eyes as I run my brush through the nightmare that is my hair and contemplate once more about getting some work done on my huge nose. I—

I can't do it! It's so frickin' terrible! Give me a second, I need to go wash the stink off my fingers.

Okay, I'm back.

Anyhoo... Don't. Just... don't.

While I've read "I gazed into the mirror" a bazillion times, never have I read it where it worked for the story. And no one in the history of ever has wondered how, "a woman of thirty-eight" does anything. Most people of thirty-eight can't even remember how old they are, much less pine about it like an eleven-year-old child dying for the day they can officially call themselves a teenager.

So what to do? Time and effort.

Figure out alternate ways. Be creative. That's kinda your job.

> "Sally! I love what you've done to your hair!" Jane beamed at me as I approached.
>
> Betty nodded her agreement. "I have to admit, red works on ya, girl."
>
> "Thank you both," I said with a grin as I slid into the booth with them. "The new color does make me feel like a woman reborn."

Whatever.

As with everything, think before you write. And then think while you're writing. Oh, and think after you've written it, you know, when you're editing. Basically… think.

Describing the Narrator in First Person isn't easy, and since they're the character that's in every single scene, that's an issue. You must figure out a way to describe them, and as close to the beginning of the story as you can. Otherwise, you leave their description to the reader's imagination. Not a bad thing, in and of itself. But if you do that, you should then pretty much avoid describing the Narrator all together.

Why? Well, it can cause issues if say, you never described the color of your Narrator's hair through the first two ACTs, and so I've been picturing her hair as blonde this whole time, and then in ACT III during the climactic scene, you write something like:

> The villain reached down, threaded his fingers through my neon purple hair, and yanked me to my feet.

Yeah, that's probably going to pull me out of the story and make me say, "What? I thought she was blonde!"

Describing the appearance of your Narrator in First Person is difficult. But that's okay. You now know, and so you can make sure you do a fine job of it.

Now that you have some information to gnaw upon while thinking about whether you should use First Person for your story or not, let's move this discussion away from advantages and disadvantages and look at some pointers to writing First Person effectively.

When it comes to the actual writing of First Person, there's a few things you need to be mindful of to make sure your reader remains engaged in the story.

The biggest issue aspiring writers miss with First Person is how hard it is to…

Create a Strong Narrator Voice

The fact is, to get all the bonuses out of First Person Narration, the writer needs to make sure they create a very strong and relatable Voice from their Narrator. Keep in mind, this is the character the reader is *inside*. Everything the reader sees, feels, and experiences is done so through the Perception of this Narrator. If the reader can't make a strong connection to the Narrator, they'll never finish reading the story. And if they never finish reading this story, they'll never even start any of your other stories.

Think back to that example about poor misunderstood Professor Stevens. Did you like that Narrator? How would you feel about reading an entire story told by that Narrator?

I personally would hate it, and would've stopped reading a few paragraphs in. Life's too short to read bad writing.

Go back a bit further to the example with the first few pages of the story I did for Sony's *EverQuest Next*. You either didn't mind the way I truncated and repeated sentences, used incorrect grammar, etc., or you hated it. If you didn't mind it, it probably added some interesting dynamics to your read, making the story more interesting by connecting you to that strange little Narrator creature in a strange little way. If you hated it, no matter how short I had made that story, you never would've finished reading it.

So yeah, Voice really is that important.

In First Person, the entire story hinges upon the shoulders of the Narrator. You must spend time developing your Character's Voice, it's the only Voice the reader will hear on every single page.

This means you, the writer, must have a solid grasp of the Narrator's motivations, beliefs, perceptions, attitudes, feelings, etc. about the world they live in. It's through this filter the reader will be experiencing the world of the story.

Spend time with your Character before you start writing your story. Get to know them. The better you do, the more they'll feel like a three-dimensional person, and the more the reader will be able to relate to them.

Consistency with the Narrator's Voice is the key. And this is a multi-threaded process.

First, you need to be consistent with the Narrator's Perceptions of the world around them. They can't be wishy-washy. This doesn't mean they can't grow and change. In fact, growth and change are a must. But they can't be like the Narrator from the Professor Stevens example, constantly misrepresenting everything they see.

It also means you need to be consistent with your Prose. *How* a First Person story is written is just as important as *Why* the Narrator does what they do.

This means being consistent with how you craft your sentences, paragraphs, and scenes. Holding your Narrative Tense (which I've already told you is the number one mistake all writers make). Because, that's all part of their Narrator Voice.

Take this series as an example. I chose to write the *Drake's Brutal Writing Advice* series in a very conversational tone. Nothing formal. Just you and me sitting down for a chat.

And it makes my creative writing/editing brain scream with rage.

First, OMG! Are you kidding me with all the sentences that start with And, But, Again, Still, Because, However, etc.?!?!?! Oh, and First! Let's not forget First!!! Lots of sentences starting with First!

And while *thank God* this isn't how I write creatively, unfortunately, it *is* how I talk. You should be able to see the difference from the few examples of my actual creative writing I've included here.

So why am I doing it this way?

I speak on these topics professionally, standing in front of a room filled with hundreds of people. I try very hard to be an engaging public speaker. But here, things have changed. I'm not there with you. Of course I'm not. Or am I? Was that rustling noise you heard a moment ago the house settling, or me shifting my weight? No. Just the house. Still, writing in the same manner that I speak to the audience on stage collapses some of the distance created between you and I by the fact that you're reading a book.

My point here is, I'm consistent with my Narrator's Voice throughout this, even if it makes my creative writing brain hurt.

It's also the reason I try and stay on the goofy side throughout this. Sure, it helps break up the monotony of learning grammar. But like with fiction, I need to connect you to the Narrator. In this case that Narrator is me. And like all humans, I want people to like me. Lord knows I could use a friend. But it goes much deeper than that. By connecting you to the Narrator of this series, it makes you more open to what that Narrator is saying. If I can get you to like this Narrator, then by extension, you'll have the desire to like what this Narrator is saying.

Creative Fiction is exactly the same.

You want to viscerally connect your reader to your Narrator. It'll not only open up all those advantages I've gone through, but it'll make the reader *want* to continue reading the story. They'll *want* to see what happens to this Narrator they've grown to like. They'll *want* to see them succeed.

And that brings us to one of the most touchy topics when discussing First Person…

FIRST PERSON SHOULD BE LIMITED TO ONE NARRATOR

This is going to be the most controversial topic I've covered so far. Mostly because there are so many writers who have hitched their wagons to First Person as if this was some type of Narrative war, and they were forced to choose a side.

And every time I run into one of these writers all I can do is shake my head and marvel over their stupidity.

There are no *sides* to Narrative. And there certainly is no Narrative war. Each Narrative has grammatical strengths and weaknesses that simply exist. They're real, and a writer should consider all these and weigh them against the story they're about to tell so they can make a *choice* of which Narrative to use for that *particular* story.

It's why I have stories published in nearly every single Narrative type that exists: First Person Present Tense, First Person Past Tense, Second Person Present Tense, Third Person Omniscient Past Tense, Third Person Free Indirect Discourse Past Tense, and Third Person Limited Past Tense. (Yes, I very much favor Past Tense.)

But the reason I've used so many is, I let the story decide which Narrative is best, then I use *that* Narrative for *that* story.

If you're a writer who feels you *must* write in a certain Narrative, then you're an idiot. *You* shouldn't be a part of this equation. Picking a Narrative should be reliant upon the type of story you're telling, not your personal opinion on which Narrative *you* enjoy.

And hopefully I've done my job throughout this series to convince you that the story is the master. If not, well… you can lead a horse to water, and all that…

Still, stepping down off my soapbox and getting back to my point. I've already mentioned this, but I want to hammer home why limiting your story to One Narrator is the best thing for First Person.

As I've discussed, First Person is best suited for a simple story that'll be told by a Single Narrator. If you have a story that's more complex than what one Narrator can tell, you need to seriously consider using Third Person, as that's what it was designed for.

Having a Single Narrator in First Person creates all those advantages I've discussed. It creates a reality that's very comfortable for the reader, and one that takes very little effort for them to slip into. It builds a cohesive and visceral connection between the story and the reader.

That being said, the title of this section does include the word "*should*". As in, you *should* use only One Narrator. It doesn't say you *must*.

If you're determined to use multiple Narrators within your First Person story, you're absolutely free to do so.

But forewarned is forearmed. So, let's chase this rabbit for a moment.

First, let's take a step back and look at the big picture. Regardless of which Narrative I'm using, I have a pretty hard and fast rule when it comes to my Narrators.

> **I will not use a Narrator in a story unless that Narrator has their own complete, and personal Plot Arc.**

Meaning, if I'm going to use a character as a Narrator, they'll have a **Setup Phase** to their story that is *uniquely theirs*. They'll have a **Build Phase** to their story that'll raise tension and complications for them *personally*. This personal Build Phase will lead to a defined **Conflict** that's *uniquely theirs*. And, they'll be forced to overcome that personal Conflict with their own personal **Climax Phase**.

Understand what I mean. I'm talking Story Structure here.

Normally, with a single Narrator, the **Story Plot Arc** *is* the **Narrator's Plot Arc** — the two are one in the same. In other words, there's one Story Plot Arc, it belongs to the Narrator, and it looks like this:

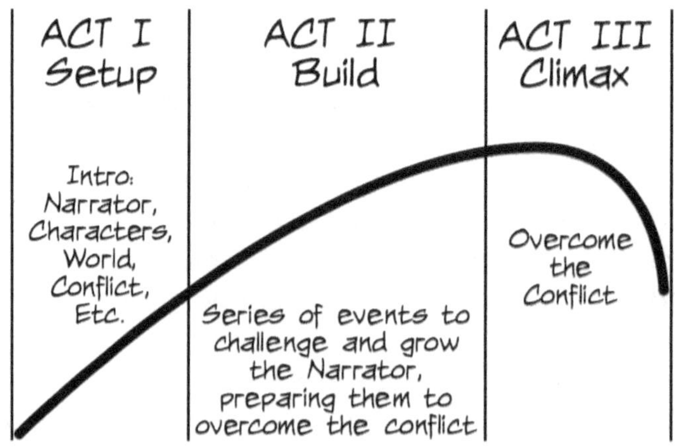

Basically, the Narrator's story *is* the story. Again, simple. *Hunger Games*. Katniss' story is the only story being told. She's the one all the Setup is about, she's the one who is challenged and grows, and she's the one who overcomes the conflict at the end of the story.

However, if I'm going to add a second Narrator, things get exponentially more complex. Because, with two Narrators I'll need three Plot Arcs.

"Three!" You interject. "Don't you mean Two?"

No, and stop interrupting me. I'm not smart enough to explain all this crazy theoretical Story Structure stuff *and* deal with your interjections.

With two Narrators, a story of mine will have *three* Plot Arcs. There will be one Plot Arc for each of the two Narrators. Each of these Plot Arcs will be personal to each Narrator. And each of these Plot Arcs will be something that each Narrator must overcome to be satisfied with why they are in this story.

The complexity comes into play with the fact that each of those two individual Plot Arcs must also be irrevocably tied to the larger Story Plot Arc. This larger Story Plot Arc needs to be different from both of the individual Narrator's Plot Arcs. However, it needs to also be reliant on the individual Narrator Plot Arcs. Meaning, if *either* of the two individual Narrator's Plot Arcs fail, then the larger Story Plot Arc also fails. Here's what it looks like:

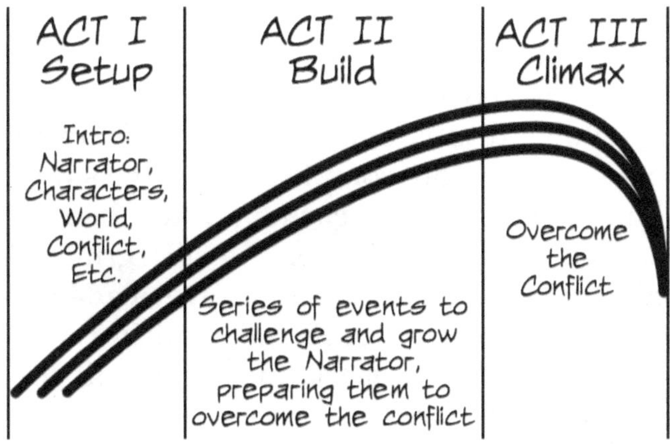

Understand, all three of these Plot Arcs must go through the same processes, just separately. In other words, all three will need a Setup Phase where I'll introduce things and setup what the Conflict of each individual Plot Arc is. All three will need a Build Phase where I'll challenge and grow the Narrators both separately to prepare them for their personal Conflicts, as well as grow them together so they can overcome the Conflict of the larger Story Plot Arc. And I'll have to create a Climax Phase for all three that will need to be overcome. This will not only have to include an individual Climax that each Narrator will have to overcome to defeat their own personal Conflicts, but I also will need to connect those two Overcomes somehow, tying them into how the larger Story Plot Arc Conflict is overcome.

Ahh… complexity, my old friend. How I do love thee.

But this is what makes a complex story. And the reason these complex stories are normally told using Third Person.

Just in case you're terrible at math, yes, the above means if you have three Narrators, you'll have four Plot Arcs. Five Narrators = six Plot Arcs. Etc.

Now, don't confuse a Narrator with a Secondary Character. You can have as many incredibly strong and wonderfully interesting Secondary Characters as the story needs, and none of your Secondary Characters have need of their own personal Plot Arcs. Each of these amazing Secondary Characters are there to help shape and affect either the Narrator Plot Arcs, or the overall Story Plot Arc.

Not that they can't have their own personal Plot Arc. I'm simply saying they don't need one.

So, if you follow my methodology, adding Character Narrators becomes exponentially more complicated for the story.

"So?" you interject. "Giving each Narrator their own Plot Arc doesn't mean I can't use First Person." A silly grin comes to your face. "In fact, using your definition above has made me even more excited to write a Multi-Narrator First Person Story!"

Yes, I get that once you start understanding the beauty of story complexity it gets your creative juices flowing. But all that complexity will not help your First Person story, only hurt it.

Why? Because the issue with Multi-Narrators in First Person is not fixed by making sure each have their own Plot Arc. The issue comes in the fact that every time you Shift to a new Narrator within First Person, you break the reality of the story you have created—that your reader is inside the head of your Narrator.

You see, the problem is, each time you create an additional Plot Arc using a new First Person Narrator, you're asking the reader to viscerally connect to each Narrator at the same level. And this is where First Person Narrative starts to break down, because in doing this, you're breaking the reality of the story you created.

Remember, the reality you create for the reader within a First Person Narrative story is that the reader is watching this story from *inside* the Narrator's head.

When you have multiple First Person Narrators, what you're doing is muddying the waters. You're spreading the reader's desire to care, and instead of enhancing the enjoyment for the reader, most times, you make them care less.

Bottom line is, First Person is not designed for multiple Narrators. That's Third Person's domain.

So why do so many writers attempt to use First Person this way? Well, most of the time they don't. They do a far worse crime, in my not so humble opinion.

Most times when I see a multi-Narrator First Person story, what I find is there is only one Story Plot Arc. And it's a simplistic Story Plot Arc to boot, one that honestly should've been told by one Narrator.

In other words, there's one Story—one Setup Phase, one Build Phase, and one Climax Phase. And even though this is a simple story, one that easily could have been told from one Narrator, for whatever reason the writer has chosen to bounce between two (or more) Narrators to tell this one simple tale.

The biggest reason this is such a crime is that it's redundant. You're only telling one story. Why would you want to weaken the telling of that one simplistic story be forcing the reader to care about multiple Narrators?

The answer I normally get is that these writers feel it strengthens the reader's connection to the story because the reader gets to see the story from multiple perspectives.

Unfortunately, doing this tends to have the opposite effect.

Look, you may think having two Narrators telling the same story helps because you get to filter the story through two different Perspectives. And it might. I'm sure there are stories that could absolutely benefit from this. However, normally it doesn't.

Think about it this way. Every story is restricted by how many words will be used to create it. When you have two Narrators who are telling the same story, this means you only get half the words to viscerally connect the reader to each Narrator. Don't you see the advantage it would give to use *all* those words to viscerally connect the reader to *one* Narrator? How much deeper you could make the connection between Narrator and reader?

And the deeper this connection, the more the reader will care about that one Narrator's plight.

The more the reader cares about the Narrator's plight, the more they will enjoy the story.

The more they enjoy the story, the more chance you have of getting them to tell all their friends what a wonderful writer you are, not only spreading your glory, but ensuring they will purchase your next tale as well.

Besides, if you have two characters traveling together, both doing the same things, why do you even need both? Either cut one of them and let the story be told by one Narrator, or make one a strong Secondary Character. This allows the story to be told by one Narrator, but still be influenced by that strong Secondary Character.

Both of these options will normally create a deeper connection between the reader and what they're reading, as opposed to diluting things with multiple Narrators.

And the final issue that arises when you use Multiple First Person Narrators is that it's always jarring for the reader to switch from one head to another. No matter how perfectly you make the transition, there will *always* be a moment, no matter how short, where the reader has to think, "Wait? Where am I? Oh, right, I'm in this other guy's head now."

Personally, I never want my reader to struggle trying to figure out who they are within a story. I want them to watch the movie I paint on their imagination.

Having more than one First Person Narrator will *always* cause a reader to trip, even if it's for a microsecond. There's no way around it.

And this all falls back to that reality First Person creates. The reader is inside a Narrator's head. Pulling them from that head and forcing them into a second head is simply jarring. No matter what you do to mitigate this, it'll always be felt by the reader, and pull them from the story.

In conclusion, my advice, as always, is for you to *think* about what you're doing, and why you're doing it, before you do it. It's that simple.

If you're intent on using Multi-Narrators in First Person, just make sure it's the correct choice. For me, there's no way I would do it, because I know for a fact that Third Person will do a better job for the story. But if you've looked at Third Person thoroughly, and are convinced your story can't be told in that Narrative, then… well… have at cha.

Now that I've shown you some of the major advantages and disadvantages of First Person, let's shift gears to the actual grammar side of things and look at some…

Tricks and Tips When Writing First Person

All that theory I just discussed is great, and if you start using it within your First Person Narration, you'll start to create a very immersive read for your stories. However, that's not all there is to know. Nor is this stuff going to magically appear in your writing because you've read this book.

It all comes down to my opening mantra—Time and Effort. One-million words!

Like all aspects of writing, it's going to take you time to master writing First Person.

However, as you write those one-million words, here are some final tips and tricks you need to keep in mind whenever you're using First Person.

I think the biggest mistake aspiring writers make with First Person is…

Overusing Exposition

Look, we want to take full advantage of the fact that our Narrative is all coming directly out of our Narrator's head. But every time you do so, you're using what is called **Exposition**. Exposition is a very important reason why First Person works so well for certain types of stories. It also creates a trap for any writer who is not paying attention to the bigger picture. If over used, it can overburden the story with self-centered Telling that doesn't move the plot. Some people call this, "Falling too deeply into the Narrator."

Let me give you a real world example:

If you've ever been to a party and got stuck next to a guy who rambles on for hours telling you *everything* he sees that's wrong with the new season of *The Walking Dead*, you know what this feels like. You're listening to someone who exhausts your interest in the topic in just a few minutes (if you were interested at all) but then goes on and on and on and on…

This is what a reader feels every time your Narrator gives them more information than they want about any specific topic.

And avoiding this is trickier to do than you might suspect. Mostly because this is subjective. If you show something you've written to three people, one is going to say you have way too much Exposition, one is going to say you have the correct amount, and the third is going to say you didn't put in enough.

It all comes down to remembering to write tight. And this is a balancing act of biblical proportions. But at the end of the day, you're the writer, which means you'll have to make the decision as to what the perfect amount shall be.

Let's take a second look at that story I'm currently writing, the one with the girl who enters Café Jax. Only this time, I'm going to fall a little too deep into her Exposition.

> It was chilly, even though it was August. I hated the cold. Growing up in Florida was probably the reason for that. I mean, I wore shorts year-round there. Why I had ever agreed to move up here to this ice-filled hell-hole was beyond me. Why couldn't something be done about it? We have technology, right? We've been to the moon, for crying out loud. Can't we figure out a way to make our planet a little warmer? We could call it Warmer Global, or some such.
>
> Anyway, the street was deserted, even though it was about three in the afternoon. Like, freaky deserted. Where was everyone? I missed the hustle and bustle of Miami. I never felt alone there, and I already hated the feeling of isolation I felt in this place.
>
> Across the road from me sat Café Jax—an ancient rust-colored brick building with a stained red and white stripped awning and an eerie wooden statue sitting beside its front door. What the hell was that thing even supposed to be? An Indian?

> An old white man? A child molester? I really had
> no idea. Whomever had been commissioned to
> create such a monstrosity should be hunted down
> and stoned to death. It took my mind back to
> when I was fourteen. My dad's best friend had
> stayed with us for a week. He never did anything
> inappropriate, though I could tell he wanted to.
> He was always ogling me in a very creepy manner.
> Much like this weird statue. Totally inappropriate!
>
> Still, the windows promised "Old Fashioned
> Shakes & Malts" as well as "Awesome Burgers &
> Fries", and since I hadn't eaten a thing since early
> that morning, they had my full attention.

Sure, we want to let the reader know how our Narrator feels about the world around her, and look for organic opportunities to drop in backstory. But what we *don't* want to do is add so much detail as to make the reader unable to understand what the story is about.

In the above, is this a story about Miami? Moving Away? Homesickness? Global Warming? Child Molesters? There's so much information, it's hard to keep track of it all.

By the way, so you don't have to flip back to read the original, here it is:

> It was chilly, even though it was August, and the
> street was deserted, even though it was about
> three in the afternoon. Across the road from
> me sat Café Jax—an ancient rust-colored brick
> building with a stained red and white stripped
> awning and an eerie wooden statue sitting beside
> its front door. What the hell was that thing even
> supposed to be? An Indian? An old white man? A
> child molester? I really had no idea.
>
> Still, the windows promised "Old Fashioned
> Shakes & Malts" as well as "Awesome Burgers &

Fries", and since I hadn't eaten a thing since early
that morning, they had my full attention.

The Narration paints the scene, allowing the reader to see it. It also paints this through the filter of the Narrator's perception, and keeps everything personal to the Narrator. All those other details from my exaggerated example, however, are not needed for the story. This scene is here for one simple purpose—to get the Narrator on the path she needs to be on so she can enter the story. The Narrator is newly arrived in this town, and she needs information as to where to go next. Meaning, from a story standpoint, I needed a scene for her to receive this information, and I made the decision that she would get this information at a diner while eating lunch. This is still the setup portion of this story, so it's going to be a little slow and boring by default. Knowing this, I try to add tidbits of detail that are both interesting, as well as help the reader begin to build their relationship with the Narrator.

To me, that little bit about the creepy statue does this. It shows that this Narrator has a quirky side, which is all I wanted to show at this moment.

Again, it's subjective. Meaning, it does this *in my opinion*. The comment about the little creepy statue may not help you connect to the Narrator in any way, and that's fine. It's my name that'll be on the cover of this project, so all glory if it succeeds, or blame if it fails, rests upon my shoulders, not yours.

Hopefully you can see the difference between the two pieces, and understand my point. When writing First Person, don't be the boring guy at the party going on for hours and hours about a topic your reader has no interest in. You must be ever vigilant in balancing enough Exposition to make connections against adding too much Exposition and boring your reader.

One way to help mitigate some of this is to keep a lookout for…

INTERNAL EXPOSITION THAT CAN BE TURNED INTO DIALOGUE

Remember, all Narration within First Person is technically inner monologue. Some of that must remain in the Narrator's head. However, the reality is, dialogue always feels more like a Show than a Tell, even if it's not. Because of this, turning Exposition Narration into Dialogue can be a wonderful Band-Aid to help mitigate overusing Exposition within your Narration.

> Sally smiled at me over her cup of tea. "So, what's been up with you?"
>
> A long slow sigh escaped my lips, and all I could do was shake my head. Was she kidding me? Where could I begin? My life had been insane ever since I'd become a covert operative fighting against the secret Martian invasion. The hours spent training with alien weapons and technology. The terror of knowing if the world found out about this invasion it would cause panic on a global scale. Trying to juggle all this secrecy with my hot steamy romance with Dylan.

If you're in a scene that's already primed as a dialogue scene, why all the inner monologue? It just don't make no sense.

> Sally smiled at me over her cup of tea. "So, what's been up with you?"
>
> A long slow sigh escaped my lips, and I shook my head. "Are you kidding me? Where to begin?" I smiled wondering if she could handle what had become my reality. But I needed to tell someone. If not, I would eventually curl up in a ball and die. "Well, to tell you the truth, I've become a covert operative for the government."
>
> She grunted a laugh. "You mean you're a spy now?

> Drake, you and your imagination!" She rose her cup
> to her lips.
>
> "Sort of. Aliens from Mars have invaded Earth,
> and I've been fighting a war against them while
> trying to keep this fact out of the press so it
> doesn't escalate into global panic."
>
> Tea splashed over Sally's face when she choked
> on her drink. Her eyes got big and she set her cup
> down. Though she missed the table completely and
> the fragile china shattered when it hit the floor.
>
> God, I missed Dylan.

Both have the same information. However, the second is way more interesting to read as opposed to the first.

As with everything, don't overuse this trick. Hiding Exposition as Dialogue is no substitute for ensuring that you're writing tightly, and every word you put down on paper is there to either connect the reader to the Narrator at a deeper level, or to move the story along.

Another thing to remain vigilant against is...

NOT OVERUSING "I" TO START EVERY SENTENCE A.K.A. FILTERING

It amazes me how many First Person stories are now rotting out this industry that have this one, signally-horrific writing issue. But this is something that causes tons of problems for the story, and can very easily, all by itself, ruin your story. Seriously, as stupid as this sounds, you want to avoid using "I" as much as possible when writing First Person.

Why? So you don't end up with a story like this:

> I stared at the monster in disbelief. I had no idea
> something this terrifying even existed. I always
> assumed monsters were make-believe. Stories my
> parents told me to keep me in line.

I was obviously wrong.

I flinched when the thing let out a vicious snarl and stepped closer. I spun, running as fast as my legs would carry me. I could hear the beast's sharp claws scrapping on the concrete of the sidewalk as it chased after me. I knew my only escape was the cliff, and the river below.

I poured all my remaining strength into the last twenty yards of ground separating me from the safety of the Mississippi. I was terrified I wouldn't make it. I could barely hear the creature inches behind me over the pounding of my racing heart. I could feel its hot breath upon my neck.

I felt a slicing pain rip across my back as the creature lashed out, ripping through my T-Shirt. I launched myself into the air out of sheer desperation and plummeted off the cliff. I freefell some thirty feet before I slammed into the cold embrace of the waters below.

I heard the monster above me and knew I was safe.

Now, this is obviously terrible. Don't see it? You will.

Bonus, I learned something about me just now; that was surprisingly difficult for me to write. It's not natural for me to start nearly every sentence with "I". Still, while this might be a bit extreme, it's not far off the mark from so many books I've read over the past decade.

Let's look at the four main reasons why the above is such a piece of crap.

One: if you remember way back when I started all this, I mentioned that with First Person, every time you use the Narrator's Pronoun (I, me, my, etc.), you drive a tiny mental wedge between the reader and what's being read. The fewer Narrator Pronouns you use, the easier it is for your reader to fall deeper into the story. So, right off the bat, you want to cut out as many Narrator

Pronouns as you can because it'll make the story more immersive for the reader. Always a good thing.

Here's what I do.

If I'm going to start a sentence with "I" it's only because that sentence describes something my Narrator is physically doing.

> I opened the door.
> I drew my sword.
> I ran away.

And please note: I said, "things my Narrator *physically* does."

You'll understand why in a moment, but I almost never use "I" to describe visual or audible stimuli around my Narrator, nor to tell the reader feelings or emotions.

Two: and far worse a crime, is the fact that most of these sentences are Tells. Now, there's no time to go into detail here about how to be a Showy writer vs. a Telly writer. Like I said, I plan on writing the next *Drake's Brutal Writing Advice* book on that very topic. As you may not want to wait a year for that to come out, I'll give you a quick overview now.

> With telling, the writer is merely cataloging actions, feelings, emotions, and events. Showing paints the picture of each of these, allowing the reader to experience these things for themselves.

In other words, if you write:

> I felt terrified.

You're Telling the reader how you felt. Terrified. But that doesn't allow them to experience the terror for themselves. To do that, you need to instead *describe* what it feels like to "feel terrified". Now, there are a bazillion ways to do this. Here are a few off the top of my head:

> My eyes bulged and my mouth went dry.
> I opened my mouth to scream, but no sound escaped my lips.
> Shivers rippled up my spine.
> I backed away, my mouth moving without sound.
> All thought fled my mind, and I became rooted in place.
> Of their own accord, my eyes slammed shut and a wail ripped from my lips, shattering the silence of the night.

Notice, all of them let the reader know the Narrator is feeling terror, yet in none of them did I use the word terror. Or even fear, horror, dread, fright, etc., etc. Hopefully you see where I'm going with all this. If not, wait for the next installment of this series. ☺

Three: and not the worst offense, but an offense nonetheless, is the fact that when you craft all your sentences in an identical manner, you create a very rote read for your reader. This, while not something most readers will consciously notice, does make the overall read less enjoyable.

When crafting our stories, we writers need to constantly vary our sentence structure. Meaning, don't do this:

> I walked into the kitchen. I picked up a pot. I crossed to the sink. I filled the pot with water. I returned to the stove. I placed the pot of water on the burner. I turned the burner on.

Again, I'm exaggerating to make my point. Still, you should be able to see how a long string of similar sentences becomes boring to read. It's a shame, because English grammar has everything you need to create varied sentences.

> Walking into the kitchen, I picked up a pot and filled it with water. I placed it on the stove to heat before making myself a sandwich. And I did all this using the same number of words as above.

Tighter, more interesting to read, and does not force the reader to fall into a repetitious reading rote.

Four: and the absolute worst sin rotting my example is something called **Filtering**.

Filtering is an industry term most aspiring writers have never heard, much less understand. But it's pretty easy to grasp. It all comes down to understanding the job of a sentence.

Let's take a trip back in time and sit down with my third-grade teacher, Mrs. Johnson.

Every sentence you write focuses the reader's attention on *something*. As the writer, you're in full control of that *something*, depending on how you craft the sentence. What you need to grasp is that, when you write a sentence, the *something* our reader focuses on is the *something* you *want* them focusing on.

To get technical, this something is called the **Subject** of the Sentence. The Subject of a Sentence is the person, place, or thing that is doing whatever action is being described by the sentence. To figure out what your Sentence's Subject is, just look at the verb, and then ask, "Who or what is doing that Verb?"

Basically, it works like this.

The ghost floated down the hall.

What is the action being done in this sentence? "floating down the hall"

Who or what is doing that action? "the ghost"

Easy enough, right?

Okay, what you need to know is that readers will normally focus on the Subject of a sentence. It's kind of the point of a Subject.

Going back to our last example, what is the focus of this sentence (the Subject)?

The ghost, certainly. Meaning, a reader reads this and they *see* "the ghost" first, and the "floating down a hall" last. Which is the desired effect here. The ghost is the important aspect I want the reader focusing on. What I don't want is for the reader to focus on the Narrator who is the one seeing all this.

Unfortunately, that's exactly what Filtering does... and the way most aspiring writers write for whatever reason.

In other words, aspiring writers do this:

I stared at the ghost floating down the hall.

Let's take a good look at this example, and discover why this sucks so hard.

First, let's figure out what the Subject is.

What is the action being done in this sentence? Well, it's no longer "floating down the hall". No. The action is now "stared".

Knowing this, who or what is doing that action? "I"

So, what does this sentence force the reader to focus on? Not the ghost. Not anymore. It's no longer the Subject. The focus is now on the Narrator, and their *reaction* to this ghost. The words, "I stared" is the *something* the reader will focus on first. *Then* they'll focus on the ghost. This is Filtering.

Meaning, the event that's happening is being *Filtered* through the Narrator instead of allowing the reader to experience the event for themselves.

Do you think I want my reader "looking" at my Narrator while my Narrator "looks" at a ghost? Or do you think it would be better if my reader just went ahead and looked at the ghost all on their own?

Ahh... I see by that twinkle in your eye, we just had a breakthrough. Nice.

Let's look at another example, but this time taken directly from my little monster story from before.

I could feel its hot breath upon my neck.

This sentence is Filtering, because I'm *Filtering* the sensation through the Narrator. It forces the reader to focus on the fact that the Narrator is "feeling the hot breath." What I would rather have happen instead is for the reader to feel the hot breath themselves. How do I do this? Simple. I remove the Narrator as the focus of the sentence.

The creature's hot breath licked my neck.

Let's do our Subject test again.

What is the action being done in this sentence? "licked"

Who or what is doing that action? "the creature's hot breath"

Oooo… scary!

With the Filtering removed, now you, the reader, can imagine what it feels like to have the creature's hot breath licking *your* neck. The reader is now focused on the sensation, and is more immersed in the story.

Don't get me wrong here. Filtering, in itself, isn't bad. Again, it comes down to the writer controlling the *something* the reader will focus on. Sometimes, depending on the situation, you may *want* the reader to focus on the Narrator.

I stared in disbelief as Dylan walked away. My heart broke with the realization that I would never again feel his lips pressed against mine.

Not my best example, but hopefully you get my point. I have a thing for Dylan. Er… no… wait…. My point is that sometimes you *want* the reader to focus on the Narrator or the Narrator's reaction to something, as opposed to what's causing that reaction.

In the above example, I *want* the reader to focus on the Narrator, and the disbelief they are feeling. Sure, that disbelief is coming from the fact that Dylan is walking away. But to get the most impact from the sentence, I don't need the reader to focus on Dylan, nor the fact that he's walking away. I need them to focus on the Narrator's disbelief.

I will say, focusing on the Narrator should happen rarely within your story. It's hard, but you should go through everything you write and look for all your Filtering. If it's not specifically a sentence where you want the reader focusing on the Narrator, you should rework it to cut out the Filtering. In other words, every single time you start a sentence with any of the following, it should be a red flag for you. With each of these, you should scrutinize the sentence to see if your reader is focusing on the correct *something*.

(These would have I, me, my, etc. before them)
(Past Tense / Present Tense)
could / can
decided / decide
experienced / experience
felt / feel
heard / hear
looked / look
noticed / notice
noted / note
realized / realize
saw / see
seemed / seem
sounded like / sound like
thought / think
touched / touch
wondered / wonder
was able to / am able to
watched / watch

This isn't an exhaustive list, to be sure, and for that I'm sorry. But it should give you enough to understand this issue.

Worse, this is probably the hardest thing you'll have to deal with while learning to write. It's something you'll fight in nearly every single story you write. Trust me, I know how exhausting that is. But we want to be great writers who tell great stories. And Filtering is a terrible disease that'll rot your story from the inside, ensuring the reader never has the opportunity to become fully immersed.

Avoid it like the plague. You've been warned.

Alrighty then! Putting this all together, let's see if I have the writing chops to rewrite that horribly written example, but with an eye toward eliminating as many Narrator Pronouns as possible to help the reader become more immersed in the story. I'll also attempt to be a more Showy writer and less of a Telly one, while varying my sentence structure to help avoid a rote read. And I'll do all this while eliminating as many Filtering issues as humanly possible.

The monster crept from the shadows, cutting off my only exit. My eyes bulged and my mouth worked without sound. How could something so terrifying even exist? Yes, my parents had tortured me with scary tales of the Swamp Demon that supposedly hunted these lands, but surely they'd only told me those tales to frighten me into being a good little boy.

Fairytale or no, the beast before me was very real indeed, complete with saliva-drenched fangs and glowing red eyes.

A vicious snarl ripped from the creature and I flinched. It snapped me from the catatonic state I'd been frozen in. As the beast stepped toward me, I spun and ran.

The beast's sharp claws clicked on the concrete sidewalk as it gave chase. Closer. Closer. I begged my legs to move faster. But to where? I was trapped between a nightmare and a thirty-foot drop to the chilly waters of the Mississippi. Since one was certain death, I headed for the cliff.

I poured all my remaining strength into the last twenty yards of ground separating me from the relative safety of the river. My heart thumped so loud in my chest it nearly drowned out the growls of the creature just inches behind.

The Demon's hot breath licked my neck. Something snagged the back of my T-Shirt. Hot agony sliced through my side.

It had me!

Panic overrode primal instincts and I launched myself into the air. The air whistled in my ears as I freefell into darkness. The ice-cold water slapped me hard before sucking me into its depths. Lungs burning, I fought against the strong current. Bursting through the surface, the sweetest

> breath of air I'd ever tasted filled my lungs.
> Howls and hisses from the cliff above were all
> that chased me as the current swept me downriver.

Meh. It'll do for an example. ☺

If this were a real piece I was writing, I'd add in more description so the reader could better visualize the scene, etc. However, the point here is to show you the difference between starting sentences with "I" vs. not starting them with "I". Hopefully, you can see not only the difference, but why the rewrite is so much more immersive than the original.

And finally, to make your First Person Narration shine, you need to always…

MAKE IT PERSONAL!!!

A little refresher before I hit this last topic, because this one is all-encompassing, and kind of the reason for using First Person.

I started by discussing that First Person is a Limited Narrative. A Limited Narrative means everything the reader sees, feels, experiences, etc. is coming from the Narrator's head.

This has nothing to do with the Narrator's Level of Awareness, as you can have a First Person Narrator be restricted to only telling the story from their head, but still allow that Narrator to have either a Limited or an Omniscient Level of Awareness about the future. Meaning they are either learning what happens next at the same time as the reader (Limited Level of Awareness) or they've already lived through the events of the story and know how it all ends (Omniscient Level of Awareness).

Understanding the fact that First Person is being told from inside the Narrator's head is vitally important if you're going to take full advantage of all the things First Person can do for a story. But none of it will work if you don't make everything personal to the Narrator.

The Narrator is the key.

Yes, you must create the perfect Narrator for your story.

Unfortunately, this is relative to your individual story. If the story needs a strong Narrator, make them strong. If it needs a sympathetic Narrator, make them sympathetic. If it needs a Narrator who is an asshole, always accusing the poor, innocent reader of interrupting their train of thought, then make them so.

I can't help you there, as every story is different. My advice returns to the fact that it all comes down to you thinking about what the story needs instead of letting chance decide if you're doing the correct thing.

Time and Effort, with the emphasis here on Effort.

The world of a First Person story exists only as presented through the Narrator's eyes. Remember the finger-glasses? If you can see it through your finger-glasses, you can write it.

Everything is also being filtered through the Narrator's Perception. If the Narrator feels someone's a jerk, then you must write that someone as a jerk. If the Narrator hates the cold, then cold things will probably merit more comments. If your Narrator is paranoid, then their comments need to be focused upon things that drive that paranoia. If the Narrator only looks at a man's groin, and never his eyes, then your Narration must be written that way—she must be a letch, and the first thing she notices should be what the man's body looks like, not the color of his eyes.

No Head Hopping in First Person. The story is coming from inside the Narrator's head, so there's no way your Narrator can know what's going on inside the other character's heads. Now, this has nothing to do with multiple Narrators. But as I discussed, having multiple First Person Narrators brings its own set of problems to your story.

All this is important when crafting First Person. However, to really make First Person shine, you must go one step further.

You must attempt to make everything as personal to the Narrator as you can.

> I stood in my backyard. It was winter, and snow
> covered the roof of the two-story home I'd grown
> up in. The pool had been drained. The trampoline

> had been placed into storage. A foot of snow
> sat on top of my father's old covered grill. The
> forest surrounding the house was filled with bare
> branches.

Sure, the above paragraph is all description, and we need it. We need it so the reader can *see* the scene. However, the above is a total waste of words.

Why? Because, while it does paint the scene, it does nothing to connect the reader to the scene on a personal level.

Keep in mind, the Narrator in the above is in *his* backyard. A backyard *he* grew up in. That is *his* pool. *His* trampoline. *His* father's grill. The forest surrounding that house is the forest *he* explored as a child.

Within First Person, it's not good enough to simply describe things so your reader can see them. You must look for organic ways to viscerally connect the reader to what is being seen as well.

> I stood in the backyard where I'd spent my entire
> childhood. The pool that housed the pirate battles
> and sea monster attacks. The trampoline where
> I competed for Olympic gold. The surrounding
> forest I had spent countless days exploring,
> pretending it was the deep dark jungles of Africa.
> The grill my father used each summer to serve up
> hamburgers, chicken, and ribs tastier than any I'd
> had since.
>
> But all that was left now were the memories,
> cold and empty as the winter gripping the world
> around me.
>
> Snow covered the roof of the two-story house.
> Icicles lined its eaves. The pool had been drained.
> The trampoline placed into storage. A foot of snow
> sat atop the covered grill. The forest was filled
> with trees that seemed as lifeless as my soul.

There's a huge difference between describing the world for the reader to see, and viscerally connecting the reader to the world being described through the Perception of your Narrator.

Now, remember my caution about falling too deeply into the Narrator and overusing Exposition. It's a difficult task balancing the fact that you need to make your descriptions personal vs. bogging your story down with overwritten Exposition. What you want to do is make sure all this extra detail is relevant to the story, and not wasted words. And this will take you years to master.

One-Million Words of Time and Effort. ☺

To give you some insight inside my writer's brain, let me explain what I was thinking when I wrote the above example. As I wrote it I was imagining a slice-of-life story where the Narrator had returned home for his father's funeral. The Narrator had left under strained circumstances, and he'd never taken the time to reconcile with his father. I imagined this scene was where he had returned home after years away and began to realize that he'd returned home too late.

If you look at the narrative, it all has purpose. All the childhood memories are fond ones, meant to conjure up images of a happy home. That way, once I shift into the cold reality of the scene, the description of the world could stand in stark contrast to those warm memories. If I was really writing this as a story, as opposed to making it all up on the fly, I would continue to build upon this, ensuring there was a payoff that moved the story. Really drive a wedge into my reader's heart over the pain and loss this Narrator feels about his broken relationship with his now dead father.

Hopefully, you know your story better than I knew the above example.

My point is, know your story, your Narrator, how they feel about the world around them, their desires, fears, loves, etc. Show this to your reader in ways that are personal to the Narrator so the reader gets a deeper connection to both the story and the Narrator, and you'll create stories people will want to read.

And that's about all I have to say about First Person.

Let's now take the briefest of moments to look at…

Second Person Narrative

I don't plan on spending much time on Second Person because it's a Narrative that's rarely used in Speculative Fiction. However, there are a few cool things about it, and I've had one story published in Second Person, so it'd be a shame if I didn't at least touch upon it.

In a Second Person Narrative story, the Narrator is a very strange beast indeed. A lot of people assume the reader is the Narrator, but I feel this is incorrect.

The Protagonist is the reader, of that there's no doubt. However, the Narrator is more of a Puppet Master, controlling the reader's thoughts and actions. A weird third-party entity hiding in the shadows with their hand stuck up your ass.

And like my analogy, this creates issues with readers. It's the reason so many adults don't enjoy reading Second Person stories.

In First Person, the reader is listening to a Narrator tell them a story about something that Narrator has done. If done well, you can get the reader to suspend disbelief that they are reading a book, and become viscerally connected to the Narrator.

In Second Person, the reader is being controlled by the Narrator of the story. It's this reason that makes the *buy in* more difficult. The reader *knows* they're not the barbarian hero or the psychic teenager in the story. They're simply suspending their disbelief by saying, "Okay, I'm the psychic teenager." Where this reality breaks is when that psychic teenager does something the reader knows they wouldn't do.

> You creep into the dimly-lit morgue, attempting to discover where the strange groaning noise is coming from.

Um… no. I wouldn't enter a dimly-lit morgue, thank you very much. Especially if there was a strange groaning noise coming from it.

Now, younger minds have less of an issue with this than adults. It's why there are so many "scary" Middle Grade books written in Second Person. With the above example, a younger reader is more apt to accept the actions they're forced to do and just roll with it.

Still, even with this issue, if done correctly, and written for the correct audience, Second Person can be a very effective tool to deliver some types of stories.

As with First Person, the reader is not watching this story unfold in the same way they would if this was on a movie screen. On a movie screen the viewer (reader) can see all the characters, including the Narrator.

In Second Person, the reader is watching this story unfold *literally* through their own eyes. It's as if the reader's eyes are the Imaginary Camera.

I know you're happy I drew the Puppet Master Narrator pulling the Readers strings as opposed to having his hand shoved up the Reader's ass. You're welcome.

Because of where this Imaginary Camera is, the reader sees, hears, feels, and understands everything through their *own* Perceptions. The rub is, all these Perceptions are given to the reader by the Puppet Master Narrator. The reader is forced to accept these Perceptions whether they want them or not.

To tell the story, the Puppet Master Narrator uses second person Pronouns such as you, your, etc. In addition, just like First Person, the Narration (all the words that surround the dialogue) are extensions of the Protagonist (reader). However, as the Puppet Master Narrator can force whatever they wish upon the poor reader, sometimes you may want to use Inner Monologue, while other times you may not.

Case in point:

> You can't believe this is happening. *The dead can't come back to life,* you think. *There must be another explanation.*

This works. But so does:

> This can't be happening. The dead can't come back to life. There must be another explanation.

It really just depends on what you are trying to do. Since you are the Puppet Master Narrator, and the reader is your Puppet, do with them as you wish.

The fact remains that Second Person is much like First Person in so many ways. To that end, let me quickly burn through several topics I've already discussed, and say, "Just like First Person" a lot.

As with First Person, Second Person is a Limited Narrative. Meaning, your Second Person Protagonist is the Camera, so you can only write things that are physically there for your Second Person Protagonist to see, hear, or experience. My finger-glasses trick works perfectly for this.

Because of this Limited Narration, it's easy to stay inside the Protagonist's head, since you simply need to stay inside the reader's head.

It's easy to convey feelings and emotions. because, well, not only are you still inside their head, you get to force whatever feelings and emotions you want upon the reader.

It's easy to create that strong familiarity bond since the reader is the Protagonist. You guessed it, inside their head.

It's easy to build that empathy that's needed so the reader cares about the story. Because... inside their head.

It's easy to stay consistent with Tone and Style. Same. Head.

Narration can be less formal, though it does need to be at the level of your targeted reader. In other words, if you're writing for a Middle Grade audience (8 to 12 years of age), you want to ensure your Narrative utilizes relevant connotation by employing diminutive, as opposed to grandiose, verbiage.

Err… I mean, write your story using words your targeted reader will be comfortable reading.

Basically, every advantage First Person gets from being a Limited Narrative, Second Person gets as well.

This means the disadvantages First Person has from being a Limited Narrative will plague Second Person also.

Information Dumps can become an issue. Stay vigilant against them.

There's no way for your reader to know what any other character in the story is thinking, unless those characters either say things aloud, or act it out.

You must limit yourself to one Protagonist. Oh, and this is a must, not a suggestion. Seriously, you can't have multiple Second Person Narrators. Ever. You have only one reader, and that reader can be only one Protagonist.

With those out of the way, let's look at a few things in which Second Person does get a bit squirrelly with.

You could say Second Person can have an Unreliable Narrator, but it's not exactly the same as First Person. *All* Second Person Protagonists are Unreliable, period.

Why? Since your reader doesn't know anything, and are simply being controlled by a Puppet Master Narrator, they fully expect to be lied to. I mean, would you trust a guy who had full control of all your thoughts, emotions, and actions?

It's also the reason Second Person stories *must* have a Limited Level of Awareness. Again, the reader has no idea what will happen next. How could they? Due to this, Omniscient is not available in Second Person.

Another huge difference is with the inability to Describe the Protagonist in Second Person.

In First Person, it's *difficult* to describe your Narrator. In Second

Person, however, you *can't* describe your Protagonist. Ever. Seriously. If you ever even hint about your Protagonist in any way, you'll destroy your story.

Use he, and every single female reader is alienated.

Use black skin, and all other skin tones are alienated.

Use blond hair, and all other hair colors are alienated.

This doesn't just apply to physical appearances, either. Religion, sexual orientation, political or social views—basically, all those topics your mother warned you to never speak about in mixed company are off limits when writing Second Person.

Mention them, and you lose any reader who is different.

This is also the reason creating your Puppet Master Narrator's Voice is so difficult. You have options, but you want to make sure those options enhance the telling of your tale.

Most of the time, I find an invisible Puppet Master Narrator works. However, say you're writing a Middle Grade Horror story. How cool would a creepy Puppet Master Narrator's Voice be.

In the end, my advice is the same as always. Time. Effort. Think about the type of story you're telling, and try and find a Puppet Master Narrator's Voice that would enhance that story.

The last strange thing about Second Person is that it should be told in Present Tense.

In Second Person, you're controlling the reader. They must read lines like, "You do this. You do that." When this is done in the *Right Now* moment of Present Tense, it's much easier for the reader to suspend disbelief. They are, after all, reading the story *Right Now*, so it's not a stretch to allow themselves to fall into the events being described.

However, when you write Second Person in Past Tense, your story is now competing with the reader's actual memories.

> Last night you crept into the dimly-lit morgue, attempting to discover where the strange groaning noise was coming from.

Um… no. Last night I was safely at home watching reruns of *I Love Lucy*.

And before you cut me off again, I get that I didn't need to add the "Last night" bit, but I'm making a point here. It's much easier for the reader to be told what they are doing *Right Now*, as opposed to *Back Then*, so if you're going to write in Second Person, I recommend you do so using Present Tense.

So you have at least one real example of Second Person in action, here's the first few paragraphs from my short story, *Wishing You Weren't Here* (Available in both eBook and audio book (read by yours truly) from Amazon.)

You reach out to the tape recorder sitting on the table before you. Letting your finger caress the "play" button for a second, you press it down. A crackling-pop stabs into your ears as the machine starts. The gears of the cassette turn for the first time in decades and the squeaks of plastic rubbing plastic fill the dark room you are hiding in.

An old man's voice, rough and dry, reverberates through the speakers. "So, am I just supposed to start talking?"

The loud screech of metal scraping across a concrete floor forces you to turn the volume down. You glance at the door to the room. Even as thick as it is, you know it won't protect you for long. You turn your attention back to the tape player as a younger man's voice spills from it.

"Just give me a moment please, James, and we will begin." The man clears his throat.

The thing to keep in mind is, if you're going to write in Second Person, you'll pretty much use all the ins and outs of First Person, but replace "I" with "you."

Now, let's move forward and delve into the Narrative that's been my bread and butter for decades now…

Third Person Narrative

Welcome. I'm happy you've made it this far. I really am. Now… prepare yourself.

> I will proclaim to the world the deeds of Gilgamesh. This was the man to whom all things were known; this was the king who knew the countries of the world. He was wise, he saw mysteries and knew secret things, he brought us a tale of the days before the flood.

I won't deny it. Third Person is my baby. My love. Well, one aspect of it, anyway. And I hope to open your eyes to all the magic it holds. The other two aspects of Third Person are outdated pieces of crap best left to rot in the graves of history. But lucky for you, I'm not overly opinionated, or anything. No one cares for people like that. ☺

Anyhoo… Let's dive into this.

Just like First Person, some variation of Third Person has been around since the Dawn of Storytelling. In fact, at least when it comes to *written* fiction stories that have survived the ravages of time, Third Person holds the record for being the oldest Narrative we've ever found. While there are older "religious" texts that have survived, the oldest physical copy of a fiction story is called the *Epic of Gilgamesh*, which is a series of Sumerian poems and tales about a Sumerian king who went on a quest for immortality. The version I'm referring to was written on twelve clay tablets around 2,100 BC. Yeah, over 4,000 years ago. Think about that. Moses is attributed for writing the first five books of the Bible, and he lived sometime between 1,500 and 1,300 BC. So the tablets holding the *Epic of Gilgamesh* are some 600 years older than the oldest parts of the Bible!

More interesting to me is the story itself, or more accurately, the structure used to write this story. The Story Structure of this tale follows The Hero's Journey. Yes, that Hero's Journey. The one that's still the predominant story structure used to this very day!

Fascinating, I know. But that's history. And you aren't here for a history lesson. You're here to learn how to improve your craft of writing. So let's do that instead.

In all Third Person stories, the Narrator is a Character who is telling the story. This Narrator could be a Character inside the story, or they could be a Character who isn't inside the story. They could even be the writer of the story, and not a Character at all. Basically, every single Narrator type I discussed in the *What is a Narrator* section is available to you within the confines that is Third Person.

In the excerpt I used to open this section, the Narrator who is telling the tale of King Gilgamesh is obviously not someone in the story. They are a Storyteller Narrator.

For the reader, a Third Person story is as close as you can get to having the same experience as watching a movie on the big screen. Just like on a movie screen, the viewer (reader) can see all the characters, including the Narrator if that Narrator is a Character within the story.

The reason for this comes from the fact that, unlike First and Second Person, the reader is watching this story unfold through an **Imaginary Camera** that's *not* inside any particular Character's head. This Imaginary Camera is free-floating, able to see much more since it's not trapped inside a Character.

And here's your first hint as to why there's such a difference between the aspects of Third Person—it all comes down to how the writer uses this Imaginary Camera. Much more on this as I progress.

To tell a Third Person story, the Narrator uses third person Nouns and Proper Nouns such as Character Names, and/or third person Pronouns such as he, she, it, they, etc.

Now, when it comes to the Tense a Third Person story can be told in, things get a little bit more limited than what you have with either First or Second Person. To remind you of what Tenses are (I know how scatterbrained you can be), here's a quick recap.

There are two Narrative Tenses, Past and Present. And both control time as it relates to the Reader, not the Narrator. If the Story is being told as if it has already happened, it's being told in Past Tense. If the Story is being told as if it's happening right now, it's being told in Present Tense.

Remember, this has nothing to do with the Narrator's Level of Awareness. You can have an Omniscient Narrator tell either a Past or Present Tense Story, just as you can have a Limited Narrator tell either a Past or Present Tense Story.

Returning to our topic, I stated when writing in First Person, Past Tense normally works better, both for the writer and the reader. Though Present Tense is commonly used in today's publishing industry.

I also stated when writing in Second Person, Present Tense is the way to get the reader to buy into the story. Though you can use Past Tense and still make it work.

Third Person is different.

For Third Person you really, really should write in Past Tense, and Past Tense only. Let me stress that. Write Third Person in Past Tense. Seriously.

Not that it can't be done in Present Tense. It can. And it can be done effectively. I mentioned this book earlier, but here's an excerpt from J.M. Coetzee's *Disgrace*.

> He is mildly smitten with her. It is no great matter: barely a term passes when he does not fall for one or other of his charges. Cape Town: a city prodigal of beauty, of beauties.
>
> Does she know he has an eye on her? Probably. Women are sensitive to it, to the weight of the desiring gaze.
>
> It has been raining; from the pathside runnels comes the soft rush of water.
>
> 'My favourite season, my favourite time of day,' he remarks. 'Do you live around here?'
>
> 'Across the line. I share a flat.'
>
> 'Is Cape Town your home?'
>
> 'No, I grew up in George.'
>
> 'I live just nearby. Can I invite you in for a drink?'
>
> A pause, cautious. 'OK. But I have to be back by seven-thirty.'
>
> From the gardens they pass into the quiet

> residential pocket where he has lived for the past twelve years, first with Rosalind, the, after the divorce, alone.
>
> He unlocks the security gate, unlocks the door, ushers the girl in. He switches on the light, takes her bag. There are raindrops on her hair. He stares, frankly ravished. She lowers her eyes, offering the same evasive and perhaps even coquettish little smile as before.
>
> In the kitchen he opens a bottle of Meerlust and sets out biscuits and cheese. When he returns she is standing at the bookshelves, head on one side, reading titles. He puts on music: the Mozart clarinet quintet.

There's nothing wrong with the above. I think J.M. Coetzee did about as good a job as can be done writing Third Person Present Tense. However, as this Tense is so foreign to most readers, and so rarely used to boot, you may have found a few sentences in the above awkward to read.

My point is, why write something that causes the reader to be uncomfortable with what they're reading? I've already stated how hard it is to gain readers.

The writer, however, gets the short end of this stick. Holding this Tense is incredibly difficult, and forces the writer to work especially hard. Since the Tense isn't natural, you'll be fixing your Tense Shifts continuously. Another issue comes from the fact that most Third Person stories won't allow you to hold to a strict Present Tense. Sometimes, you'll have to slip into Past Tense whether you like it or not. Look at this one sentence again:

> From the gardens they pass into the quiet residential pocket where he has lived for the past twelve years, first with Rosalind, then, after the divorce, alone.

"Pass" is a Present Tense Verb, meaning the sentence starts in Present Tense. However, "has lived", "first with", "then, after" are all in Past Tense. And they need to be, because all that stuff happened before the story that's happening Right Now. But that's the trap of Third Person Present Tense, there will be times you need to Shift into Past Tense. (It's also the trap of using Present Tense in First Person as well.)

Another issue with trying to force Third Person to hold a Present Tense is that it'll fight you, forcing you to create some very awkward sentences. You can overcome these, but you'll have to work at it.

But the biggest offender to me is when I read, "says". As in:

> 'It was nice,' she says, draining her glass, rising. 'Thanks.'

I don't know, perhaps I'm just crazy, but seeing the word "says" always throws me out of a book. It's one of the reasons I can't read First Person Present Tense either.

My biggest question to anyone contemplating using Present Tense when writing Third Person is Why? Even when it's done perfectly, it doesn't add anything to the story. It doesn't make it more immersive. It doesn't make it more interesting. It doesn't build tension better. It adds no benefits that I can see. It literally does nothing good, and most readers find it very off-putting to read. So, why even use it at all?

Well, as they say, there's a Story for every Narrative.

One story I think worked really well in Third Person Present Tense was a wonderful little tale written by paleontologist Dr. Robert T. Bakker called *Raptor Red*. This story is about a Raptor and is set back in the days of the dinosaurs. However, this story doesn't humanize the animals, as in, they don't walk and talk like the dinosaurs in *Ice Age*. They are written exactly as Dr. Bakker imagined they would've lived back then, so it's written more like an animal documentary you'd see on Animal Planet.

However, since the animals in that book are living in the Right Now, not really thinking about the past, nor planning for the future, the Present Tense Narrative works. As the Raptors can't tell the audience their story, having the third-party Narrator that comes with Third Person bridges the gap between the reader and the animal characters.

Hence, the perfect story to be told in Third Person Present Tense. But this is way more the exception, and far from the rule.

To better illustrate my point, let's look at a sample of my own writing. First I'll give it to you in Third Person Past Tense, which is how the piece is written. Then I'll rewrite it so that it's in Third Person Present Tense. From there, we can discuss.

Here's an excerpt from a novel I'm currently writing:

> General Alzadysta shook his head, exasperation entering his voice. "We all know why we cannot kill her. It would be—" The Torijan's words were cut short as the largest Kithian Valimane had ever seen approached the general. At least a half-hand taller than the tallest lionman, standing nearly eye-level with the winged general, this new Kithian locked eyes with Alzadysta for several moments before the Immortal inclined his head. "I see you, Malkin Kanon," he said.
>
> The Kith returned the nod. "And I see you, Alzadysta."
>
> The lionman's voice was little more than a growl, and Valimane had trouble understanding his garbled words. Looking over his shoulder, the beastman glared at the Mamokian king. "Your fears do not concern me, *Gold Man*," he said. "We shall be long gone before *Mother* arrives." The disdain lacing the title left no doubt as to his feelings. Returning his attention to the general, Malkin removed the medallion from around his neck. "And we have no need of your protection any longer." He spat the words out like a curse as he dropped the Tarsith to the ground at the Immortal's feet.
>
> When Malkin stepped back, the other Kithian leaders approached one after the other. Each

removed their necklace with a snarl before adding it to the growing pile before the general.

Once the last pendant had been deposited on the ground, Malkin Kanon stepped forward again. "The last of the Grays lay dead, but one Blue escaped us," he said. An angry glare filled the creature's eyes. "Flew off before we could sink claws into it."

And here it is again, but in Present Tense.

General Alzadysta shakes his head, exasperation entering his voice. "We all know why we cannot kill her. It would be—" The Torijan's words are cut short as the largest Kithian Valimane has ever seen approaches the general. At least a half-hand taller than the tallest lionman, standing nearly eye-level with the winged general, this new Kithian locks eyes with Alzadysta for several moments before the Immortal inclines his head. "I see you, Malkin Kanon," he says.

The Kith returns the nod. "And I see you, Alzadysta."

The lionman's voice is little more than a growl, and Valimane struggles to understand his garbled words. Looking over his shoulder, the beastman glares at the Mamokian king. "Your fears do not concern me, *Gold Man*," he says. "We shall be long gone before *Mother* arrives." Disdain laces the title, leaving no doubt as to his feelings. Returning his attention to the general, Malkin removes the medallion from around his neck. "And we have no need of your protection any longer." He spits the words out like a curse as he drops the Tarsith to the ground at the Immortal's feet.

Malkin steps back, and the other Kithian leaders approach one after the other. Each remove their necklace with a snarl before adding it to the growing pile before the general.

Once the last pendant is deposited on the ground, Malkin Kanon steps forward again. "The last of the Grays lay dead, but one Blue escaped us," he says. An angry glare fills the creature's eyes. "Flew off before we could sink claws into it."

First and foremost: That was amazingly, mind-numbingly difficult to write. I had to edit the living crap out of it multiple times to catch everything that needed changing. Now admittedly, this is due to the fact that I don't write this way. But neither does anyone else, for the most part. So, as a writer, you have very few examples to lean upon. It also means your learning curve on writing in this style is going to be longer than normal.

I struggled to make sure every single sentence stayed in Present Tense. As I have said, I'm not going to go over Verb Forms in detail in this book, but that's exactly why I struggled with the above. I had to scrutinize every Verb in every sentence, and it took me several editing passes to get them all right. Though, truth be told, I'm not 100% sure I did get them all. I could've easily missed a few.

But let's take this further. When a reader reads:

"Your fears do not concern me, *Gold Man*," he says.

The, "he says." feels like a typo. It's not natural. So, as with all typos, when the reader hits this they're pulled out of the story.

Writing this in Present Tense also created some awkward sentence structures, forcing me to rework the sentence.

The lionman's voice was little more than a growl, and Valimane had trouble understanding his garbled words.

This works well in Past Tense, but I couldn't change it to Present Tense without reworking it.

> The lionman's voice is little more than a growl,
> and Valimane struggles to understand his garbled
> words.

I couldn't use the word trouble. It just didn't translate into Present Tense within the confines of this sentence. Not that the rewrite is bad. It simply caused me to work harder than normal.

And that's a huge issue with writing Third Person, or even First Person, in Present Tense, it forces the writer to work extra hard to avoid creating awkward sentences because it limits the choices you have.

Now keep in mind, I'm editing a previously written piece. If I was writing this from scratch, I feel it would be even more difficult to come up with sentences that didn't feel awkward in Present Tense. To me, it makes everything feel like a Tell. And there's nothing less immersive than writing a story that's one big Tell.

But the worst offender to me here is, where's the advantage? Sure, I pulled it off. I changed its Tense and I feel the rewrite reads just as good as the original. But is it more immersive than the Past Tense version? Is there more tension? Is it more interesting to read? In my not so humble opinion, no. I can't see any advantage, but the disadvantage of how much extra work it was will haunt me till my dying day. Seriously. To you, it may seem as if my train of thought is unbroken. But I had to take a full six months off from writing after switching that to Present Tense! There was a time there, a very dark time indeed, where I was frightened I may never have the strength to write again.

Lucky for you, I found that strength and was able to return and finish writing this book.

Bottom line is, think about it before you use Present Tense. To me, I would never step into these treacherous waters unless there was an incredibly solid, story-driven reason for me to do so.

Thinking something like, "Oh, since no one writes this way it'll mean my stuff will stand out as unique." is not only wrong, it's career suicide.

As most readers find it more enjoyable to read, stick with Past Tense when writing Third Person. It's more natural to both read and write. It's what readers expect. And honestly, it's what the industry expects. Seriously, it's going to be very difficult to sell a story that's written in Third Person Present Tense. Acquisition Editors are readers as well. If your choice of Tense annoys them, chances are they won't purchase your book. As it's already unbelievably hard to break into this industry, why would you ever want to make that even more difficult by writing in a Tense that's problematic?

With all that said, from here on out everything I'm going to teach about Third Person is being done with the assumption that you'll be writing in Past Tense. You want to write in Third Person Present Tense? Go ahead. I showed you it can be done, and done well. But you're on your own, bub. I want no part of it.

Unfortunately, this is also as far as I can take Third Person as a single topic. It's too complex. Too varied. And within these variations, there's a wide chasm separating each Third Person type from the other.

I can, however, break Third Person down into three main types, all of which I've mentioned a few times already: Third Person Omniscient, Third Person Free Indirect Discourse, and Third Person Limited.

These are all considered Third Person, follow many of the same rules, and each have similarities to the others. At the same time, they couldn't be more different.

Case in point: Third Person Limited is the *most* immersive Narrative that exists, while Third Person Omniscient is the *least* immersive Narrative that exists.

From here on out, I'm going to talk about each of these types separately. Let's begin by going through each of these quickly and see how they handle who the Narrator can be, as well as that Narrator's Level of Awareness, beginning with…

Narrators in Third Person Omniscient

Third Person Omniscient is the oldest form of written storytelling. If you've read more than three books in your life, you've probably seen this Narrative in action.

(Side note, because I'm the proverbial jerk, I must say again if you don't consider yourself a reader, please don't attempt to become a writer. Just… don't.)

In a Third Person Omniscient story, there's a third-party Character telling the story. This third-party Narrator is someone who is *NOT* in the story. Let me stress that. In Third Person Omniscient, the Narrator is *NEVER* a Character in the story.

While this does limit your choices of a Narrator, your options are still pretty wide open. In fact, you can use most of the Narrator types I discussed in the *What is a Narrator* section. The Narrator could be you, the Writer, a Commentator, an Interviewer, a Storyteller Narrator, and the list goes on.

Honestly, the only Narrator types not available to Third Person Omniscient are Narrators who restrict the telling of the story.

In other words, they can't be a Character inside the story they're telling. Think more God-like when it comes to a Third Person Omniscient Narrator.

> When the gods created Gilgamesh they gave him a perfect body. Shamash the glorious sun endowed him with beauty, Adad the god of the storm endowed him with courage, the great gods made his beauty perfect, surpassing all others, terrifying like a great wild bull. Two thirds they made him god and one third man.

Since this Narrative is Omniscient, the Narrator must be someone who has access to everything. The entire world; all the people, all the things within it, and all the events and their outcomes, past, present, and future. Basically, the Narrator needs the ability to tell the story without any limitations.

I mean, Omniscient is in the title, for Pete's sake.

Keeping with this, the Narrator for a Third Person Omniscient story *must* have an Omniscient Level of Awareness.

Again, Omniscient. In title. The sake of Pete. Whoever the hell Pete is.

This Narrative is all-encompassing. Which is honestly the only hard rule within Third Person Omniscient. If it's broken, it means you've moved away from true Third Person Omniscient, and are now writing in Third Person Free Indirect Discourse. Pretty simple.

Let's now take a quick gander at…

Narrators in Third Person Limited

There's no doubt in my mind that Third Person Limited is the Narrative of today when it comes to Speculative Fiction. Unfortunately, it's the youngest in this game, and like my personality, I'm not sure if you could even call it mature, yet. It's still evolving, growing, and the best writers of today are still experimenting with new ways to make it shine. In fact, as far as my research has uncovered, this book may be the first attempt to define it. At least, define it as I use it.

First!

Don't get me wrong, the nomenclature of Third Person Limited has been around for decades. But in my not so humble opinion, it's always been used erroneously. As I've stated a few times now, in my travels, every time someone is teaching what they call Third Person Limited, they're in reality teaching Third Person Free Indirect Discourse.

"Oh, yeah!" You interject. "You skip that one."

Interruptions… *Big Sigh*

Yes. Patience Padawan. There's a method to my madness… or at least that's what I told the State Shrink when she came by last week. She bought it, so no psych ward for me this year. Haha!

Third Person Limited is the hardest of the Third Person Narratives to master, mostly due to the fact that it's not well defined by the industry. But also because, well, it's damn difficult to pull off. For some reason, the nuances of this Narrative seem to elude most aspiring writers. Hopefully, when the dust settles and the blood dries, I'll have done my job and you'll walk out of here better from the experience. If not, I blame you. What? You can't hold me responsible when there's a high probability I'm criminally insane.

> Hello, there! Mrs. Johnson here again. Drake's third-grade teacher. Once again, Drake is going to be a naughty boy and teach you something in a way I don't approve of. No. I don't approve of it one bit at all!

Thank you, Mrs. Johnson. You're excused. Oh, before you go. It was I who filled your pencil sharpener with glue. Bwahahahaha!

As with Omniscient, in a Third Person Limited story, there's a third-party Character who is telling this tale. The difference is, this third-party Character is *absolutely* a Character within the story. In fact, they must be.

The easiest way to wrap your mind around Third Person Limited is to think of it like this:

> Third Person Limited is written exactly like First Person, only using third-person Nouns and Pronouns.

Much more on this in a moment. For now, I'm talking Narrators.

The biggest difference between Third Person Limited and all other Narrative styles is with the Narrator's Level of Awareness. Whereas in all other Narratives you can have a Narrator with a Limited or Omniscient Level of Awareness, with Third Person Limited you *must* use a Limited Level of Awareness to pull this Narrative off. The future *must* be undiscovered country. The Narrator and the reader *must* be learning what's going on at the same time.

Look, this may all sound confusing, but it's not. Think about their names. Third Person *Omniscient* is told by an *Omniscient* Narrator with an *Omniscient* Level of Awareness, while Third Person *Limited* is told by a *Limited* Narrator with a *Limited* Level of Awareness. See how it all lines up?

Bonus for Third Person Limited: it gets *all* the advantages First Person brings to a story, but less of its disadvantages. Yummy!

Turning our attention to the final Third Person Narrative type, let's now look at the…

Narrators in Third Person Free Indirect Discourse

There's a very high chance this is the first time you've ever read anything concerning Third Person Free Indirect Discourse. I assure you, I didn't make this one up. It's a real grammatical term. However, for whatever reason, probably its stupidly long and asinine name, it's never taught. Or even talked about. Or invited to parties. It certainly has never been given any award in recognition for its contributions to literature. Which is a shame since almost every single Third Person Speculative Fiction book ever written uses this Narrative type.

Seriously. I'd be willing to bet that almost every book you've read that was written in Third Person was written in Third Person Free Indirect Discourse. I'd even go so far as to say that if you're currently writing in Third Person, you're writing in Third Person Free Indirect Discourse. And yet, you've never even heard of this Narrative type before! I know this is probably shocking for you to hear, since you've been happily wallowing in your own ignorance, but that's okay. Hush. Huuuush. Lay your head down my shoulder and daddy'll make it all better.

Alright… I admit. That got a little weird even for me.

Still. Poor Third Person Free Indirect Discourse. Always the bridesmaid and never the bride.

Since the evolution of storytelling fascinates me, I like to think of Third Person Free Indirect Discourse more as the prototype that birthed the love of my life, Third Person Limited.

Basically, Third Person Free Indirect Discourse has been around for at least a few hundred years. It exists because writers of Speculative Fiction quickly learned that First Person has some hard limitations that can ruin a story, and Third Person Omniscient sucks ass in the immersion department.

Writers in the past wanted more. Something better.

Now, this wasn't some organized event. There was no *writing summit* where Baum, London, Sinclair, Burroughs, Fitzgerald, Mitchell, Steinbeck, Hemingway, Heinlein, Asimov, etc. got together and started discussing ways to write Speculative Fiction in a more immersive way. Though, if something like that *had* happened… oh, to be a fly on that wall!

Wait? What was I talking about? Oh, right. No. It wasn't an organized event. Third Person Free Indirect Discourse evolved because the above writers, and many, many others, wanted new and improved ways to write stories. So, they experimented while they wrote. Breaking rules. Tweaking methods. Pushing their craft as they attempted to discover new ways to use English grammar to deliver more interesting and immersive stories.

Or perhaps they didn't. Perhaps they simply wrote with a devil-may-care attitude, and what they created has given us the raw materials to continue pushing grammar in new ways. I wasn't around back then! Why do you keep thinking I have all the answers? For all you know, I could be a madman frothing at the mouth!

However it happened, it definitely shaped how we write today. And as a writer, the more you learn about the differences between these Narrative types, the better you'll be able to use them to push your own writing.

As I've been teaching Creative Writing, I've noticed that aspiring writers have a hard time grasping what I mean when I say Third Person Free Indirect Discourse. But honestly, it's not that difficult.

I'll go into more detail in a moment, but here's my definition of it:

> It's one-part Third Person Omniscient, so you have a disembodied third-party Narrator who is *not* in the story.
>
> It's one-part Third Person Limited, so you also have a very grounded Character Narrator who *is* in the story.

And you simply Shift back and forth between these two Narrators willy-nilly as you see fit.

Let me give you an example of Third Person Free Indirect Discourse so hopefully you can understand what I'm talking about here. One of the best examples of Third Person Free Indirect Discourse in action is Thomas Harris' *Silence of the Lambs*.

Here are the first two pages of this book.

> Behavioral Science, the FBI section that deals with serial murder, is on the bottom floor of the Academy building at Quantico, half-buried in the earth. Clarice Starling reached it flushed after a fast walk from Hogan's Alley on the firing range. She had grass in her hair and grass stains on her FBI Academy windbreaker from diving to the ground under fire in an arrest problem on the range.
>
> No one was in the outer office, so she fluffed briefly by her reflection in the glass doors. She knew she could look all right without primping. Her hands smelled of gunsmoke, but there was no time to wash-- Section Chief Crawford's summons had said now.
>
> She found Jack Crawford alone in the cluttered suite of offices. He was standing at someone else's desk talking on the telephone and she had a chance to look him over for the first time in a year. What she saw disturbed her.
>
> Normally, Crawford looked like a fit, middle-aged engineer who might have paid his way through college playing baseball-- a crafty catcher, tough when he blocked the plate. Now he was thin, his shirt collar was too big, and he had dark puffs under his reddened eyes. Everyone who could read the papers knew Behavioral Science section was

catching hell. Starling hoped Crawford wasn't on the juice. That seemed most unlikely here.

Crawford ended his telephone conversation with a sharp "No." He took her file from under his arm and opened it.

"Starling, Clarice M., good morning," he said.

"Hello." Her smile was only polite.

"Nothing's wrong. I hope the call didn't spook you."

"No." *Not totally true*, Starling thought.

"Your instructors tell me you're doing well, top quarter of the class."

"I hope so, they haven't posted anything."

"I ask them from time to time."

That surprised Starling; she had written Crawford off as a two-faced recruiting sergeant son of a bitch.

This example is obviously written in Third Person. All the Characters are being referred to by either their names, or by third-person pronouns such as he or she. But it neither falls into the category of Omniscient, nor Limited, because it has elements of both.

Look again at the opening line.

Behavioral Science, the FBI section that deals with serial murder, is on the bottom floor of the Academy building at Quantico, half-buried in the earth.

The first sentence of the first paragraph is "detached", told from an Omniscient perspective. It's a piece of stage setting in which Starling doesn't appear until the next sentence. It's even separated from the rest of the paragraph by being written in Present Tense. *Gasp!* Tense Shift in a New York Times Bestseller! Oh, the horror. *The horror!*

It feels Omniscient. It smells Omniscient. It *is* Omniscient. This line is being told by some disembodied entity who isn't a Character within the story, and this Narrator is talking directly to the reader. Third Person Omniscient.

However, every line after the first line is from Starling's limited perspective, written using Past Tense. Let's look at a line from the dialogue section.

"No." *Not totally true, Starling thought.*

This is no longer being told from the perspective of a disembodied third-party Omniscient Narrator. This is now being told by Starling herself. The line and her inner monologue are "Limited". In doing this, she has become the Narrator.

That's Third Person *Free* Indirect Discourse. The writer is *free* to Shift from an Omniscient Narrator to a Limited Narrator as they feel they should. Eh? See what I did there? Eh? It lines up? *Free. Free.* Eh? Lines up? Eh?

As you continue to read the wonderful story that is *Silence of the Lambs*, this **Shifting** between a third-party Narrator and a Character Narrator continues to happen. Sometimes the story is being told by an Omniscient Narrator who isn't in the story, others by one of the Characters within the story, etc. And Harris does a masterful job of doing all this Shifting in a way that becomes nearly invisible to the reader.

The more you read books written in Third Person, the more you'll realize that nearly every single one of them are written in Third Person Free Indirect Discourse.

To me, Third Person Free Indirect Discourse is the catchall between strict Third Person Omniscient and tight Third Person Limited.

As I've stressed throughout, there's no one Narrative type that's perfect for all stories. This is very true within Third Person. So, while yes, my love *is* Third Person Limited, it's *not* the perfect Narrative type for all stories. The fact that it's so Limited means it could very easily ruin some stories.

Silence of the Lambs is the perfect example of this.

Had this story been written in true Third Person Limited, as I like to write, it would've lost the ability to Shift from an Omniscient Narrator into Starling's head, Crawford's head, Hannibal's head, Buffalo Bill's head, etc. And that would've hurt the telling of this particular tale.

Plus, strict Third Person Limited was literally a baby back in the late 80s when Harris was penning *Silence of the Lambs*. It's only been evolving here in the last 50ish years or so. I blame the Fantasy Genre for much of it. Writers like Robert Jordan and Ursula Le Guin pushing boundaries, attempting to make Third Person more and more Limited in the hopes of making their fantasy stories more immersive.

Still, the maddening thing about this for me is, there's no way to teach Third Person Free Indirect Discourse. Shifting between the disembodied third-party Narrator and a Character Narrator is done at the writer's discretion. The writer, using *their* skills combined with *their* gut instincts (let's call this "Talent", for lack of a better word), decides when to Shift and when not to.

Since there are no rules when to Shift within Third Person Free Indirect Discourse, this Narrative is a hodge-podge of… *whatever*.

That's not to say this Narrative is bad, it's simply that, while most Speculative Fiction is written in this way, it's probably not by design. It's *way* more likely that this is the predominant Narrative since most aspiring writers don't know any better. I've stated several times now that most writers don't choose a Narrative, but instead write in the Narrative their favorite books are written in. Since, by far, this is the predominate way to write Speculative Fiction, aspiring writers simply fall into Third Person Free Indirect Discourse without even realize what they are doing.

This, in and of itself, isn't a bad thing. In fact, what I'm describing here some people might call the **Author's Narrative Voice**. And that would absolutely be an accurate description. However, as you've hopefully come to see, that doesn't mean this Narrative is guaranteed to help the story you're writing. It still has its advantages and disadvantages.

This ability to Shift willy-nilly doesn't make your job easier. It actually makes it *way* harder. Because, for all this Shifting to work, it means the writer must rely heavily on their *Talent*. And since it takes an average of five to ten years to gain this *Talent*, which is five to ten years longer than most aspiring writers are willing to devote to this craft, *Talent* is something that tends to be lacking.

One-million words. That's how many words you must write, edit, and throw away before you'll develop the *Talent* you need to write anything worthy of being read.

Time. Effort.

Getting back on track, let's end this "quick" overview of Third Person Free Indirect Discourse by finishing our discussion of the Narrators available within this Narrative, as well as what those Narrator's Level of Awareness should be.

This Narrative type, as you can probably guess, is unique. Again, it has to do with the fact that there are few hard-and-fast rules here combined with the fact that you'll be Shifting between at least two Narrators simultaneously.

Let's begin with the Character Narrator first. If you look back at the *Silence of the Lambs* example again, you'll notice that the Character Narrator in that piece is Clarice Starling. Meaning, when the story isn't being told by the disembodied third-party Narrator, it's being told by Clarice Starling.

For the Character Narrator, you can use any Character who is in your story. This could be the Protagonist, the Antagonist, or a Secondary Character much like a Peripheral Narrator.

Pretty simple.

When it comes to the disembodied third-party Narrator, your choices are not as open as you might assume. While, yes, *technically* you can use any type of Narrator you can possibly imagine—all the ones I discussed in the *What is a Narrator* section—there's one that works better than all the others.

Since using Third Person Free Indirect Discourse means Shifting between at least two Narrators, using an **Observer Narrator** as the third-party Narrator is very advantageous.

Remember, the goal of an Observer Narrator is to become

invisible to the reader. Because you're going to Shift a lot in this Narrative, having an invisible third-party Narrator makes the Shifting much easier for the reader to accept without being pulled out of the story. It allows the reader to forget about the third-party Narrator and focus more on the Character Narrator.

Look back at the *Silence of the Lambs* example and you'll notice the third-party Narrator Harris used is absolutely invisible—it's an Observer Narrator. This Narrator only states the facts, never imputing their own comments or opinions. Comments and opinions are reserved for the Character Narrator.

As for a Level of Awareness, I feel you could make this third-party Narrator either Omniscient or Limited and be successful, depending on the story you're telling.

However, when it comes to the Character Narrator you Shift into, who *is* inside the story, I would recommend that you stick to a more strict Limited Narrator. Meaning, your Character Narrator should be *Limited* to having no idea what's going to happen in the future.

Again, check out the *Silence of the Lambs* example and you'll notice this is the case. Starling has no idea why Crawford called her in, and is a bit nervous over this fact.

Now that you have the basics of these three Third Person Narratives, let's delve into the depths of each, starting with…

Third Person Omniscient

Let me start by getting up onto my proverbial soapbox: Third Person Omniscient is a dead Narrative and should *not* be used in today's Speculative Fiction.

"Then why the hell are you talking about it?"

You overstep yourself, sir! Er… madam! Whatever you are! This is *my* book. *I'm* the only one allowed to be rude here. Just kidding. I love being a punching bag.

But to answer your question, the reason you must understand Third Person Omniscient is so you can build your own Narrative style upon it (if you're going to use the traditional Third Person Free Indirect Discourse), or so you can understand how Third Person Limited is implemented.

Third Person Omniscient is absolutely the *least* immersive Narrative that exists. You can't push the reader further away from the story than you can with this Narrative.

Let's break this down a bit further, to make sure you understand what I'm saying here.

The reason for Third Person Omniscient's piss-poor ability to be immersive is, there's a third-party Narrator, who is not a part of the story, but is standing between the reader and the story.

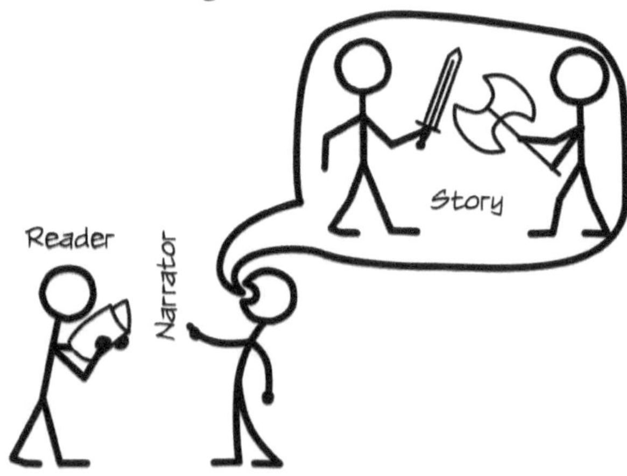

As I've shown through our discussion of the different types of Narrators, you can mitigate this intrusion, or you can enhance it, depending on how you handle this third-party Narrator. But as my wonderfully artistic drawing shows, you can never eliminate it completely.

"Actually, I find your art a bit on the simplistic side," you chide. "But now that I have your attention, I'd like to point out that there's also a Narrator standing between the reader and the story within First Person."

Wow! Call me impressed. You've finally made an intelligent interruption. And I'll just pretend you didn't say that about my artistic ability.

Yes, there's a Narrator standing between the reader and the story when using First Person. But it's different. In First Person, the fact that there's a Narrator standing between the reader and the story can be nearly eliminated by using all the tricks I discussed, such as culling out your "I's" and eliminating any unneeded Filtering, always making the Narrative personal, using a Narrator with a Limited Level of Awareness, etc. All reasons why First Person, when done well, is a close second when it comes to immersing the reader into the story—it has the ability to viscerally connect the reader to the Character Narrator.

In Third Person Omniscient, however, there are no options for eliminating the Narrator. The Narrator is ever present, and ever felt by the reader.

Worse, there's no way to viscerally connect this ever-present Narrator to the events of the story, because the Narrator is *not* in the story.

Actually, what I stated here is a half-lie. The half that's true is the fact that there's no way to viscerally connect the reader and the Narrator. There *is* a way, however, to mitigate the Narrator's effect upon the story, and that's to use an Observer Narrator.

Remember, the goal of an Observer Narrator is to make the Narrator invisible. But as we discussed, using this type of Narrator means the Narrator can never add anything to the story either. If you're going to write in Third Person Omniscient, having an invisible Narrator means you'll have a very bland Narrator indeed. One the reader never even notices. Meaning, your story better be amazing!

The reason an Observer Narrator works so well in Third Person Free Indirect Discourse is the fact that you still have the ability to viscerally connect the reader to the Character Narrator. In true Third Person Omniscient, you can *NEVER* Shift into the head of a Character Narrator, so you don't have this ability. A huge reason I feel Third Person Omniscient is a dead Narrative.

(I know what I just said made you fume. But hold your interruption. I'll explain why in just a moment.)

Still, some people believe reincarnation happens. Third Person Omniscient may be exactly what your story needs. If so, good on ya. You've chosen wisely. So long as you thought it through, I'm satisfied.

As an example, *The Lord of the Rings* is written in Third Person Omniscient using an Observer Narrator. Meaning, you never "notice" who is telling this story as you read it. The Narrator is simply stating facts as they happen, never intruding or allowing themselves to be noticed. If you feel your story would benefit from this type of Narration, then this is the right choice for that particular story. But keep in mind all those other things I mentioned about *The Lord of the Rings*, and why I feel some people find it difficult to read.

Time. Effort. And all that. Choose wisely.

Still, in today's world of readers who demand a more dynamic and immersive tale, an Omniscient Narrative is not the type most readers want.

Today's readers demand a more immersive experience, something Third Person Omniscient simply can't deliver. Hence, Third Person Free Indirect Discourse and Third Person Limited.

So why *would* you use Third Person Omniscient?

I'm glad you asked. As with all the Narrative types, this one has both advantages and disadvantages. Let's start in a more positive light and discuss the fact that it's a…

VERY TRADITIONAL NARRATIVE

Once upon a time there lived an inquisitive author who spent his entire life studying how stories were constructed. It fascinated him to discover why some of them worked, when others didn't. And even though this author was a complete idiot, for some reason people loved it when he taught them all the things he'd discovered during his studies.

There's no doubt how this Narrative came to be. It's the way stories have been told since the dawn of time, and you can't get any more traditional than Third Person Omniscient.

Why is this an advantage? Two reasons: reader comfort and how quickly it hooks the reader into the plight of the story.

Reread the above example. How easy was it to slip into, and become interested in what will happen next? I mean, what I wrote was stupid, and yet, halfway through the first line I probably had you hooked.

What aspiring writer wouldn't be interested by an "inquisitive author who spent his entire life studying how stories were constructed?" Who's the complete idiot now?

And that's power. Power to hook the reader almost from the very first line, or at the least, within the opening paragraph.

I'm sure this is why Harris wrote the first line of *Silence of the Lambs* the way he did. It's a powerful opening line that hooks the reader quickly.

Here are a few more opening paragraphs that'll hook ya fast to show you what I mean:

> Once upon a time there dwelled on the outskirts of a large forest a poor woodcutter with his wife and two children; the boy was called Hansel, and the girl Gretel. He always had little enough to live on, and once, when times were bad, they had to get by with one piece of bread and butter each. One night, as he was tossing about in bed, full of cares and worry, he sighed and said to his wife, "What's to become of us? How are we to feed our poor children, now that we have nothing more for ourselves?"

Or:

> A very long time ago, in midwinter, when the snowflakes were falling like feathers from heaven, a beautiful queen sat sewing at her window, which had a frame of black ebony. As she worked, she looked sometimes at the falling snow, and it happened that she pricked her finger with her needle, so that three drops of blood fell upon the snow. How pretty the red blood looked upon the dazzling white! The queen said to herself as she looked it, "Ah me! If only I had a dear little child who had skin as white as the snow, lips as rosy as the blood, and hair as black as the ebony window frame."

Or:

> There was once a fisherman who lived with his wife in a pigsty, close by the seaside. The fisherman used to go out all day long a-fishing; and one day, as he sat on the shore with his rod, looking at the sparkling waves and watching his line, all of a sudden, his float was dragged away deep into the water. When he reeled in his line, he pulled out a

golden fish. But the fish said, "Pray let me live! I am not a real fish. I am an enchanted prince. Put me in the water again, and let me go!"

As you can see, in each of these (and dozens more I could have used but didn't—you're welcome) by the end of the opening paragraph the reader is as hooked as that poor ole fish prince.

Side note before we go on. This "quick hooking ability" that having an Omniscient opening paragraph brings to the story is why so many stories start out this way.

As you'll see when you get there, Third Person Free Indirect Discourse is a sliding scale that encompasses everything from nearly Third Person Omniscient to nearly Third Person Limited.

With a story like *Silence of the Lambs*, the story stays pretty fluid, utilizing both the third-party Narrator as well as the Character Narrator throughout. There is a ton of Speculative Fiction that follows this method.

However, in the Fantasy Genre, you find the opposite. These stories may still use a third-party Narrator, but most of the story stays inside the Character Narrator. Authors like Robert Jordan and Brandon Sanderson, who are so amazing at writing in an incredibly limited manner, still understand the power of an Omniscient opening paragraph to start off a novel, chapter, or even a scene. The quicker you hook your reader, the better your odds of that reader reading your entire book.

Here's the opening to Robert Jordan's *Eye of the World*, the first book of his *Wheel of Time* series.

The Wheel of Time turns, and Ages come and pass, leaving memories that become legend. Legend fades to myth, and even myth is long forgotten when the Age that gave it birth comes again. In one Age, called the Third Age by some, an Age yet to come, an Age long past, a wind rose in the Mountains of Mist. The wind was not the beginning. There are neither beginnings nor

> endings to the turning of the Wheel of Time. But
> it was a beginning.
>
> Born below the ever cloud-capped peaks that
> gave the mountains their name, the wind blew
> east, out across the Sand Hills, once the shore
> of a great ocean, before the Breaking of the
> World. Down it flailed into the Two Rivers, into
> the tangled forest called the Westwood, and beat
> at two men walking with a cart and horse down the
> rock-strewn track called the Quarry Road. For all
> that spring should have come a good month since,
> the wind carried an icy chill as if it would rather
> bear snow.
>
> Gusts plastered Rand al'Thor's cloak to his back,
> whipped the earth-colored wool around his legs,
> then streamed it out behind him. He wished his
> coat were heavier, or that he had worn an extra
> shirt. Half the time when he tried to tug the cloak
> back around him it caught on the quiver swinging
> at his hip. Trying to hold the cloak one-handed did
> not do much good anyway; he had his bow in the
> other, an arrow nocked and ready to draw.

Notice, the first two paragraphs are completely in Third Person Omniscient. But the final paragraph is limited to Rand al'Thor. In fact, outside of a very few minor Shifts, the rest of this chapter is solidly written from Rand's very Limited Narration.

Hence, this is Third Person Free Indirect Discourse. It's a very tight version, to be sure. Definitely very close to the Third Person Limited side of the scale.

But that's the beauty of Third Person Free Indirect Discourse. You have two points, and you have the ability to find the sweet spot that'll enhance the telling of your story. *Silence of the Lambs*, probably due to the brutality the reader is exposed to, is told higher on the Third Person Free Indirect Discourse scale, staying closer to the Omniscient side of things. And *Eye of the World*, due to the fact that Fantasy readers want to be as close to the action as they can get, is told lower on the Third Person Free Indirect Discourse scale, staying closer to the Limited side of things.

But I seem to have slipped into teaching Third Person Free Indirect Discourse.

Let's return to Third Person Omniscient and look at another advantage with the fact that it…

CALLS LESS ATTENTION TO THE NARRATION

This is a strange aspect that all Third Person Narratives have in common, and one you may disagree even exists. But a huge advantage Third Person has over First Person is that it's easier for a reader to forget they're even reading words, and instead see only the images the words conjure up in their mind.

It's why people can so easily lose track of time when reading well-written Third Person Narrative.

Sure, First Person can, and does, do this. I'm not saying it doesn't. I'm simply stating it's easier for the writer to accomplish this using Third Person.

Why do I feel this way?

Well, it all goes back to my theory on why First Person is a close second behind Third Person Limited when it comes to immersion—and that's the dreaded "I".

As I've stated, we've been consuming First Person stories since we were children. In every case, these stories are someone else telling us what they've seen and done. Mentally, we've been programmed to accept this fact every time we read the word "I."

However, in Third Person, you're following a character named Drake or Sally. For some reason, probably because we're only exposed to this type of Narration when we're reading literature, it's easier for our brains to suspend disbelief and fall completely into the story, literally becoming Drake or Sally.

I have no examples to prove this to you, it's simply my theory on how the different Narrative types affects a reader's mind. But I do believe it. And I feel it's an advantage for Third Person.

Getting back to Third Person Omniscient, and yet sticking with the Narration aspect of it, another wonderful advantage this Narrative has is the fact that it's…

NOT WRITTEN FROM THE CHARACTER'S PERSPECTIVE

This may sound strange after hearing me dote on First Person and Third Person Limited over how awesome it is to tell a story from the perspective of a Character Narrator who is inside the story. But remember, I'm not trying to prove which Narrative is the best. I'm simply trying to show you versions of each so you can combine this new information with your own imagination and write better stories.

Each Narrative type will be best for a certain type of story. Limited Narratives work magic inside action-oriented stories where immersion of the reader is important. But since there are a bazillion different types of stories out there, some will have Narratives that work for them, while other Narratives will destroy them.

So why is a third-party Narrator an advantage? Since the story is being told by a Narrator who isn't in the story you have the power to give this third-party Narrator their own method of speaking to the reader, instead of being limited to one of your Characters.

For example, say you're writing a story where the main Protagonist is a three-year-old child. How horrible would it be to read an entire novel written through the perspective of a three-year-old? Here's where I would normally write some crazy example to make my point. But let's be real; no one wants to read anything written from the perspective of a three-year-old.

Who am I tying to kid here? You know there's no way I'm gonna pass up the opportunity to write something as messed up as this!

Drake walked into the monster's cave. He looked at the monster and said, "You're ugly!" And monster said, "No, you're ugly!" But Drake's mom was there,

and she said, "Well, no snack for you, young man."
(She was talking to the monster.) She gave Drake
a peanut butter sandwich. But the monster got
no snack, because it didn't eat all its vegetables.
And Drake thought, orange you glad she didn't
say banana? Then He-Man showed up and, "By the
power of Greyskull!!!" But the monster was now
Drake's friend, so they went to the beach and
built a sandcastle!

Within the true Limited Narratives (First Person and Third Person Limited) you want to use the Narrative as an extension of the Character Narrator, so the Narration needs to have their Voice, use words they would use, follow speech and thought patterns natural to that Character Narrator.

The reason Third Person Omniscient has an advantage here is, there's a disembodied third-party Narrator telling the story. Meaning, you can write the story using that Narrator's voice, instead of some demented toddler.

Drake waddled into the kitchen on his stubby
little legs. His mother was at the counter making
lunch. He loved to imagine she was some horrible
monster, and he was invading its cave.

Looking at his mother, Drake laughed as he said,
"You're an ugly monster!"

"No, you're an ugly monster!" His mother teased
back with a big smile. But the smile slipped from her
lips as she set a peanut butter and jelly sandwich
on the table in front of Drake's highchair. "No
snack for you today, young man, because you didn't
eat all your vegetables last night."

A joke popped into Drake's head he had heard
on T.V. that morning and Drake giggled as he
remembered the punchline. *Orange you glad she
didn't say banana?* He hated bananas, and would

> rather have no snack than one of those.
>   This reminded him that after lunch his mother was taking him to the beach where he could build himself an awesome sandcastle. Hopping into his chair, Drake said, "By the power of Greyskull!" then began devouring his sandwich.

Much easier to read, not to mention something that's actually coherent.

Say your story's Protagonist is a tentacled demon. Or a vicious serial killer. Or worse, a politician. There's no easy way to viscerally connect a reader to any of these horrible creatures.

Creating a third-party Narrator who shall be telling the tale however, might give you what you need to accomplish this.

Another advantage this Narrative has over the others is the fact that it's a…

TRULY OMNISCIENT NARRATIVE

This is definitely one of those double-edged sword thingies, and one that needs to be weighed very carefully against the story you're telling so you understand how this will affect things.

What I mean by a "Truly Omniscient Narrative" is this Narrative is all-encompassing. The Third Person Omniscient Narrator knows *everything*.

The advantage this brings is that there are no barriers between the reader and the events of the story. Everything can be told to the reader, past, present, and future, in the hope of telling a more interesting and enjoyable story.

> Drake reached for his gym bag. On the handle of the bag sat a massive black and red spider, but he didn't notice the little guy because he was too busy staring at Dylan's bare, sweat-covered chest. Unfortunately for Drake, Dylan was straight. Even more unfortunate for Drake, he would not

discover this fact until they had been married for three years and were adopting their second child.

Poor Drake. Alone and heartbroken. Again. But this does a wonderful job of illustrating the danger that comes into play by giving too much information to the reader. Just because the Narrator knows everything, doesn't mean the reader needs all this information. Or even wants it.

Imagine if my above example was a love story. How terrible would it be to read a romance novel that ends with Drake finding the person he thinks will be the love of his life, but the reader has already been told this will end poorly? It would be horrendous, and I doubt any reader would continue reading it. The suspense has been taken away from the reader.

Another case in point: *The Lord of the Rings.* Remember, many who attempted to read this massive epic tale became casualties to the "Started but Didn't Finish" plight due to the sheer amount of non-story related information that's piled upon them.

And the walking… oh, dear God! The walking!!!

Worse, as you should be able to guess from the above example, too much information can destroy any chance of building tension. In this example, Drake not knowing that Dylan's straight is now information the reader has. Once the reader knows something, it doesn't matter whether the Character knows or not, there's no tension attached to the fact.

Now, you can build a different type of tension, certainly. Tension the reader will feel as they attempt to anticipate when the axe will fall. And depending on the story you're telling, this may be the exact type of Tension you want. But it's not the same, and needs to fit the type of story you're telling.

Because of this, not only can Third Person Omniscient be tedious to read, it can become very tedious to write. Bloated, uninteresting scenes can become an issue quick, especially in Sci-Fi and Fantasy, due to the insane desire of the writer to give the reader, "All the wonderful flavor of this interesting world I've created!"

Remember, you're writing *stories*, not roleplaying games. Keep things tight, only giving the reader things they must know to enjoy the story.

Additionally, while the above example can *technically* be called foreshadowing, in Third Person Omniscient, foreshadowing will normally feel like a big-ole-Tell.

Foreshadowing is a powerful tool Third Person Narratives can implement fairly easily. Within First Person, foreshadowing is much more difficult, if not downright impossible to use.

Still, foreshadowing is meant to be a vague hint of a possible future. If you come right out and tell the reader what will happen, that's not foreshadowing. That's called a *Spoiler*!

But I digress. Let's look at the next topic, something that's another blessing as well as a curse, which is the fact that this Narrative creates…

A Healthy Distance Between the Reader and the Story

Due to the fact this Narrative is so good at distancing the reader from the events of the story, it might be the perfect thing for the story you're trying to tell.

Say you're writing a story that has a horrible traumatic event such as murder, rape, etc., but this event is something that, for whatever reason, you don't wish the reader to be immersed in. Writing your story in Third Person Omniscient will mean your reader won't be forced to live through the gory, graphic details of said event.

Now, if you've ever read any of my work, you might guess pretty quickly that this is a hard pill for me to swallow. My fans don't call me fifty-shades of red for nuthin'.

For me, and the stories I tell, I absolutely *LOVE* putting my readers in the most uncomfortable, traumatic situations I can imagine.

It's *DRAMA!!!*

It also builds empathy between the reader and my Character Narrator, since, if I do it right, the reader is so immersed that they'll feel they have lived through the horrendous event themselves.

But that's the stories I tend to tell. Your mileage may vary.

If you're not telling the same types of stories as I am, you may want to protect your fragile readers from such horrors. And this is more than acceptable, and the reason I list this amongst Third Person Omniscient's advantages.

Just know, this is the heart of why this Narrative is the least immersive Narrative in this game. So, using it will absolutely protect your readers. But it'll also mean you'll have to work all that much harder to make sure those readers are still invested in the story.

Again, all I care about is that you put in Time and Effort, think about the story you're going to be telling, and pick a Narrative that'll be best for that story.

The final advantage I want to discuss is one that's unique to Third Person Omniscient. For this is the only Narrative that can be used for…

CROWD NARRATIVES

If you're telling a story where one of the "Characters" within your story is going to be a crowd, such as a mob, an army, a whole village, or even the emotions of an entire nation, there's really no other way to do this outside of a disembodied third-party Omniscient Narrator.

Now, please don't misunderstand me here. I'm not talking about one small remote scene. I'm talking about having a "Character" who is a crowd. If all you need to do is show a crowd's emotions for one small scene, you can do so and still stay in a very Limited Narrative by simply sticking to what the Character Narrator can see.

> Drake couldn't believe how quickly the normally docile Comic-Con crowd had turned on him. They had all risen from their seats and were approaching the stage, wielding whatever they could find to use as weapons. Pencils, pens, notebooks, laptops, a realistic-looking prop Legend of Zelda sword. Several had even broken off chair legs. Those

> were the ones he truly feared. They were the
> ones with real vengeance in their eyes.
> And all he had said was, "Star Wars is overrated."

Since all the above is kept within the Character Narrator's perception, this is still written in a Limited Perspective. Everything in the above Drake can see. It's all limited to Drake.

What I'm talking about here is when you're going to use a large group on an ongoing basis as a Character within the story.

Here's an example written in Third Person Omniscient.

> Attitudes had changed. People were tired of
> the status-quo. The hate. The murders. The
> segregation. It had worn everyone thin. *The
> incident* was the breaking point. From that day
> forward, nothing was the same. Neighbors who
> had fought neighbors for generations were going
> out of their way to love one another.

Or some such.

As with everything, take the time to understand why you would need such a "Character", and how you're going to use them throughout your story. While writing the above example, my mind was exploring how I could tell an entire story in this very distant, crowd mentality manner. I came up with bupkis. But that's not surprising since I create stories that are extremely Limited to the Character Narrator.

However, this does open up the opportunity to talk about the differences between the three different Third Person Narrative types.

As I've said, Third Person Free Indirect Discourse is when you Shift between Omniscient and Limited. So, let's revisit the above example, but add a bit:

> Attitudes had change. People were tired of
> the status-quo. The hate. The murders. The
> segregation. It had worn everyone thin. *The*

> *incident* was the breaking point. From that day forward, nothing was the same. Neighbors who had fought neighbors for generations were going out of their way to love one another.
>
> Drake remembered well where he was the day of *the incident.* Alone, in his room, watching reruns of *Queer Eye for the Straight Guy,* and crying like a baby with the realization that wearing cargo shorts and ironic T-Shirts with a geek-culture reference was no longer in fashion.

We start in Omniscient, then Shift into Limited. The very definition of Third Person Free Indirect Discourse.

So, while I can't wrap my brain around how to write an entire story from a crowd perception, it can be effective in setting things up before slipping to a more Limited form of Narrative. Again, this is the power of Third Person Free Indirect Discourse.

Continuing with this side path, let me take this example further and show you what I mean by sticking to a strict Third Person Limited. In the above two examples, I start out very wide—a third-party Narrator talking to the reader. However, Third Person Limited doesn't get a third-party Narrator. It only gets the Character Narrator. So, if I was to write the above in Third Person Limited, I might do something like this:

> Drake couldn't believe how much people had changed. He assumed that, like him, people were tired of the status-quo. The hate. The murders. The segregation. It had definitely worn Drake thin. *The incident* was the breaking point. From that day forward, nothing was the same. Neighbors who had fought neighbors for generations were going out of their way to love one another.
>
> *I couldn't be happier,* he thought when the world appeared to have matured overnight.
>
> He remembered well where he was the day of

> *the incident.* Alone, in his room, watching reruns
> of *Queer Eye for the Straight Guy,* and crying
> like a baby with the realization that wearing cargo
> shorts and ironic T-Shirts with a geek-culture
> reference was no longer in fashion.

As you can see, the shift to a true Third Person Limited means I no longer have access to that disembodied third-party Narrator. *Everything* must be Limited to the Character Narrator, exactly like you would if you were writing First Person. This adjustment is slight, but it does create a difference. And it's this subtle difference that's going to force the reader to experience the story in different ways.

Funny thing is, there are some interesting way to accomplish this. Let's look at one final piece, also written in Third Person Limited"

> Drake remembered well where he was the day of
> *the incident.* Alone, in his room, watching reruns
> of *Queer Eye for the Straight Guy,* and crying
> like a baby with the realization that wearing cargo
> shorts and ironic T-Shirts with a geek-culture
> slant was no longer in fashion.
>
> Attitudes had changed. People were tired of
> the status-quo. The hate. The murders. The
> segregation. It had worn everyone thin. *The
> incident* was the breaking point. From that day
> forward, nothing was the same. Neighbors who
> had fought neighbors for generations were going
> out of their way to love one another.

If you are as clever as I think you are, you noticed that the second paragraph in the above is *identical* to that very first example—the one I stated was written in Third Person Omniscient.

But as I said, this is Third Person Limited, not Third Person Omniscient or Third Person Free Indirect Discourse.

So, why is one of the example Third Person Free Indirect Discourse, and this one not?

It comes down to tricking the reader's perceptions. Just by changing the order of the paragraphs, leading with Drake, you make the second paragraph Third Person Limited because the reader assumes they are still inside Drake's head as Drake reflects on how *the incident* affected the world around him.

And sometimes that's all you need—for the reader to continue believing they have never left the Character Narrator's head.

More on this when I dive into the depths of Third Person Limited.

Let me finish Third Person Omniscient with the last advantage it has, but which is also the single worst thing that aspiring writers can totally botch when writing in any of the Third Person Narratives, which is the…

ABILITY TO SPREAD THE STORY BETWEEN MULTIPLE CHARACTERS

Since Third Person Omniscient is being told by a third-party Narrator who is *NOT* in the story, but has all the facts of the story, this means this Narrator knows the reasons behind the actions of every single Character within said story.

And this is a pretty powerful thing, indeed.

It means you can use all these motivations to help the reader understand the story you're telling at a deeper level.

However, the thing aspiring writers overlook is, you aren't inside any of these Characters' heads. You're only inside one head, and that's the third-party Narrator. The guy who is not in the story.

Now, depending on which type of third-party Narrator you use, that third-party Narrator may be able add in their own thoughts and comments (Commentator Narrator, Interviewer Narrator, Storyteller Narrator, etc.). Or they may not be able to (Observer Narrator). But you absolutely can't be inside any of your Character's heads.

If my above statement has finally made you snap, vowing to

burn this book as a sacrifice to anarchistic writing, skip on down to the chapter titled *Breaking the Rules*.

I, however, will stand by my statement that in Third Person Omniscient, you cannot be inside the head of any character in the story.

In fact, it gets even more limiting than this when it comes to the Characters in your story, because to really make Third Person Omniscient shine, you should focus on one Character at a time. I call this Character the **Focal Character**.

Here is an excerpt from J.R.R. Tolkien's *The Lord of the Rings*:

> 'Don't be alarmed! I mean just this: I will tell you what I know, and give you some good advice - but I shall want a reward.'
>
> 'And what will that be, pray?' said Frodo. He suspected now that he had fallen in with a rascal, and he thought uncomfortably that he had brought only a little money with him. All of it would hardly satisfy a rogue, and he could not spare any of it.
>
> 'No more than you can afford,' answered Strider with a slow smile, as if he guessed Frodo's thoughts. 'Just this: you must take me along with you, until I wish to leave you.'
>
> 'Oh, indeed!' replied Frodo, surprised, but not much relieved. 'Even if I wanted another companion, I should not agree to any such thing, until I knew a good deal more about you, and your business.'
>
> 'Excellent!' exclaimed Strider, crossing his legs and sitting back comfortably. 'You seem to be coming to your senses again, and that is all to the good. You have been much too careless so far. Very well! I will tell you what I know, and leave the reward to you. You may be glad to grant it, when you have heard me.'
>
> 'Go on then!' said Frodo. 'What do you know?'

Let's break this example down a bit.

As I've said, *The Lord of the Rings* is written in Third Person Omniscient using an Observer Narrator. As you can see in the above, the Narrator stays invisible, never adding in their own comments or opinions. They simple state the facts of what's going on.

This is the purest, and most traditional form of Third Person Omniscient, and the style that was used to tell stories for thousands of years.

Note also that we're never inside any of the Character's heads. In other words, there's no inner monologue because we can't hear inside the Character's minds. If you did that, it would mean you were writing in Third Person Free Indirect Discourse.

Sure, we're told what some of the Characters are thinking, like with the line:

> He suspected now that he had fallen in with a rascal, and he thought uncomfortably that he had brought only a little money with him.

But this doesn't place us inside Frodo's mind. It stays firmly with the third-party Narrator's telling of the tale. It's still just the facts of the story. Facts the third-party Omniscient Narrator has access to.

However, take this a step further and you'll notice the Narrator only does this for Frodo in this scene. He doesn't tell us what any of the other Characters are thinking. Everyone else's Narrative is simply things Frodo can see.

That's because in this scene, Frodo is the **Focal Character**. Meaning, the Narrator will tell us his thoughts and reasons, but not those of the other Characters. Having a Focal Character is as immersive as Third Person Omniscient can get.

The thing Third Person Omniscient can do, however, is have different chapters or scenes with different Focal Characters. Tolkien does this throughout this book. During this part, Frodo is the Focal Character. In other chapters, you'll find that Strider is the Focal Character. And so on.

The interesting thing is, these chapters are grouped together. Meaning, Frodo is the Focal Character for a large block of continuous chapters before we switch to another Focal Character. And after the switch, we stay with that new Focal Character for another large block of chapters.

Again, this has to do with what was traditional during Tolkien's day.

Very different from how I write, where I switch to a different Character Narrator every time I switch to a new chapter. I never have the same character twice in a row. But back in Tolkien's day, that was considered bad form.

Again, Speculative Fiction evolves.

My point here is to expose the demon that haunts so many aspiring writers who use Third Person. And that is…

HEAD HOPPING

I'm going to go into **Head Hopping** here, and try and explain it as best as I can. However, please keep in mind that Head Hopping is a disease that destroys all three forms of Third Person.

Head Hopping is when you allow the story to enter any and all character's minds who happen to be in the scene. It's a terrible thing that shouldn't be used in any of the three types of Third Person Narratives. Head Hopping is a terrible thing that'll ruin your story without you ever even noticing.

Why? Because writers who Head Hop do so because they feel it adds to their story. They think they're right. So, when they reread their own work, the Head Hopping is a good thing to them.

Unfortunately, it's not a good thing for your readers. And here's why.

You, the writer, love all your characters. The main ones, the secondary ones, even the tertiary ones like that weird homeless guy the Protagonist only glances at once while walking down the street and then is never again mentioned for the remainder of the story.

You love them all because you created them. It's natural. I get it.

However, you're the only one who does.

There's not one single reader on this planet who will ever give a crap about your entire cast, outside of you. Not even your mother.

Look, I know there are lots of aspiring writers out there who feel the more heads they can put their reader inside, the more immersive their story will be. I meet these types every single year. But this is absolute bovine scatology.

All seriousness aside, you must understand why Head Hopping ruins stories.

The fact is, a reader can only care about so much. They have only enough love for a few Characters. When you Head Hop into every Character in your story, what you're doing is spreading the story too thin. Not only are you wasting words, words that could be used to viscerally connect the reader at a deeper level with the important Characters, you're asking the reader to do the impossible—care about all the Characters in the story as much as you do.

It fails every single time.

The funny thing is, when done correctly, none of the Narrative types allow for Head Hopping. Not First, Second, nor any of the Thirds.

We just discussed Third Person Omniscient, and the fact that you're not supposed to be inside any of your character's heads. Sure, you follow a Focal Character, and the third-party Narrator can let the reader know what that Focal Character is thinking and how they feel about the world around them, but you should do this from the third-party Narrator's mind, and not the mind of the Character in the story. So, no Head Hopping there.

You'll see in a moment why Third Person Limited should be written exactly like First Person. Meaning, whoever your Character Narrator is during a chapter, that's the only head you're in, period. So, no Head Hopping there.

Third Person Free Indirect Discourse is really the only gray area. Since this is the Narrative Type 99.9999999% of aspiring writers are using if they're writing in Third Person, this is where the vast majority of this Head Hopping issue crops up.

Still, keep in mind, Third Person Free Indirect Discourse is a hybrid of the other two Third Person Narratives. Yes, you're Shifting between a third-party Narrator and the Character Narrator. Yes, you can have Multiple Character Narrators. However, to allow your readers the best opportunity to build a visceral connection to your Character Narrator, you really should run things just like it's done with Third Person Omniscient and have just one Focal Character per chapter or scene.

Meaning, in any given chapter or scene, you can Shift between your third-party Narrator, and only *ONE* Character Narrator.

This will all make sense after I break down Multiple Characters in just a moment.

For now, just realize when writing in any of the Third Person Narrative types, you want to limit yourself to the absolute minimum number of Character's minds you can be inside and still tell your story. Head Hopping is bad.

Going back to *Silence of the Lambs*. Starling is the Character Narrator used 90% of the time. We do get a taste of Crawford, Hannibal, and Wild Bill, but only because the information we glean from those Narrative Shifts is vital to the story being told. Most of the time, even in scenes where several of these Characters are together in the same room, Harris only Shifts between the third-party Observer Narrator and Starling.

Case in point: In the sample of *Silence of the Lambs* I used earlier, both Starling and Crawford are in the same room, talking to each other. However, Harris never Shifts into Crawford's head during that chapter. Only Starling's. We don't Shift into Crawford's head until we get a chapter that's dedicated to Crawford. And then, during that chapter, we only Shift between the third-party Narrator and Crawford. Since 90% of the chapters use Starling as the Focal Character, this builds a strong visceral connection between the reader and Starling. Most of the story stays inside her perspective, which is exactly what the story needs, since Starling is the Protagonist and the one struggling to answer that story's Major Theme.

In most Third Person Free Indirect Discourse stories, you

can probably limit yourself to only Shift between the third-party Narrator and *ONE* Character Narrator. *Harry Potter and the Sorcerer's Stone* is a wonderful example of this. In that first book, Harry is the only Focal Character for the entire story.

It all comes down to those two words I keep repeating. Time. Effort.

Head Hopping will ruin your story. You've been warned.

Alrighty, then. I think that's enough chitchat for a Narrative that's dead and buried. Once again, skipping Third Person Free Indirect Discourse, let's dive into the mysterious realm of…

Third Person Limited

Oh, Third Person Limited. How do I love thee? Let me count the ways.

Immersion.

Immersion.

Immersion.

Immersion.

Immersion.

Oh, are you still here? That was probably embarrassing for you to watch, huh? Sorry.

I really do love Third Person Limited. However, before I head down this path, I want to make a few things very clear. First, I'm not against First Person. As you've seen, I've written a lot in First Person. In fact, I'm currently writing an entire novel series in First Person. It's a wonderful Narrative. However, for me, it always comes down to the type of story I'm telling.

I think about the story, its complexity, what I feel would be the best way for the reader to experience the story, and *then* I choose my Narrative.

Time. Effort.

As I've stated, First Person will break a complex story. If you need Multiple Character Narrators, must tell things from different times or places, etc., or the story has Subplots or Parallel Plots that need to be expertly threaded throughout, Third Person is your Huckleberry.

And if you want to immerse your reader using all the advantages that First Person brings to this fight, Third Person Limited shines like no other.

Since my dark, epic fantasy stories tend to be *very* complex, and I strive to make them as immersive as possible, I've written more in Third Person Limited than any other Narrative type.

It's as simple as that.

However, there's one other major misnomer I want to crush right here and now.

I've already stated that I feel people have been confusing Third

Person Limited with Third Person Free Indirect Discourse for decades, and I truly believe this. Now let me see if I can prove why.

I've already gone through Third Person Omniscient, and shown you that to hold to this Narrative, you must use a disconnected third-party Narrator who isn't in the story. Strick? Absolutely. And something most writers today find terribly limiting. Which is why it's almost never used in today's Speculative Fiction.

Going to the other extreme, we find Third Person Limited. It, too, is strict with its Narrators. Because, and what I'm about to say will go against everything you've ever been taught about Third Person (hush, Mrs. Johnson!!!), Third Person Limited has no third-party Narrator.

Let me say that again:

> Third Person Limited has *no* disembodied third-party Narrator.

None. Zero. Zip. The Narrator in Third Person Limited is the Character Narrator. Period. Meaning, you write Third Person Limited *EXACTLY* the way you write First Person. The only difference is, you use Third Person Nouns and Pronouns. Before you brand me a heretic, please give me a second, and I'll show you what I mean.

To better illustrate my argument here, let's take a trip down memory lane and look at all the Narrative Types as a whole.

In a First Person story, the Character Narrator is the person saying "I". The reader "watches" the story unfold through an Imaginary Camera that's literally inside the Character Narrator's head. Finger-glasses, remember?

This creates a very strong link between the reader and the Character Narrator. Unfortunately, every time you use the word "I", you remind the reader they are *not* the Character Narrator. This makes this the second most immersive Narrative, in my not so humble opinion.

In Third Person Omniscient, there's a third-party Narrator who stands firmly between the reader and the story.

This does a wonderful job of keeping the reader separated from the action, and why this Narrative type is the worst for immersion.

With true Third Person Limited, one could argue that the reader isn't the Character Narrator either. And I can understand this argument. In all Third Person Narratives, the Imaginary Camera is Free-Floating, taking the reader with it.

However, the difference with Third Person Limited is, the Imaginary Camera is only the "eyes" of the reader.

In all other aspects; emotions, feelings, thoughts, motivations, desires, etc., the reader is *inside* the Character Narrator's head *to the exact same degree* as they are in First Person.

In both First Person, and Third Person Limited, the mind of reader and the mind of the Character Narrator are linked!

They are one.

Now, my finger-glasses trick doesn't work for Third Person Limited, since the Imaginary Camera is hovering outside the Character Narrator's head. But imagining that this Imaginary Camera is *tethered* to your Character Narrator's mind is a great way to think about how all this works.

The reader's "eyeballs" are free-floating around the Character Narrator, but in all other aspects, the reader is *inside* the Character Narrator.

And remember, the Imaginary Camera is "free-floating", so you can spin this Imaginary Camera as needed to tell your story. Just constantly stay aware that it's forever attached to your Character Narrator's mind via its tether.

The reason this is an important thing to grasp is because, just like First Person, when your Character Narrator leaves the room, your Imaginary Camera has also left the room. The Imaginary

Camera (the reader's ability to see) and the Character Narrator's ability to see are one in the same. So, unless the Character Narrator leaves his eyeballs behind, you can't let the reader see anything your Character Narrator can't see.

Just like First Person.

Once you grasp this concept, which you should have no problem doing, considering my amazing artistic ability, you'll have no issues with avoiding Head Hopping.

In Third Person Limited, *visually*, you can only describe what the Character Narrator can see. Since the reader in all other aspects is inside the Character Narrator's mind, *emotionally*, just like First Person, you can only describe what that Character Narrator is thinking, experiencing, and feeling.

The reason I feel this makes Third Person Limited more immersive than First Person is twofold.

One, in First Person the Imaginary Camera is the Character Narrator's eyes. This limits the reader's ability to "see" the story as easily as they can "see" the world around a Third Person Limited Character Narrator through their free-floating Imaginary Camera.

This free-floating Imaginary Camera means the reader can see more of the story, including being able to see the Character Narrator. For action, this is a wonderful thing.

Since I tend to write stories that have tons of action, it's easier (and more exciting, immersive, etc.) to allow the reader to see *all* the action, including the actions of the Character Narrator. With the Imaginary Camera free-floating, it gives me the ability to move and adjust this Camera as needed, so I can immerse the reader into what they're seeing from any angle.

In First Person, since the Imaginary Camera is locked inside the Character Narrator's head, it means instead of "Showing" the reader the Character Narrator's actions, you tend to be forced to "Tell" the reader what "I" am doing. Remember, finger-glasses.

The second reason Third Person Limited rules in immersion is a bit more esoteric. I won't fault you if you feel I'm wrong here, but from what I've discovered while studying how readers are affected by what they read, for whatever reason, Third Person Limited allows readers to *become* the Character Narrator much more easily than they can with a First Person Narrator.

I suspect this is due to the fact that since we've been consuming stories using "I" since the day we could understand human speech, we've been preprogrammed to always know that "I" is not "me". However, when the Character Narrator is being referred to as Drake or Sally, he or she, it's easier for the reader to suspend disbelief and become said Character Narrator. Probably because we only consume these types of stories when we're specifically reading books, and not every time one of our stupid friends tells us the stupid crap they did last weekend after they got stupid drunk.

Now, I'm specifically talking about Third Person Limited here. This is absolutely *not* the case with either Third Person Omniscient or Third Person Free Indirect Discourse. When it comes to immersion, First Person can slaughter either of those two beasts.

Still, I haven't proved my point as to why there is no third-party Narrator in Third Person Limited.

Or have I?

I stated that you should write Third Person Limited exactly as you would write First Person. In First Person, you never Shift into a disembodied third-party Narrator. So… same is true with Third Person Limited. You remain "limited" to just the Character Narrator.

Seriously. They are written identically. Don't believe me? Let's put it to the test.

Here's the example I used to make my points throughout the First Person section, the one where the girl enters Café Jax.

> It was chilly, even though it was August, and the street was deserted, even though it was about three in the afternoon. Across the road from me sat Café Jax—an ancient rust-colored brick building with a stained red and white stripped awning and an eerie wooden statue sitting beside its front door. What the hell was that thing even supposed to be? An Indian? An old white man? A

child molester? I really had no idea.

Still, the windows promised "Old Fashioned Shakes & Malts" as well as "Awesome Burgers & Fries", and since I hadn't eaten a thing since early that morning, they had my full attention.

Out of habit more than need, I looked both ways down the empty street before crossing to the café.

Inside, red-leather-topped stools sat in a neat row before a counter filled with all the knickknacks one needs when eating burgers and shakes. Matching booths lined the walls under the windows, with free-standing tables filling the space between. It had that homey, nineteen-fifties retro look, though I doubted it was retro at all. More accurate, this was what the place looked like when it was built in the nineteen-fifties, and it hadn't changed by a hair since.

Lucky for me, the windows hadn't lied—the food was pretty good. Though the cute boy who served me was better. About my age, he had tussled brown hair, matching warm brown eyes, and that strong thin body reserved to young men on the cusp of manhood. Perhaps a year or two too young for me, but I was only looking for some eye candy.

As shy as he was cute, it was all I could do to get him to talk. Not that I'm Ms. Outgoing or anything. But it'd been a long trip, and I was hungry for both food and a little conversation from someone born within the same decade as me.

"You lived here long?" I asked when he brought out my food.

To me, this is tight and personal. I avoid Filtering, and use as few "I" sentences as possible. The reader feels a strong connection to the Narrator, has Empathy for why she's the way she is, is written in the Narrators voice, keeping it consistent with Tone and Style, and is being told by a Limited Narrator who is Unreliable, learning things at the same time as the reader. Everything I feel First Person should be.

Now, here's the exact same piece, but written in Third Person Limited.

It was chilly, even though it was August, and the street was deserted, even though it was about three in the afternoon. Across the road from Sasha sat Café Jax—an ancient rust-colored brick building with a stained red and white stripped awning and an eerie wooden statue sitting beside its front door. *What the hell is that thing even supposed to be? An Indian? An old white man? A child molester?* Sasha really had no idea.

Still, the windows promised "Old Fashioned Shakes & Malts" as well as "Awesome Burgers & Fries", and since she hadn't eaten a thing since early that morning, they had her full attention.

Out of habit more than need, Sasha looked both ways down the empty street before crossing to the café.

Inside, red-leather-topped stools sat in a neat row before a counter filled with all the knickknacks one needs when eating burgers and shakes. Matching booths lined the walls under the windows, with free-standing tables filling the space between. It had that homey, nineteen-fifties retro look, though it was probably not retro at all. More accurate, this was what the place looked like when it was built in the nineteen-fifties, and it hadn't changed by a hair since.

Lucky for Sasha, the windows hadn't lied—the food was pretty good. Though the cute boy who served her was better. About her age, he had

> tussled brown hair, matching warm brown eyes, and that strong thin body reserved to young men on the cusp of manhood. Perhaps a year or two too young for her, but she was only looking for some eye candy.
>
> As shy as he was cute, it was all Sasha could do to get him to talk. *Not that I'm Ms. Outgoing or anything.* But it'd been a long trip, and she was hungry for both food and a little conversation from someone born within the same decade as her.
>
> "You lived here long?" Sasha asked when he brought out her food.

Look closely and you'll note that I all I did was change nouns and pronouns. I to Sasha, me to she, my to her. The only other change was to take the two lines that were über personal, the one about the Indian statue, and the one about her not being Ms. Outgoing, and change them into Inner Monologue by italicizing them.

Why use the Inner Monologue? Two reasons.

First, in Third Person Limited, I'll concede that just like First Person, all Narrative is *technically* an extension of the Character Narrator.

However…

It's also still *technically* Third Person. Meaning, Inner Monologue does not feel awkward when added to a Third Person story.

Remember, Inner Monologue feels odd in First Person. Not that it can't be done. It can. It's simply redundant since all First Person Narrative reads like Inner Monologue. Meaning, this is a trick that's not available to you if you write in First Person. Point for Third Person Limited!

Second, the bonus this brings to Third Person Limited is, whenever I write a line that's extremely personal to the Character Narrator as Inner Monologue, it draws more attention to it, and therefore has more impact upon the reader. It makes them feel like they are even deeper inside the Character Narrator's mind.

This is a powerful tool, allowing me to create an even more visceral connection between the reader and the Character Narrator.

Getting back to the topic at hand. When done correctly, you'll write Third Person Limited exactly the same way you write First Person. The two are interchangeable when done well.

To drive this point home, I'll do one more experiment. Here's the opening of the Epic Fantasy piece I'm currently writing in Third Person Limited. Let's see if I can just as easily change it to First Person.

Here is the Third Person Limited version:

> *Have I sworn allegiance to the just, or simply to the victorious?*
>
> This question clawed at Valimane Dray's mind as he passed his gaze over the imposing group assembled in a loose circle beneath the Temple of Wisdom. Ten in total, including himself and Tyelay.
>
> *Can the righteousness of our cause truly cleanse my soul of what I've done this day?*
>
> He could not say. The bile resting in the back of his throat was less ambiguous. Soot and ash congealing in his sweat conspired to irritate the skin beneath his armor, exasperating the dark cloud saturating his thoughts.
>
> Those in attendance stood around a central Sending Stone, and spoke in hushed whispers.
>
> Waiting.
>
> *I hate waiting.*

And now let's see if I can pull it off in First Person:

> *Had I sworn allegiance to the just, or simply to the victorious?*
>
> This question clawed at my mind as I passed my gaze over the imposing group assembled in a loose circle beneath the Temple of Wisdom. Ten in total, including myself and Tyelay.

> Could the righteousness of our cause truly cleanse my soul of what I'd done this day?
>
> I could not say. The bile resting in the back of my throat was less ambiguous. Soot and ash congealing in my sweat conspired to irritate the skin beneath my armor, exasperating the dark cloud saturating my thoughts.
>
> Those in attendance stood around a central Sending Stone, and spoke in hushed whispers.
>
> Waiting.
>
> I hated waiting.

So, this is a bit different from before. I still only changed nouns and pronouns. However, I did have to adjust my Tense in a few spots. I'll not going into Verb Forms in this book, but let's take a look at why I had to change some of the Verb Tenses in this piece.

When writing in Third Person Past Tense, all Narration is written in Past Tense. However, any dialogue, including Inner Monologue, is written in Present Tense. Look back at the first example. Note that all the Inner Monologue is written in Present Tense.

Since this rewrite is written in First Person Past Tense, and I don't use Inner Monologue with First Person, I was forced to change all that Inner Monologue to Narrative, meaning I needed to change it from Present Tense to Past Tense.

Which is why:

> **<u>Have</u>** *I sworn allegiance to the just, or simply to the victorious?*

Became:

> **<u>Had</u>** *I sworn allegiance to the just, or simply to the victorious?*

Still, my point is made. Outside of very minor things (nouns, pronouns, perhaps a tiny bit of Verb Tense), First Person and Third Person Limited are written in a nearly identical manner.

So why did I use First Person for the Café Jax story, and Third Person Limited for the epic fantasy story? Valid question.

With the epic fantasy story, the biggest reason is, it's complex as hell. Four Character Narrators, time shifts, Parallel Plot Arcs, Subplot Arcs, etc. As I've said, First Person will ruin a story if it's complex. It just doesn't work.

So, based solely upon the complexity, Third Person Limited is the vehicle I want my reader riding in for this tale.

As for the other story, my reasons are many. One is that First Person is the predominant Narrative type for the Targeted Genre the Café Jax story falls into. Yes, I bent to the industry. Sue me. I like to eat food, and food costs money, and the industry only pays you money if you play by their rules.

But only slightly less important was I felt the story was enhanced by what First Person brings with it. It's also an incredibly simple story. Basically, all the things I've already discussed when we spoke of First Person.

Again, the story should always help you pick the proper Narrative. And in this case, I feel it did.

Now, I notice you've been squirming in your seat, trying in vain not to interrupt me. I didn't allow you, because I already know what you're going to say. You're going to say that BOTH of the times I switched the First to Third Person, the Third Person still feels like there was a third-party Narrator telling the tale.

And yes, I could concede that fact. I won't. But I could. Still, it'd be inconsiderate of me to at least not chase this rabbit for a bit.

Yes, I can see where the following line would feel like there's a third-party Narrator:

> *Could the righteousness of our cause truly cleanse my soul of what I've done this day?*
> He could not say. The bile resting in the back of his throat was less ambiguous. Soot and ash congealing in his sweat conspired to irritate the skin beneath his armor, exasperating the dark cloud saturating his thoughts.

The, "He could not Say.", the description of the things irritating him, etc. all feel like there could be a third-party Narrator telling all this.

However, there's not. You see, it's all personal to the Character Narrator *in the moment*. This is an incredibly subtle thing, and probably the hardest thing to master within Third Person Limited. But all of it is written in a way that's coming directly from the perception of the Character Narrator. It's all personal to him, and not some third-party Narrator. Again, just like First Person.

You still have a question sitting in your eye. "But if it feels like there's a third-party Narrator, why are you so insistent on teaching it as if there is no third-party Narrator in Third Person Limited?"

Perhaps it's just getting into the correct mindset. Or, perhaps I'm being too hypercritical here. Still, for me it's easier to wrap my poor ole country-boy brain around the fact that there's no third-party Narrator to Shift into. This means I only get the Character Narrator to play with, and forces me to stay tight to that one Narrator. This keeps me focused on the prize—writing Third Person Limited in the same way as I would write First Person so I can leach all the advantages First Person has, but keep the advantages of Third Person at the same time.

To help illustrate this one more time, let's take a look at the opening of *Silence of the Lambs* again.

> Behavioral Science, the FBI section that deals with serial murder, is on the bottom floor of the Academy building at Quantico, half-buried in the earth. Clarice Starling reached it flushed after a fast walk from Hogan's Alley on the firing range. She had grass in her hair and grass stains on her FBI Academy windbreaker from diving to the ground under fire in an arrest problem on the range.
>
> No one was in the outer office, so she fluffed briefly by her reflection in the glass doors. She knew she could look all right without primping. Her

hands smelled of gunsmoke, but there was no time to wash-- Section Chief Crawford's summons had said now.

The opening line, "Behavioral Science, the FBI section that deals with serial murder, is on the bottom floor of the Academy building at Quantico, half-buried in the earth." is really the only thing that makes this Omniscient. The rest is Limited to Starling's Perspective. But since there's both Narrative types, this falls into the realm of Third Person Free Indirect Discourse.

To change this and turn it into true Third Person Limited would be mind-numbingly simple. All that needs to happen is to make everything personal to the Character Narrator. Now, this is one way I might do it. I'm certain you could figure out other ways.

> Clarice Starling was out of breath by the time she entered the Behavioral Science section of the Academy building in Quantico. She was flushed after her fast walk from Hogan's Alley on the firing range and her descent via stairs all the way to the bottom floor, the home of agents who dealt with serial murder. She had grass in her hair, and grass stains on her FBI Academy windbreaker from diving to the ground under fire in an arrest problem on the range.
>
> No one was in the outer office, so she fluffed briefly by her reflection in the glass doors. She knew she could look all right without primping. Her hands smelled of gunsmoke, but there was no time to wash-- Section Chief Crawford's summons had said now.

By simply removing the opening line and burying it inside Starling's personal perception of the world around her, I removed the third-party Narrator.

Let's test this against my First Person theory, and see if it can be rewritten into First Person by just changing its Nouns/Pronouns.

> I was out of breath by the time I entered the Behavioral Science section of the Academy building in Quantico. I was flushed after my fast walk from Hogan's Alley on the firing range and my descent via stairs all the way to the bottom floor, the home of agents who dealt with serial murder. I had grass in my hair, and grass stains on my FBI Academy windbreaker from diving to the ground under fire in an arrest problem on the range.
>
> No one was in the outer office, so I fluffed briefly by my reflection in the glass doors. I knew I could look all right without primping. My hands smelled of gunsmoke, but there was no time to wash-- Section Chief Crawford's summons had said now.

Look, this is all very technical stuff, and I know I'm splitting hairs here. Perhaps you are reading the above and thinking to yourself that I'm stupid, that you don't see a difference. And that's fine. I admitted at the start of this whole thing that I see things differently than most. But I still believe the better you understand these miniscule differences, the better your writing will become.

I'm also not saying my rewrite is better than Harris' original version. It isn't. It's simply different. I've already stated that I feel *Silence of the Lambs* would not work as well if written in Third Person Limited. I'm simply using it as an example to make a point. That's all.

But this is the essence that is Third Person Limited. Write it exactly as you would First Person, keeping all the Narration personal to the Character Narrator.

Let's look at some more advantages that Third Person Limited has in common with First Person, starting with…

EASY TO STAY IN THE NARRATOR'S HEAD

"Just like First Person…" I've said it a lot already, and I'm going to say it even more throughout the remainder of this topic. If this annoys you, I do so apologize. Then again, I've never really concerned myself with your feelings, so… ☺

Still, I can't stress enough that when done right, Third Person Limited has all the advantages of First Person, with way less of its disadvantages.

To that end…

Just like First Person, there's no easier way to stay inside your Character Narrator's head than to realize that everything you write *must* come from the perspective of that Character Narrator.

This is harder than it sounds. You must truly embrace what it means to be the Character Narrator. Everything must be from their perspective. Let's look at two examples from the Epic Fantasy saga I'm currently writing so I can show you what I mean.

I have two chapters that both start at the same moment in time, with the description of the early morning sunlight. However, since each is from a different Character's Perspective, they feel different. Not only do I use a different Style and Tone for each, each of these Character Narrators view the world around them in a different light. And I need to show this through the writing.

This first excerpt is from the perspective of a warrior who is now a slave and has been sold to fight as a gladiator. He's violent, angry, and isn't really enjoying life at the moment.

> Tilting his head, he narrowed his eyes as the day's first rays of sunlight breached the bars of the tiny window set high in his cell wall. Dust motes churned about in the orange light, practicing their slow advances and feints above the dingy floor.

Notice the words I use, particularly the Verbs. "He **narrowed**", "sunlight **breached** the bars", "dust motes **churned**", "practicing their slow **advances and feints**". These are all brutal, violent, militaristic ways of looking at the morning sunlight. But it holds to this Character's Voice, Tone, and Style. It shows the reader how this Character sees the world around him.

Here's the same basic thing, but from the perspective of a seventeen-year-old farm boy who has never been in a fight in is life.

> Sunlight poured through the glazed window set above his bed, washing over him. The cool air of his bedroom tickled his bare arms. He wished for nothing more than to curl under his warm blankets and let sleep retake him, but he was already late in rising. Lifting his arms high over his head, he stretched and made a half-hearted attempt to wipe the crusties from his eyes. He peered out at the blurry view offered through the window's wavy, semitransparent glass.

Now the light is "**pouring**" in and "**washing**" over him. The air is "**tickling**" his arms. His blankets are "**warm**". A much different Character Voice, not to mention Tone and Style. But this Character does not see the world in the same way as the first guy. So, I need to show this through the writing.

While both paragraphs describe these Character Narrators seeing the same early morning sunlight, they couldn't be more different.

And that's the key to Third Person Limited, especially when you're going to use Multiple Character Narrators. Write from your Character Narrator's head, because that's where the story is coming from. It's also how you separate one Character Narrator from another, as well as making each a unique Character that the reader can build a visceral connection with.

And… just like First Person… in Third Person Limited it's very easy to…

CONVEY THE NARRATOR'S FEELINGS AND EMOTIONS

Seriously. In Third Person Limited, your reader is *inside* your Character Narrator's mind. Just like First Person!

Sure, the Imaginary Camera is free-floating like some deranged drone circling around the Character Narrator. But this is only the *visual aspect* of what the reader gets from the story. For everything else, the reader's brain and the Character Narrator's brain are one brain.

Understanding this is understanding the power of Third Person Limited.

As we've discussed, with Third Person Omniscient, even though we focus on a Focal Character, the reader is kept at arm's length from the story. With Third Person Free Indirect Discourse, you are free to Shift between a third-party Omniscient Narrator all the way down into the mind of a Character Narrator within the story. (Hopefully, keeping things limited to one Focal Character per chapter, and not every single Character that's mentioned in the story. Head Hopping is bad, umkay?)

"Limited" is in Third Person Limited's name.

When you're writing in Third Person Limited, you lose the ability to Shift up into a third-party Omniscient Narrator. You also lose the ability to Shift into any other character outside the Character Narrator.

Think back to my Finger-Glasses example. Now, the "eyes" are free floating here in Third Person Limited. But just like First Person (and real life), you have no ability to know what anyone around your Character Narrator is thinking or feeling.

Just like First Person, a Third Person Limited story is *limited* to being told strictly from one Character Narrator's perspective at a time.

But this means you're free to deeply explore everything about that one Character Narrator's feelings and emotions, allowing the reader to experience them as well. I'm not going into all the details here again, since I already went into great detail with this topic when I discussed the same thing in First Person. It really is the same.

And… just like First Person, the limited nature of this Narrative means that you…

CREATE A STRONG BOND BETWEEN THE READER AND NARRATOR

Yup. And since I've already discussed this as well, I'll just point you back to First Person.

In fact, let's save some time here. Not only does having a Limited Narrator build that strong bond between the reader and the Narrator just as it does in First Person, it also:

→ Builds Empathy, because the reader understands *why* the Narrator does what they do.
→ Means the Narration can be in the words of the Narrator, making it easy to keep a consistent Tone and Style.
→ Can have an Unreliable Narrator, so the Narrator and reader are both learning things at the same time.

Just as all the above happens with First Person.

Seriously. Go back and reread the First Person section of this book and simply change "First Person" to "Third Person Limited" as you read and you'll grasp how close these two Narratives are.

However, while all the above is wonderful, and makes both First Person and Third Person Limited very powerful tools for telling stories, that marks the end of the road where First Person and Third Person Limited are twinsies.

Let's now discuss some things that First Person can't compete with, starting with Third Person Limited's number one advantage, the ability to have…

MULTIPLE CHARACTER NARRATORS

Hurry, hurry, hurry! Step right up and see the most amazing sight on this great big green Earth of ours. Multiple Character Narrators without causing your readers grief!!! That's right, folks. I'm talking Narrators here, and having more than one of 'em! Only five cents a ticket to see this marvel of creation with your very own ocular orbs!

Er…or something like that.

Anyhoo… Yes, a huge advantage Third Person Limited has over First or Second Person, and even Third Person Omniscient, lays in the fact that you can have Multiple Character Narrators seamlessly, without making the reader feel that you've broken the reality of your story. (Why doesn't Third Person Omniscient have this? Because you only get the one disembodied third-party Narrator within Omniscient. Sure, you can have Multiple **Focal Characters**, but those aren't Narrators, now are they? As for Third Person Free Indirect Discourse, it does share this advantage, but since we're not there yet, hold your roll!)

Within Third Person in general, readers are not thrown off by Multiple Leading Characters because they're kind of expecting it. And since this expectation is there, when you add in a second Character Narrator within Third Person Limited, provided you do it correctly, the reader won't be jarred by the effect, and will simply keep on keeping on.

However, please understand what I mean by, "provided you do it correctly."

To understand the first aspect of having Multiple Character Narrators, let's chase a rabbit for a bit.

In my local writing class this month, after I read something I wrote to illustrate a point, one of my students asked, "I've seen other people italicize Inner Monologue like you did there. But why do it? It's annoying to me. And since I don't like it, I don't use it in my stories."

On the topic of **Standardized Formatting**, I hear this kind of thing *a lot* from aspiring writers. I don't understand it, but there are a bazillion aspiring writers out there who feel they can ignore the "normal" way to format inside a novel. They might do this because, like my student from above, they *personally* don't like the look of it, or perhaps because they want to be different in an attempt to set themselves apart from the pack, or maybe they're an anarchist at heart, and can't stomach following rules of any type.

Whatever. It doesn't matter why. All that matters is that they're wrong. And stupid. And their mothers dress them funny. ☺

It's important that you understand *why* we format things inside a novel the way we do. It's even more important that you follow those Standardized Formats.

Standardized Formatting has nothing to do with the story, nor the writer, nor with being creative, nor with doing things that make the writer feel comfortable.

Standardized Formatting has to do with explaining something to a reader *WITHOUT* having to explain anything to the reader!

Case in point:

> Drake looked at the student, annoyance threatening to overwhelm his sanity. *Why do aspiring writers fight Standardized Formatting so much?* He sighed, taking a moment to reign in his anger. Through clenched teeth he answered, "Reasons."

In the above, when the reader reads the line, *Why do aspiring writers fight Standardized Formatting so much?* they know it's Inner Monologue (something said inside Drake's mind). So, *as* it's being read by the reader, they *imagine* it's being said in Drake's mind. Why? It's written in italics. They don't struggle trying to figure out *how* it was said within the confines of the story. They *know*, because the italics "shows" them *visually* how it was said. Same when they hit, "Reasons," they know this line is being said out loud. Because this is fiction, readers know that any words inside "" are being said out loud. (Sort of fiction, anyway. It really did happen to me this week in the really real world.) It's why we don't write:

Drake walked into the room where Sally was sitting. "Hello, Sally," Drake said out loud by forcing air from his lungs in a controlled manner past his voice box which he controlled with very subtle muscle movements so Sally could understand what he was saying.

Sally smiled at Drake. "Oh," she responded, also out loud using her mouth and voice box to make the sounds audible in the same way Drake had done. "Hi, Drake. How are you today?" This she also said out loud. It was a question, meaning she varied the words with slightly higher pitches to indicate that she would like for Drake to answer her.

Ugg…. Readers know when they're reading fiction that anything between a set of these babies "" are words that are being said out loud in the same way they know any sentence that ends in a ? is a question.

And thus, the reason we italicize Inner Monologue.

Sure, I could have written:

Why do aspiring writers fight formatting so much? he thought.

Or:

"Why do aspiring writers fight formatting so much?" he thought.

Or even:

Why do aspiring writers fight formatting so much? he thought.

But why? Adding, "he thought" in this scenario is redundant, because the italics visually "show" the reader that this is him thinking. Adding "" around the inner monologue is misleading, because when the reader starts reading the line they're going to assume it's being said out loud. Then, when they finally get to the end of the sentence, they'll discover they've been tricked, the dialogue was actually Inner Monologue. HA! Stupid Reader!!! Got cha! But do you really think it's a good idea to make your reader feel stupid? And the last way is just confusing. It looks like a typo because the "h" is not capitalize in he, and there's a sentence that just says, He thought. What's that all about?

Ensuring the read isn't confused is the reason Standardized Formatting exists. Another history lesson for you, Standardized Formatting started to come into practice over the first few centuries following the invention of the printing press. Now, just so you don't think to yourself, "Oh, well, then it's relatively new!" Printing presses were first invented around 1440 AD. Yeah, they started creating Standardized Formatting a long time ago. Some things, like italicizing Inner Monologue, aren't as old—only in the last hundred years or so. Still, since today's fiction industry has almost totally adopted italicized words to mean words that are said inside the character's mind, and readers have bought into this fact since it gives them a visual clue about what they're reading, you should use it and stop complaining.

It doesn't matter what your personal opinion is about it. You're irrelevant to this discussion. It's all about the reader.

HEY! I've heard that same phrase from someone before. Oh, right! Me! Neat.

Why chase this Standardized Formatting rabbit? Because having Multiple Character Narrators means you need to format things in a specific way so the reader can anticipate the Shift into a new Character Narrator. They need a *visual clue* so they can anticipate what you're about to do.

Keep in mind, I'm only talking Third Person here—Omniscient, Free Indirect Discourse, and Limited. None of the other Narratives should even have Multiple Narrators. However, even within Third Person, you should limit yourself to using only one Character Narrator or Focal Character per scene or chapter. So, just like First Person, if you start a scene or chapter inside one Character Narrator's head (or by focusing on one Focal Character), you must remain with that Character *for the entire scene/chapter.*

Side note: writing both Character Narrator and Focal Character is becoming exhausting. From here on out I'm going to just use Character Narrator, since I'm discussing Third Person Limited Here. But please, if you're writing in Omniscient or Free Indirect Discourse, understand the rules are the same for the Focal Character.

Before you can Shift into a new Character Narrator's head, you must give the reader a visual clue to let them know you might be doing so. If you don't, they won't be expecting it, and they'll be thrown out of your story, which ruins the story for the reader. *cough* Abraham Lincoln Vampire Hunter *cough*

Sorry, dang! Something got caught in my throat. Weird. Not even sure where that came from since I'm typing here. Anyway, I'm okay now.

When writing Third Person Limited, there are two accepted ways to visually show the reader you might be Shifting into a different Character Narrator. One, a scene break. Two, a chapter break.

Let's start with a chapter break, as it's the simplest to understand.

A chapter break is where you end one chapter, and begin the next chapter. Do I need to explain this further? I didn't think so.

When you begin a new chapter within Third Person, you're absolutely free to begin that new chapter inside a new Character Narrator's head. No reader will fault you for it.

A scene break is a bit more complex. These happen inside a chapter, but are "shown" to the reader with a visual clue by ending one scene, skipping a few lines, perhaps even adding a nifty piece of artwork, and then starting a new scene. Something like:

And with that final blow, Drake had single-handedly slain the entire invading army.

Drake lounged on his throne as he glared down at the defeated kings who had come to swear fealty to him.

With the first line, this is obviously the end of a massive battle scene. However, the next line starts somewhere else. A new *scene*. But the reader has a visual clue in the fact that I ended one scene, skipped a few lines, added a nifty piece of artwork, and then started a new scene.

They knew I was leaving Kansas behind to go to a new place, which is kinda the point of a "Scene Break".

Now, I kept the Narrator the same from one scene to the second. However, as I'm talking about having Multiple Character Narrators here, let's look at a scene break that Shifts to a new Character Narrator.

> And with that final blow, Drake had single-handedly slain the entire invading army.

> Sally stared at Drake in disbelief as he rolled and flopped out in the open grass field. For the past hour, he'd been swinging a stick he'd found. She assumed he was fighting some massive imaginary army only he could see, but it could just as easily have been a dragon or a demon for all she knew. She shook her head. "What a moron."

It can be a bit more jarring, and needs to be handled with bit more care, but you're absolutely free to begin a new scene inside a new Character Narrator's head. If done well, no reader will fault you for it.

Another thing to keep in mind every time you start a new chapter/scene inside a new Character Narrator's head is, *YOU JUST STARTED A NEW CHAPTER/SCENE INSIDE A NEW CHARACTER NARRATOR'S HEAD!!!*

You must do this in a way that grounds the reader to this new Character Narrator *as fast as humanly possible*. You must **Set the Scene!**

The last thing you want is for your reader to be confused, assuming they're still in the last guy's head only to discover two pages later that they're now in some new guy's head. HA! Stupid Reader. Gotcha again!

No. Not good at all.

For me, I like to mention the Character Narrator's full name either in the opening sentence of a new chapter/scene, or as close as I can. This gives the reader yet one more visual clue as to whose head they're now in.

If you look at my above example, I begin the new Scene with the name of the new Character Narrator—Sally. This means there's absolutely no time delay between the start of the scene, and the moment the reader discovers they're in a new Character Narrator's head.

Pretty sweet.

Going back to the epic fantasy novel I'm currently writing, let's look at the opening paragraph of the first five chapters:

CHAPTER ONE

Rolling onto his back, Klain lay on the hard slab that formed his bed. It had been a cold night, though the Human slaves probably suffered more from the chill than he. Flexing his claws, he ran their sharp edges through the heavy fur covering his arm as he glared at the stone ceiling. Thick wooden support beams stretched out above him like the fingers of a giant hand. Foreboding. Oppressive. A constant reminder of his master's hold upon his wretched life. A life that had never been his.

CHAPTER TWO

Arderi Cor sat up in bed with a start. Breathing hard, he gazed wide-eyed around his tiny bedroom without seeing anything. It had been the same type of dream for several moons now, ever since the strange happenings at last harvest's Salintine festival. While the details differed from night to night, the terror did not. Nor did the outcome. In every one, the Siers had Tested him... and he had failed.

Chapter Three

A relentless sun hung high in a cloudless blue sky. Klain panted hard, sweat running in rivulets beneath his fur. Fatigued from the combat he had survived so far, he knew he would be given no reprieve until either all those slated to fight him were dead...

Or I am!

Chapter Four

Reality roiled into a kaleidoscope of colored lights swimming across Malant Cor's field of vision.

Chapter Five

Clytus Rillion stood on his seat screaming with the rest of the nearly one-hundred-thousand spectators packed into the Grand Coliseum. In all his seasons attending the Games, never had he witnessed such a spectacle.

Note, in each of these, I give the reader the full name of the Character Narrator as soon as possible. Giving the full name is just a gimmick I use. I've always found it difficult to give the reader the last name of my Character Narrators, so I came up with this ploy as a way of doing this organically. I've kept this consistent for decades now, so my readers can rely on me to continue this trend. You can figure out your own gimmick.

Still, look at how fast I let the reader know whose head they're in. In two of them, the first words are the new Character's name. In the other three, it's either the first or second sentence. Very little time for my reader to become confused over something as stupid as them wondering whose head they're in.

Another thing I try to do in the opening paragraph is to set this new Character Narrator's **Voice, Tone, and Style**. This helps the reader drop into that Character's mindset even faster.

This is much subtler, and a lot more difficult, than simply shoving the Character's name into the reader's face. It harkens back to what I showed you between the two Character Narrator's describing the sunlight coming into their respective rooms. But let's expand upon this a bit more.

Looking at the first example, when I Shifted to the Sally Narrator, "disbelief" is very close to the beginning. I used this particular word to cast doubt on what the reader had read in the previous scene. Also, I described what Drake was doing in a very different manner than how he saw what he was doing. The Drake Narrator saw himself as heroic and mighty. The Sally Narrator saw Drake as an idiot. This "Tone" difference helps the reader make the mental transition without much work on their part.

Let's look again at the first paragraphs of my current work in progress, and break this down a bit.

CHAPTER ONE

Rolling onto his back, Klain lay on the **hard** slab that formed his bed. It had been a **cold** night, though the Human **slaves** probably **suffered** more from the **chill** than he. Flexing his claws, he ran their **sharp** edges through the **heavy** fur covering his arm as he **glared** at the stone ceiling. **Thick** wooden support beams stretched out above him like the fingers of a giant hand. **Foreboding**. **Oppressive**. A constant reminder of his **master's** hold upon his **wretched** life. A life that had **never** been his.

Notice this paragraph paints a picture of things being rough. Elements of the scene are described as hard, cold, suffering, sharp, etc. The words I chose for this opening paragraph create a Tone for the reader to experience. One that's not the most pleasant. However, all this agony is laced with, if not calmness, at the very least acceptance. This is a character who is in a bad situation, but who is resigned to this fate.

CHAPTER TWO

Arderi Cor sat up in bed with a **start**. Breathing hard, he **gazed** wide-eyed around his tiny bedroom **without seeing** anything. It had been the same type of dream for several moons now, ever since the **strange** happenings at last harvest's Salintine festival. While the details differed from night to night, the **terror** did not. Nor did the outcome. In every one, the Siers had Tested him... and he had **failed**.

Shifting to Arderi in the next chapter, the reader gets a completely different Tone. He's not in a cell, but in a bedroom, so the room is different. Now, over the next few paragraphs I describe this room, but that's not the immediate Tone I want my readers to feel. It's more important to me they feel panic, a strangeness of the unknown, and the pressure of failure—all things I hit them with right here in this opening paragraph.

CHAPTER THREE

A **relentless** sun hung high in a cloudless blue sky. Klain **panted hard**, **sweat running** in rivulets beneath his fur. **Fatigued** from the combat he **had survived** so far, he knew he would be given **no reprieve** until either all those slated to fight him were **dead**...
Or I am!

Shift again, and my readers discover they're back in Klain's head. The Tone here has changed from what they felt in Chapter one, however, to that of exhaustion and a resolve to live to fight another day. It's also difference from what they left behind in the Arderi Chapter.

CHAPTER FOUR

Reality roiled into a kaleidoscope of colored lights swimming across Malant Cor's field of vision.

Okay. Since this is limited to one line, it's a tough one to use as an example. Let me give you the next few paragraphs so I can talk about the Tone I used here.

Reality **roiled** into a kaleidoscope of colored lights **swimming** across Malant Cor's field of vision.

It's like opening my eyes under water, yet everything looks crisp and clear. I just cannot tell what anything is!

"Now, Malant, **focus**. **Bend your mind** and see the room around you." Sier Sarlimac, Malant's primary instructor, stood in front of him—if a **disembodied** head and hands **floating** in a **sea of colors** could be called *standing*. "Tell me what I'm holding."

The scene before Malant was **off-putting**. Strain as he might, he could see **no difference** between the multitude of **swirling** colors that made up the room, and anything his teacher might be holding in his hands.

The Tone I wanted the readers to experience here is one of confusion, struggle, etc. I want the reader to be disoriented here. So, I wrote this in a confusing way, forcing that confusion upon my Character Narrator.

Is the above confusing? I think so. However, if you were to continue reading for a few more paragraphs, you'd find the Character Narrator, and by extension the reader, begins to grasp what's going on. And I do this through the Tone I set. Oh, and this is a very different Tone from the first three chapters, so that dichotomy helps the reader break from the old Character Narrators, and more easily slip into this new Malant Character.

Here's the final one.

CHAPTER FIVE

Clytus Rillion stood on his seat **screaming** with the rest of the nearly one-hundred-thousand spectators **packed** into the Grand Coliseum. In all his seasons **attending** the Games, never had he witnessed such a **spectacle**.

As with the other chapters, I **Set the Scene** over the next few paragraphs, describing what everything looks like for the reader. Still, there's a Tone even in this short opening paragraph. Excitement, chaos, noise, crowds, etc. All of which are very different from anything the reader has read so far. This allows the reader to make a seamless transition into this new Clytus Narrator's head.

Visual and Tonal clues must be given to your reader to effectively Shift between Multiple Character Narrators. You'll do this by utilizing Standardized Formatting and paying attention to the Tone you create at the beginning of each chapter/scene.

That, however, is far from the end of this discussion.

Since I've given you the beginnings to several of my chapters, I want to really hammer home the biggest difference between Third Person Limited and Third Person Free Indirect Discourse.

Remember at the start of this topic where that arrogant asshole had the audacity to rewrite the opening of the New York Times Bestseller *Silence of the Lambs*? Oh, wait. That arrogant asshole was me.

Anyway...

Remember how I showed ways to take out the Omniscient, and hold it to a stricter Limited?

Well, one of the ways I like to teach Third Person Limited is with scale. You see, an Omniscient Narrative has the ability to start off Macro (big), and then work Micro (small). This is the reason so many chapters written in Third Person Free Indirect Discourse start this way.

Meaning, *Silence of the Lambs* starts with a wide shot of the FBI Academy at Quantico, and then slides into the Micro that is Starling's inner mind.

By far, this is the most common way to start a story/chapter/scene in Third Person Omniscient and Free Indirect Discourse.

This Shift is usually handled by the third-party Omniscient Narrator. Those types of stories normally start a new chapter or scene with a massive wide shot of some sort. This pulls the reader out of a specific Focal Character, gives them a new aerial view of a different location, and then brings them back into a new Focal Character.

And with that final blow, Drake had single-handedly slain the entire invading army.

It was the first warm day of spring, and the entire town of Smallberg had come out of their winter slumber. Shoppers where happy to find new wares to purchase in their favorite shops. Children were glad for the freedom of the outdoors. Even the elderly were appreciative over the fact they could lounge on their porches.

Sally had come with Drake to the town park. She stared at him in disbelief as he rolled and flopped out in the open grass field. For the past hour, he'd been swinging a stick he'd found. She assumed he

> was fighting some massive imaginary army only he could see, but it could just as easily have been a dragon or a demon for all she knew. She shook her head. "What a moron."

The above is technically still in true Omniscient. If I were to continue to slide further into Sally's mind, I would turn this into Free Indirect Discourse. But hopefully you can see why so many people like to use Free Indirect Discourse, as it gives them the ability to use a third-party Narrator to open their chapters or scenes with.

Literally, you could start your story from the edge of the Milky Way Galaxy if you wanted, slowing bring the reader into our outlying spiral arm, into our solar system, toward our star burning bright at its center, nearer to our big blue orb, falling through our atmosphere to an elongated continent set apart from the majority of the land this world had to offer, shifting to the left of this smaller land mass, as if heading for the coast, only to stay slightly inland, heading for a high, raised platform of sand-covered dirt surrounded by a ring of ugly and bare mountains, at the center of which sits hundreds of gaudily lit buildings with flashing lights covering them like some insanely designed throw rug, all the way down to a small sign cowering between two three-lane roads packed with cars, a sign that reads, "Welcome to Fabulous Las Vegas Nevada", with a frustrated looking man standing next to this sign wearing cargo shorts and a T-shirt with some humorous geek-culture-related joke upon it, and he's giving you the middle finger.

Yeah. To me, that's the essence of Omniscient.

However, I don't normally write in Omniscient nor Free Indirect Discourse. I write in Third Person Limited. So what are my options?

Well, I do the exact opposite. I start Micro (small), and then work Macro (big). I start focused on my Character Narrator, and then work out from there.

Case in Point: Look back at the opening paragraphs of the first five chapters of my current work in progress.

Chapter One starts with a dude lying on a bed looking at a ceiling.

Chapter Two starts with a kid waking up frightened.

Chapter Three starts with the dude from Chapter One panting and sweating.

Chapter Four starts with a different kid who can't see what's in front of him for some reason.

Chapter Five starts with another dude standing and screaming.

Each of these chapters begin small, with a single Character Narrator doing a single thing. I then build from that, allowing the reader to see and experience more and more, but always keeping everything being told through the filter that is the perception of the Character Narrator.

To me, that's essence of Third Person Limited. This is the change I made with *Silence of the Lambs*. Instead of starting with a wide-shot, I started off with Starling.

It's also how I begin anything I'm writing in First Person. The first line is the Character Narrator doing one simple thing. I then build the world around that first simple thing.

I guess what I'm driving at here is, pay attention to how you open your story/chapters/scenes. Time. Effort. If you want to hold to strict Third Person Limited, regardless if you're using Multiple Character Narrators or not, everything must be kept firmly inside the perceptions of said Character Narrator. I.E., you don't have a third-party Narrator.

Most writers either can't do this, or more probable, don't want to do this. Like any Narrative type, Third Person Limited's strict limitations can ruin some stories.

It's the reason the vast majority of stories are still being written in Third Person Free Indirect Discourse to this very day.

To push this topic just a tad bit further, there is one question I get asked all the time concerning Multiple Character Narrators, and that is…

WHO SHOULD BE THE CHARACTER NARRATOR WHEN MORE THAN ONE IS PRESENT?

This is a wonderful question. And while this is something that's going to be different for every situation of every book, I do feel this is something that can be answered pretty concretely. First, let me explain what I'm even talking about.

What I mean by this is; if you're writing a story where you have Multiple Character Narrators, and more than one of them are in the same scene, who should be the Character Narrator? Remember, you can only have one *active* Character Narrator per chapter or scene. If more than one is present, you can only be in one of their minds. No Head Hopping!

For this discussion, let's say we're writing a story where we have two Character Narrators, Drake and Sally. Meaning, throughout this story, we're alternating chapters between these two. Let's also say that when the story started, these two Character Narrators were in different towns.

However, as things must happen in stories, eventually Drake and Sally end up in the same room.

So, which to pick as the Character Narrator? The Character whose mind the reader will be inside? We can't be in both. We must pick one. But which?

For me, I weigh this against four different aspects, the culmination of which lets me know who my Character Narrator will be.

The first concerns the reader, and either giving them information, or withholding information from them.

Meaning, let's say the Drake Narrator has been trying to figure out something. By extension, this means the reader is also trying to figure out whatever this is. Let's say that we're going to write a chapter where Drake and Sally are talking, and something Sally says makes Drake's mind click, and he figures out whatever it is he's been trying to figure out. Now, if he says this out loud, then this information will be given to the reader regardless of which of these two are the Character Narrator. However, let's pretend that Drake figures this out, but it's something he doesn't want to say out loud. Perhaps he's hiding this information from Sally, or perhaps there's a Secondary Character who is in the same room that can't know this information. Whatever. This means that this information is only going to be available inside Drake's mind.

If this is a piece of information we want our reader to have, then we would need to choose Drake as the Character Narrator. By choosing Drake as our Character Narrator, the reader will be inside Drake's head. So, when he puts the pieces together in his mind, and figures out whatever this is, the reader will get this information by the simple fact they are inside Drake's mind.

On that same note, the opposite could be true. Let's say whatever Drake figures out is something we need Drake to figure out, so he can do whatever, but we don't want to give that information to the reader. In that case, we'd want to stay away from Drake's head for this scene, picking Sally as our Character Narrator.

In other words, thinking about what information the reader either needs or doesn't need may help you decide whose head to be inside.

The second thing I think about is worldbuilding. Worldbuilding is an interesting conundrum for me, because I always want to make sure my readers get worldbuilding information in an organic manner.

I would never write:

> Drake turned to Sally and said, "You and I are humans. And as humans, we need to breath air to survive."

Now, you're probably rolling your eyes here, but this same level of stupidity happens all the time with things like:

> Titania looked at Oberon and said, "You and I are fairies. And as fairies, we must eat pixie dust to survive."

You see, writers feel that it would stupid to tell something all humans know, like the need to breath air. However, for some reason they feel they can have other races do things that are just as stupid.

If the fairies in your world must eat pixie dust to survive, then every single fairy already knows that!!! Just like every human knows they must breathe. Why would they ever say it? Sure, your human reader may not know that, but don't give them this information in a stupid way and make your characters look dumb.

Returning to our topic, one of the things that might help me decide between opposing Character Narrators in the same scene is if there will be some worldbuilding I need to do. If so, picking the Character Narrator who doesn't know something might be cool for the reader.

Such as, let's imagine Drake lives in a fantasy world (not a stretch of the imagination by any means). And in this world, he pretty much knows everything, like the fact that Wood Sprites will eat your brain. However, Sally isn't from this fantasy world, and therefore knows nothing.

Let's say we write a scene where a Wood Sprite shows up and Drake kills it before it's even a threat. This confuses Sally, because the little creature looked so cute.

Now, if they discuss why the Wood Sprite is dangerous, then the reader will get this information no matter who is the Character Narrator. As it's all said as dialogue, it doesn't matter whose head the reader is in.

However, which Character will be filled with more wonder? Drake, who already knew this fact, or Sally, whose getting all this new information?

Move this further. Same scenario as above, but this time the Wood Sprite just flies by at a distance. This adds some huge variables now.

If Drake is the Character Narrator, he might just mention that it's there. But as it's just one, and not near them, would he think to even discuss it with Sally? I mean, you could make him, you are the writer. But would it be organic?

> The Wood Fairy flew by well out of reach. Drake paid it no mind, since he was still preoccupied with how Sally had entered his magical land. He turned to Sally. "Oh, by the way. Did you see that Wood Fairy just fly by?"
>
> Sally nodded her head. "She looked so cute."
>
> "Yeah, well, stay away from them. They're Zombie Wood Fairies and they'll eat your brain."

Not very organic, in my opinion. It kind of comes out forced. Plus, since Drake's Tone is preoccupied and depressed, the excitement of this new information gets downplayed.

If Sally was the Character Narrator, however, and she noticed it, chances are high that she would ask Drake what it was. This would open up the discussion in a more natural, organic way.

> Something flitted by. At first Sally assumed it was just a large bug, but looking closer she realized it was a tiny woman with wings. *What a beautiful creature!*
>
> Excited, she turned to Drake. "Was that a fairy?"
>
> Drake had been looking at the ground, still appearing as if someone had urinated in his Cheerios. He looked up. "Oh, yeah, stay away from those. They may look cute, but they're Zombie Wood Fairies and they'll eat your brain."

Not only does this feel more organic, the reader can get caught up in the wonder and excitement Sally's going to be feeling as she discovers this new magical world.

So, thinking about all the worldbuilding things I need to give my reader can sometimes help me choose who the Character Narrator will be.

On that same note, I also consider whose reactions will be more interesting for the reader to follow. Looking at the above example, was it more interesting to read about Sally's wonder and excitement having just entered a brand new magical fantasy world, or more interesting to be inside Drake's head as he fumes about the fact that Sally shouldn't be there?

So, think about your reader, and try and imagine which Character Narrator would be the most interesting to follow.

But all three of those pale compared to the number one reason I choose which Character Narrator to be in any given scene— *Drama!!!*

For me, if it's clear which Character Narrator is going to be the most impacted by a scene, that's normally the Character who the reader will be inside.

Let's say Drake and Sally are both Character Narrators. They have agreed to meet at a diner. Drake is going there because he has just spent his life savings purchasing an engagement ring, and he's planning on popping the big question. Sally is going there because she's met Dylan, and she's planning on breaking up with Drake.

Which side is going to experience the most drama?

Sure, it's going to be weird for Sally. She's there, picking at her Chinese Chicken Salad while she waits for the right moment to tell Drake it's over. Then, all of a sudden, Drake is down on one knee with a ring in his hands. *Awkward.*

But that's nothing compared to the pain and agony Drake's gonna feel as he holds up his offering only to have Sally shake her head and say, "Drake . . . I had no idea you were thinking of us that way. I'm so, so sorry, but I've met someone else who is way better than you."

In this case, I'm going to put my reader inside Drake's head. That way the reader can wallow in all the pain that Drake is about to experience.

Or...

Perhaps the story you're telling is different. Perhaps letting the reader feel what Drake feels in this moment would ruin your story. Still, problem solved. You know you *can't* be inside Drake's head.

Using these four things, 1) information I either want to give to the reader, or withhold from the reader, 2) do I need to give some worldbuilding items to the reader, 3) who is going to be more interesting to follow, and 4) who is going to have the most dramatic experience, should pretty much answer which character to use as your Character Narrator. Spending some Time and Effort thinking about what would be best for the reader and story will help you determine which Character Narrator to use in any given chapter or scene.

Now, let's take this Multiple Character Narrator to the next level and discuss something I touched upon during our First Person discussion…

MULTIPLE NARRATORS = MULTIPLE PLOT ARCS

I may be repeating myself a bit, but I want to at least touch on this subject here—my rule about having Multiple Character Narrators in one story. To do this, each Character Narrator should have their own unique and complete Plot Arc.

Here again, is how I see a story that would have two Character Narrators:

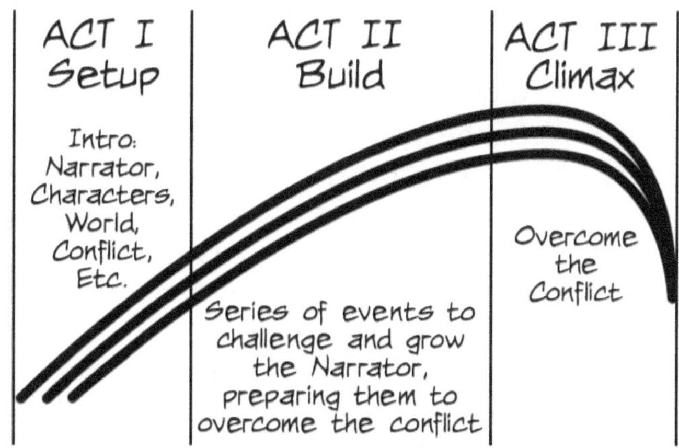

Two Character Narrators means three Plot Arcs—one for each Character Narrator, and one for the overall Story Plot Arc.

Flip back to First Person if you need a full refresher about this, but the fact is, never will I slip into some random slub's head for a scene or two. Just like First Person, doing so breaks the reality you're creating within the story.

Now, I didn't say you can't do this. I said, "never will *I* slip into some random slubs head for a scene or two." This is a rule I hold *myself* to. It can be done, and done effectively.

Brandon Sanderson did this in his debut novel, *Elantris*, a book written in Third Person Free Indirect Discourse. For most of the book, he stuck to this rule. He had three Character Narrators, each with their own personal Plot Arc, and he told this story by bouncing between these three Characters. However, things got a bit… weird… at the end of the book. As in, one of those three Character Narrators was no longer in a position where they could accurately describe to the reader what was going on around them. So, Brandon Shifted a few times, using a few Secondary Characters as Character Narrators. However, I do love that he only used them as Imaginary Cameras, and didn't waste any time attempting to build a visceral connection between the reader and these new Character Narrators. It also helped that these new "Cameras" were closely related, story-wise, to the incapacitated Character Narrator. So, it didn't break the reality of the story to a degree where the reader felt thrown out of the novel. In fact, it was seamless.

Sure, I have Multiple Character Narrators, but each has their own personally motivated Plot Arc, and each of these Plot Arcs are then tied together to a much larger Story Plot Arc.

In case you didn't do the math with my current Work in Progress, yes, in this story I have five Plot Arcs. That's a lie. I have Six.

There's a Klain Plot Arc (1), an Arderi Plot Arc (2), a Clytus Plot Arc (3), a Malant Plot Arc (4), there's a Story Plot Arc for this Novel (5), but this is Book One of a Five Book Saga, so there's also an even larger Saga Plot Arc (6).

Each of these Plot Arcs are different. Each is personal to their respective characters/books. And each is reliant on those below it. In other words, if any Character fails to overcome their individual Plot Arc, it would mean that the Story Plot Arc of Book One would fail, which would in turn then ruin the overall Saga Plot Arc.

Ah, Complexity. How I do love thee!

If done poorly, when you Shift into a Character Narrator who doesn't have their own Plot Arc, you'll hurt your story. Why? Because readers will lose trust in you.

From my experience, most writers don't Shift into Secondary Characters with the same skill as Sanderson did in *Elantris*. The normal reason I see aspiring writers Shift into a Secondary Character's head is to give the reader some information the Character Narrator has no access to. And this is just lazy storytelling. In other words, instead of figuring out how to get this piece of "important information" into the story organically, while remaining loyal to your Character Narrator, they simply have a small scene where the Bar Tender (or whomever) gets this information. Do this, and your readers will quickly realize they have no need caring about these Shifts into other Characters, and by extension this will lessen their overall enjoyment.

Again, this falls under the domain of Head Hopping. I know I'm beating this like a dead horse, but Head Hopping only hurts your story. Period.

I know you might be reading that and still saying to yourself, "This guy is wrong. I love being inside as many Character heads as I can be. And my readers will love it too!" But if that's the case, you and I will simply have to agree to disagree. And at least in my genre, I don't know of one single *successful* Fantasy book that does this. Not one. There are tons of Fantasy stories written this way, most being Self-Published. But I've never found one that was a huge seller that Head Hops.

If that's not a good enough argument to convince you that Head Hopping is bad, well… then I give up. You do your thing.

Getting back to the topic of Multiple Character Narrators, understanding *why* you should do things a certain way is vitally important to you doing this successfully. Yes, Third Person Limited is wonderful at telling a story using Multiple Character Narrators. However, make sure you give the reader all the tools they need to be comfortable with each transition. Chapter or scene breaks as a visual clue, a new Tone to separate the new from the old, and make sure every single Character Narrator you use is vital to the telling of your story so the reader will make the effort to become invested in this new plight.

My point is, having Multiple Character Narrators is a very hard thing to pull off indeed. As with all aspects of creative writing, it's something that'll take you years to master. I know this is not a popular thing to say to aspiring writers, but I highly recommend that you keep your stories simple in the beginning.

Remember, one-million words before you write anything worthy of selling. So, don't waste that "Truly Great Story Idea" you have in the beginning. You may not have the skill to write it yet. Spend the first few hundred-thousand words writing stories with only one Character Narrator. This will help you build your writing skills, without worrying over the complexities of juggling Multiple Character Narrators. Then, after you've started mastering that, you can begin writing more complex stories.

Trust me, your "Truly Great Story Idea" will thank you for being put on the backburner until you have the writing chops to tell that amazing tale.

And one last thing concerning Third Person and Multiple Focal/Character Narrators, and that the wonderful ability to…

KILL OFF CHARACTER NARRATORS

That's right, my friend. While it's nearly impossible to kill off a First Person Narrator, the act of murdering a Character Narrator in any of the three types of Third Person is surprisingly easy.

Now, I'm not saying it's easy to do without pissing off your readers—ask any fan of George R.R. Martin's *Game of Thrones* how they feel about the death of Ned Stark and you're bound to get an earful. (Oh, and *Spoiler!*)

Killing off a Character Narrator is something that must be handled with delicate care indeed. So much so, there's absolutely no way I can even begin to tell you how to do it within the confines of this book.

I can tell you that killing off a Character Narrator must be done for a very strong, story-motivated reason. A reason that's going to be unique to each writer and each story they write. I can't, however, give you any advice on how to do this without pissing off your readers. It's all going to depend on the story.

I've done it. And I'll continue to do it much to the torment of my readers. But you're on your own when trying to do this within your own stories.

My reason for bringing this up here is to simply state it *can* be done in Third Person because with Third Person there are other Narrators to finish the tale without the reader feeling as if they've been abandoned.

In Omniscient, there's a third-party Narrator telling the tale. So, killing off a Focal Character means nothing to this Narrator. They're not in the story, so after the Focal Character's death they simply keep on telling the tale.

In Free Indirect Discourse, there's both a third-party Narrator and one or more Character Narrators. So, again, killing off a Character Narrator does not mean the story is prevented from being told. The reader simply loses the perspective of that dead Character Narrator.

Both of these are the absolute easiest when dealing with Focal/Character Narrator's deaths, however.

Third Person Limited is a bit more tricky. At least, for me it is.

And the reason for this is that I won't have Character Narrator without their own personal Plot Arc. And I've already told you, if one of my Plot Arcs fail, that causes any Plot Arcs above them (Story and Saga Plot Arcs) to fail as well.

So, while yes, I will kill off a Character Narrator. In doing so I must then *organically* force one of the other Character Narrator's to take up that dead Character's Plot Arc, or in some other organic way figure out how to overcome that dead Character's Plot Arc.

Much easier said than done.

Time. Effort.

But for me, and my fan base, all that Time and Effort pays off for the story.

Enough of that. For our final stop on the advantages Third Person Limited has that First Person doesn't, I want to talk about at...

SUBPLOTS, PARALLEL PLOTS, AND FORESHADOWING

With First Person, you're very limited in how you can move through a story. For the story to work well in First Person, you should stick to one Character Narrator, start at the beginning, work your way through the story linearly toward a defined Conflict, and then reach a climax where you Overcome that Conflict. Talking the norm here. Rules can be broken.

All Third Person Narratives allow us to break from that simplistic story structure, having Multiple Focal or Character Narrators, moving back and forth through time, tell stories that happen simultaneously but in different locations, etc. In other words, Third Person allows a writer to create more complex stories.

But let's talk specifically about Third Person Limited here, though everything I'm about to say applies to Free Indirect Discourse as well.

One of the huge advantages having Multiple Character Narrators gives a story is the ability to give one Character Narrator information that a second Character Narrator doesn't get. This is awesome, because technically, you have a third party in this equation who is invisible—your reader. (Hint, this is why so many people use a Secondary Character as a Character Narrator for a scene or two. They give the reader information without giving that information to the Character Narrator.)

Let me explain.

Let's say you're writing a story with two Character Narrators. For this example, let's call them Drake and Sally.

In the first chapter, Drake is our Character Narrator. So, during this chapter, everything is told from his perspective. We keep everything personal to him, using all the tricks we've learned so far to make the story amazing. During this chapter we meet his girlfriend, Titania. She's smart, funny, attractive, and genuinely loves Drake. During Drake's chapter, the reader gets to experience all this wonderfulness with Drake, and hopefully the reader falls in love with Titania as well.

In the second chapter, Sally is our Character Narrator. So, same thing with the writing here—it's all personal to Sally. During this chapter Sally discovers that Titania is not what she appears. In reality, she's a disgusting Wood Fairy who has transformed herself to look like a tall, beautiful human woman. Unfortunately, before Sally can return with this news, she falls through a magic mirror and gets trapped in a very bad place.

Let's also imagine that throughout both chapters of this story we've introduced Wood Fairies to our readers, letting them know that these little creatures are very bad indeed. The readers learn that Wood Fairies survive by burrowing into the heads of humans and eating their brains! ZOMBIE WOOD FAIRIES!

What this gives our story is Tension. Drake is in danger, but doesn't know it. Sally knows Drake is in danger, but can't tell him. Drake also doesn't know that Sally, herself, is in danger. But the reader gets to know all these facts.

Meaning, the reader gets to feel the tension that Sally feels, unable to let Drake know he's in danger. PLUS, they get to feel the tension of Sally's own danger. PLUS, they also get to live with Drake, and be forced to deal with his ignorance. This means, if we want them to, we can make the reader begin to see double meanings with everything that sweet little Titania says. In other words, we can drive the reader to feel things we want them to feel, even though Drake is ignorant to these things.

Why is this cool?

Well, let's say we have Titania do things that make the reader totally buy into what Sally fears—that Titania is there for nefarious reasons and plans on eating Drake's brain. How cool will it be for the reader when they discover Titania is actually good, and fighting her people, attempting to save humanity?

Flip it. Perhaps we play Titania in such a way that the reader buys into the fact that she is good, and is honest about fighting her people and changing the relationship her kind has with humans. And then, in the end, she tries to eat Drake's brain.

This is just one basic example of how you can use Multiple Character Narrators to Foreshadow things within your story. Sometimes, you can use this to give the reader information that's wrong, and sometimes you can use this to give the reader a heads up on things that are true. Again, this falls under the umbrella of talent. I can't teach you how to use it, I can only show you the tool.

In much the same way, having Multiple Character Narrators also allows you to have Subplots and Parallel Plots. Again, I can only show you the tool here, but here's basically what I mean.

A lot of times, you'll use Subplots just as the Foreshadowing I showed with my last example. You can have things happen to one Character Narrator that another Character Narrator never finds out about, but ties into the overall Story Plot Arc. This means the reader knows things that one of your Character Narrators doesn't, allowing you to play with that to enhance your story.

For Parallel Plots, you can have a Character Narrator whose story either never touches the other Character Narrator's story, or doesn't touch until the very end. One reason for doing this might be to show how one Character Narrator's actions affect the others, even though neither may realize the connection.

Case in Point: Brandon Sanderson does a wonderful job of using the Subplot tool in his novel, *Way of Kings*. In this story, we meet a slave named Kaladin. He's purchased by an army at war, and he and his fellow slaves are used as cannon fodder. Now, in the beginning, the reader doesn't understand why all these slaves were purchased just to be killed. It not only seems like a cruel thing to do, but a huge waste of money. However, the reader is also following another Character Narrator named Dalinar. Dalinar is one of the people in charge of this army. Now, Dalinar is royalty, and Kaladin is a slave. They don't exactly have mutual friends to introduce them. Still, while Kaladin struggles to figure out the reason why his group was purchased just to be slaughtered, the reader gains some understanding of the other side of this equation through Dalinar's Narrative. One builds the other, both building empathy between the reader, the Character Narrators, and with the Story as a whole.

In the same novel, Brandon also utilizes Parallel Plots to great effect. There are two other Character Narrators the reader follows: Shallan, a woman with her own quest that doesn't seem at first to have anything to do with either Kaladin nor Dalinar; and Szeth, and assassin who is wreaking havoc in a completely different part of the world. Through book one of this saga, the reader pretty quickly starts to sees how the Shallan story arc will intersect with the other two. However, it's not until book two of this saga that the actions of Szeth are felt by the rest of the Narrating Cast. Meaning, through book one, his story seems completely unattached. This leaves the reader in the wonderful position of continually contemplating how all these things will come together. Readers love trying to guess where a story is heading before it gets there!

Again, I really can't tell you how to use these tools because every story is unique. Just know that they're available to you in Third Person, and look for ways to utilize them in your own work.

And honestly, reading is the way you'll learn how to use all these tools. Read. Read. Read.

Okay, so I've given you tons of reasons why Third Person Limited is superior to First Person. However, I also told you that I'm not on the side of any Narrative. None are perfect for all stories. To that end, let's take a look at some of Third Person Limited's detriments, starting with…

IT'S A LIMITED NARRATIVE

Just like First Person, Third Person Limited is a Limited Narrative. Meaning, when your Character Narrator leaves the room your Imaginary Camera has left the room as well. Anything that happens in the room once your Character Narrator is gone is off limits to the story.

This can cause issues within some stories. Let's say we're telling a story where there is a terrible secondary character—let's call this character Dylan. Let's say Dylan has a piece of information that if the reader doesn't discover somehow, the reader will never be able to understand the story. However, Dylan would never give this information to Drake, our Character Narrator.

So, how do we give the reader this information without giving said information to any of our Character Narrators?

Well… in Third Person Limited (and First Person), you can't. Not easily, anyway.

The reader only gets to know what the Character Narrator(s) know. It's *LIMITED* to your Character Narrators!

The only way for the reader to discover this is to give it to a Character Narrator. This is normally when an aspiring writer will just write a chapter using some random slob as the Character Narrator. I've already said my peace about why I feel this is bad, but you do what you want.

For me, I work hard to come up with an organic way to get this information to one of my Character Narrators, and therefore give it to my reader. It's sometimes hard. It's work. But it's kinda a writer's job to figure out clever ways of doing things. If it were easy, everyone would be selling millions of copies, and not just a select few.

Still, it's also the reason most people write in Third Person Free Indirect Discourse, where you're not limited to simply your Character Narrator, but you have access to a third-party Narrator as well.

Another thing with this being a Limited Narrative is the fact that the world around the Character Narrator must be limited to that Character's Perceptions. Just like First Person, if the Character Narrator feels another character is an ass, you can't write that character as awesome.

Going back to my *Elantris* example from Brandon Sanderson, this was expertly done. One of the Character Narrators felt a certain way about a Secondary Character, so Brandon wrote that Secondary Character to fit the mold that was the perception of the Character Narrator. However, come to find out, that Secondary Character was not what either the reader, nor the Character Narrator expected. It was a wonderful reveal, that really enhances the enjoyment of that story.

It was totally unexpected by me, because I believed the Character Narrator.

Don't get me wrong, I'm not saying Brandon lied. The hints were there. They were simply clouded by the Character Narrator's personal perceptions, which helped Brandon hide this Secondary Character's true intent. Which made the reveal an unexpected and marvelous thing, indeed.

Another option, one that First Person does not have, is with the fact that you can have Multiple Character Narrators in Third Person Limited. And when it comes to Perceptions of the world around them, this is a cool and fun thing to play with.

In other words, you can have one Character Narrator feel Drake is a fool and a second Character Narrator see Drake as amazing. If done well, this dichotomy can create wonderfully interesting levels of tension for the reader as they try to figure out which Narrator is correct in their perceptions, and which is wrong. (Hint, my money's on Drake being an idiot.)

Still, while being Limited can be a huge disadvantage to some stories, the ability to play with different perceptions is *only* a wonderful thing if you implement it effectively. Time. Effort.

Another disadvantage Third Person Limited shares with First Person is the dreaded…

INFORMATION DUMP

However, unlike First Person, which is wonderful at helping to hide Information Dumps, Third Person Limited tends to make Information Dumps stand out like a festering blister, causing readers to be revolted by their mere presence.

It's true. When writing in any of the Third Persons, you must be ever-vigilant against Information Dumps. And that's easier said than done. Especially in Third Person Limited since it still falls into the family of Third Person, and it's easy to forget that it needs to be written exactly like First Person.

Meaning, once a writer begins describing things (Setting the Scene, as I call it), they forget to keep everything personal to the Character Narrator, and instead remember that they really, really, really, love the world they've created. They dump all that detail upon the reader, heaping description upon description until the reader is so bored they couldn't care less if the world was saved by the Protagonist, or if the ultimate Evil rose to power and subjugated the populace under its iron fist.

Yes, you must Set your Scene. Meaning, you must describe what things look like to enough degree that the reader will be able to "see" what you "see". However, you must also balance this so as not to overburden your story. Unfortunately, the writer is the worst person to judge if they've been successful or not. A writer is too close to their own work, and since they made it all up in the first place, will always feel whatever information they put into their story is perfect.

The smart writer, however, knows they must rely on readers. This is one of the reasons I'm such a huge supporter of Critiquing Writer's Groups. Attend these and you'll find a group of like-minded individuals willing to read your unpublished drivel. And when they do read it, make sure you ask them specific questions. Like, "Hey, guys. So, in this chapter you just read, I describe where Gorlabs come from, their history, and why they are the way they are. How did this section make you feel? Specifically, I want to know if you feel this section held too much information, the right amount, or should I have given you more?"

Don't tell them that you think you added the perfect amount of Gorlab awesomeness, and you think you're the clever egg for coming up with Gorlabs. If you do, they'll more likely than not just agree with you because it's easy on them. No. Ask them open-ended questions then sit back and listen. If more than half the people think you have too much information, as much as it hurts your artistic pride, you need to cut some of that information back.

Again, that's part of what being a writer means—the ability to endure the pain of cutting things from your story you love, but doesn't help the reader enjoy the story.

Another major disadvantage I want to talk about within Third Person Limited that will ruin your story on the quick is…

AUTHOR INTRUSION

While Author Intrusion can technically haunt any Narrative type, it's especially bad with the Limited ones. This means First Person, Third Person Limited, and Third Person Free Indirect Discourse, though the latter is more resistant to it over the first two.

Spotting Author Intrusion is a pretty simple thing. There are a few types of Author Intrusions, like when a character says something out of character, but in line with the Author's social views:

> Dylan was a great and mighty warrior, and one who had bedded many women. Yet he was moved by the fair maiden's frustrations. "Dylan agree with pretty girl. Women should be allowed to vote."

But the most common is with Limited Narrations. Since these Narrative types should remain Limited to the Narrator telling the story, any time you give the reader information the Narrator wouldn't or couldn't know, you, the Author, have *Intruded* upon the story.

> Drake smiled. *Today was going great*, he thought. He had nailed his interview and been offered his dream job as a Dogfood Taste Tester. He was on his way home to his loving wife. Little did he know that she was having an affair with the door-to-door spatula salesman who had been stalking his neighborhood for the past month.

Yeah, I've already used this as an example once. Sue me. (Ha! It's funny because I'm a starving writer, and have no money for you to sue me over… ahh… and it's sad for the same reason. ☹)

Anyhoo… If my intent was to write the above in Third Person Limited, everything should be Limited to only what Drake knows. He doesn't know his wife is having an affair, nor does he know how long the door-to-door spatula salesman has been stalking his neighborhood. Stating any of this destroys the "limited" perspective of the Narrative, and throws the reader out of the story.

This is true for First Person, as well. Though the reason I didn't discuss it with First Person is it's much more obvious there, and so most aspiring writers don't do this as often.

> I smiled. Today was going great. I had nailed my interview and been offered my dream job as a Dogfood Taste Tester. I was on my way home to my loving wife. Little did I know that she was having an affair with the door-to-door spatula salesman who had been stalking my neighborhood for the past month.

It's very easy to spot the Author Intrusion in the above First Person example, so you rarely see anyone actually do something like this. Now, the above would not be Author Intrusion if this was a First Person piece being told by an Omniscient Narrator. Then he would know the future, so stating this would not be bad.

However, since Third Person Limited is still being written in the Third Person, and since most people write Third Person Limited incorrectly by thinking there's a third-party Narrator, Author Intrusion can creep in.

Avoiding this is simple. All you have to do is keep in mind what we've already talked about. In Third Person Limited, there is no third-party Narrator. Just the Character Narrator. Exactly like First Person. So, provided you write your Third Person Limited with all the Narration coming out of your Character Narrator, you'll avoid Author Intrusion.

And this brings us to Third Person's worst atrocity. Just like First Person, Third Person is ruined by...

FILTERING IN THIRD PERSON

I went into great detail of what Filtering is during my discussion of First Person. However, this is such a terrible thing to do to a story, one I find rotting out every level of publication from Self to Traditional, I want to go over it again here, but from a Third Person slant.

Filtering is bad.

As within First Person, every sentence you write in Third Person focuses the reader's attention on *something*. As the writer, you're in full control of that *something*, depending on how you craft the sentence. You must make sure that you craft your sentences so that the *something* your reader focuses on is the *something* you *want* them focusing on.

Remember my ghost floating down the hall?

The ghost floated down the hall.

Since "the ghost" is the Subject of this sentence, it means the reader will focus on the ghost. Exactly what I want them focusing on.

However, for some unknown reason, many, many writers would rather their readers focus on their Character Narrator. They'll inevitably do something like:

> **Drake stared as the ghost floated down the hall.**
> **Drake saw the ghost floating down the hall.**
> **Drake looked as the ghost floated down the hall.**
> **Drake peeked at the ghost floating down the hall.**
> **Drake gawked at the ghost floating down the hall.**
> **Drake listened as the ghost floated down the hall.**

Whatever. It's terrible. Just terrible. No one wants to look at Drake while he looks at *something*. Trust me, enough women have confirmed this to me over the years.

Now, a lot of folks feel they must do this to "stay in their Point of View". But you don't. The reader wants to look at the *something* that's cool! They want to look at the ghost. And provided you've done your job throughout, writing a line like, "The ghost floated down the hall." is well within the "Point of View" of your Character Narrator. They can see it, so they can describe it.

Avoiding Filtering comes down to understanding that you need to structure your sentences so that the Subject of those sentences is the *something* you want the reader looking at.

Not:

> Drake could feel the demon's hot breath upon his neck.

But:

> The demon's hot breath licked the back of Drake's neck.

Here's the example I wrote in the First Person section, but instead I've turned into Third Person Limited. (Bonus, yet one more piece I can use to show you that writing Third Person Limited is almost identical to writing First Person.)

This is the terrible way, where I'm going to Filter the story through the Character Narrator which will in turn make this a very Telly piece, indeed.

> Drake stared at the monster in disbelief. He had no idea something this terrifying even existed. He'd always assumed monsters were make-believe. Stories his parents told him to keep him in line.
> *I was obviously wrong.*
> Drake flinched when the thing let out a vicious snarl and stepped closer. He spun, running as fast as his legs would carry him. He could hear the beast's sharp claws scrapping on the concrete of the sidewalk as it chased after him. He knew his only escape was the cliff, and the river below.
> Drake poured all his remaining strength into the last twenty yards of ground separating him from the safety of the Mississippi. He was terrified he wouldn't make it. He could barely hear the creature inches behind him over the pounding of his racing heart. He could feel its hot breath upon his neck.
> Drake felt a slicing pain rip across his back

as the creature lashed out, ripping through his T-Shirt. He launched himself into the air out of sheer desperation and plummeted off the cliff. He freefell some thirty feet before he slammed into the cold embrace of the waters below.

Drake heard the monster above him and knew he was safe.

I think I'm gonna be sick.... Not only is this Filtering Hell, it's all one big ole crappy Tell! But, seriously, so many things I read are written this exact same way. For some reason, writers just don't see how this ruins a story. Even now, you may have read the above and said to yourself, "It's not *that* bad."

I assure you, my friend. It's *revolting*!

Thank heavens I already rewrote this in First Person to remove all those horrendous Filters and replace all that Tell with some yummy Show! Let's see if I can now take that same rewritten First Person piece and turn it into Third Person Limited by just changing Nouns and Pronouns.

The monster crept from the shadows, cutting off Drake's only exit. His eyes bulged and his mouth worked without sound. How could something so terrifying even exist? Yes, his parents had tortured him with scary tales of the Swamp Demon that supposedly hunted these lands, but surely they'd only told him those tales to frighten him into being a good little boy.

Fairytale or no, the beast before him was very real indeed.

Complete with saliva-drenched fangs and glowing red eyes.

A vicious snarl ripped from the creature and Drake flinched. It snapped him from the catatonic state he'd been frozen in. As the beast stepped toward him, he spun and ran.

The beast's sharp claws clicked on the concrete sidewalk as it gave chase. Closer. Closer. Drake begged his legs to move faster. But to where? He was trapped between a nightmare and a thirty-foot drop to the chilly waters of the Mississippi. Since one was certain death, he headed for the cliff.

He poured all his remaining strength into the last twenty yards of ground separating him from the relative safety of the river. His heart thumped so loud in his chest, it nearly drowned out the snarls of the creature just inches behind.

The Demon's hot breath licked his neck. Something snagged the back of his T-Shirt. Hot agony sliced through his side.

It has me!

Panic overrode primal instincts and Drake screamed as he launched himself off the edge of the cliff. The air whistled in his ears as he freefell into darkness. The ice-cold water slapped him hard before sucking him into its depths. Lungs burning, Drake fought against the strong current. Bursting through the surface, the sweetest breath of air he'd ever tasted filled his lungs.

Howls and hisses from the cliff above were all that pursued him as the current swept Drake downriver.

Which would you rather read? You know what? Don't answer that. It's subjective and your attitude has been a bit testy lately. Yeah, talking about that rude comment you made concerning my artistic abilities. And since I'm the one writing this book, I'll let you know how *I* feel. I'd rather read the second version. To me, it's immersive, showy, exciting, gripping. All the things I look for in a good book.

Once again, don't get me wrong here. Filtering, in itself, isn't bad. Again, it comes down to the writer controlling the *something* the reader will focus on. Sometimes, depending on the situation, you may *want* the reader to focus on the Narrator.

> Drake stared in disbelief as Dylan walked away.
> His heart broke with the realization that he would
> never again feel Dylan's lips pressed against his.

Still not my best example, but hopefully you get my point. I have a thing for Dylan. ☺

I mean... in the above example, I *want* the reader to focus on the Drake Narrator, and the disbelief he's feeling. Sure, that disbelief is coming from the fact that Dylan's walking away. But to get the most impact from the sentence, I don't need the reader to focus on Dylan, nor the fact that he's walking away. I want them to focus on Drake's disbelief and pain.

As with First Person, focusing on the Character Narrator should happen rarely within your story. Also, just like First Person, I try and limit myself to only using the Character Narrator's Noun and Pronouns when describing what that Character is *physically* doing.

In other words, lines like the following are okay:

> Drake's eyes bulged...
> He begged his legs...
> Drake poured all his remaining strength into...
> His heart thumped...

These are all things the Drake Narrator is doing physically. These are things where the *something* the reader needs to look at is the Character Narrator, because the Character Narrator is the one doing the *something*.

I avoid things that describe the Character Narrator paying attention to anything else that's going on. Remember, the Character Narrator is the Narrator, so *EVERYTHING* seen or heard is seen and heard by them. There's no reason to keep telling the reader the Narrator is seeing everything!!! Writing "Drake watched", "Drake saw", "Drake heard", etc., does nothing except hurt the immersion of your story.

It's hard, but you should go through everything you write and look for all your Filtering. If it's not specifically a sentence where you want the reader focusing on the Character Narrator, you should rework it to cut out the Filtering. In other words, every single time you start a sentence with any of the following, it should be a red flag for you. With each of these, you should scrutinize the sentence to see if your reader is focusing on the correct *something*.

> Drake could see/hear/etc.
> He decided
> Sally experienced
> She felt
> Dylan heard
> He looked
> Jill noticed
> She noted
> Herman realized
> He saw
> Mary seemed
> She sounded like
> Bob thought
> He touched
> Jane wondered
> She was able to
> Barry watched

Yes, same list, and still not complete.

In conclusion, Filtering, in all Narratives, will be your worst nemesis. One that'll take you years to not only notice, but carve from your writing. I promise you, it'll be one of the biggest things you can do to make your writing more interesting.

Alright. So that's a lot for you to digest. Let's wrap up Third Person Limited by looking at…

WHAT DOES THIS DO FOR YOU?

Obviously, Third Person Limited is the Narrative I love to write in most. But please understand, I don't traditionally write in this Narrative because of any personal feelings I happen to have for it.

The story I'm writing always chooses the Narrative I'll write in. So why so much Third Person Limited for me?

Since I write a lot of action stories, with plenty of fighting, chases, and heart-pounding escapes, having the Free-Floating Imaginary Camera of a Third Person Narrative is awesome. It allows me to spin that Camera around my Character Narrator as needed to keep my action as nail-biting as possible.

I also tend to write stories with Multiple Character Narrators. The Third Person family of Narratives is the only Narratives that can handle this seamlessly.

My stories tend to be complex, with multiple Subplots, Parallel Plots, time shifts, set in multiple locations simultaneously, etc. Because of this complexity, Third Person is where I need to hang my hat.

However, all the above could be written extremely effectively in Third Person Free Indirect Discourse. So why do I hold my writing to the strict rules that is Third Person Limited?

Immersion.

It really is that simple. Sure, there are advantages in having access to an Imaginary Camera that can be all encompassing. One that could give grand sweeping wide shots of my scenes before it zooms down into my Protagonist. And some stories need that advantage, which is why I have stories written in Third Person Free Indirect Discourse. This gives me the bonus of using that Narrative's ability to Shift between a third-party Narrator and a Character Narrator to help tell those stories. But for most of my dark, epic, tragic fantasy tales, I want my reader to become encased in the events of the story. To become my Protagonists. To be my Character Narrators. Feeling every painful and joyful moment of their lives. And nothing does that like Third Person Limited.

Is it a lot of work? That's the understatement of the year!

While this Narrative does an amazing job of staying inside your Character Narrator's head, conveying that Character's feelings, emotions, and perceptions to the reader, building that amazingly important visceral bond between Narrator and reader, it's a constant struggle to always remember the Narrative must be filtered through the Character Narrator's perception. It's the Character Narrator, not the writer, who is telling the tale. Setting that Character's Author Voice, Tone, and Style is crucial.

Worse, when you have Multiple Character Narrators, it means you must develop Multiple Character Author Voices, Tones, and Styles. Each of these needs to follow their own structure, creating a unique experience for each Character Narrator you have.

Time. Effort.

I didn't mention it before, but I feel the above is one thing that First Person has the edge with. First Person is easier to write compared to Third Person Limited. In First Person, you only need to do all this crazy stuff once, for one Narrator. In the Multi-Character Narrator world that is Third Person Limited, you must do this for each Character Narrator you use. And you must stay consistent with each!

It ain't easy, my friend.

In addition to maintaining your unique Character Narrators, you must stay ever vigilant against Info Dumps, Author Intrusion, Head Hopping (POV Shifting), and the ever present, and ever crappy Filtering monster.

Earlier I talked about why I chose to write one of my new novel series, the one where the girl enters Café Jax in the excerpt, in First Person. I gave you some valid story-related reasons, but the truth is, the honest-to-god truth is, I needed a F'in' break! Third Person Limited is heavy as hell! Creating complex stories takes life-consuming effort. Since that series is simple, from a story complexity standpoint, I welcome the relief of writing it in First Person. It's like a vacation!

And a writer needs to consider this as well. Your sanity and motivation are both affected by your workload.

So, again, Time, Effort. Think about your story, what you want to accomplish through the telling of it. Think about how you want the reader to interact with the story. Only then can you decide what Narrative would be best.

Third Person Limited may be my favorite to both read and write, but it might just ruin the story you're telling.

And that, my friend, brings Third Person Limited to a close. Let's now bring this Narrative discussion to its finality by talking about…

THIRD PERSON FREE INDIRECT DISCOURSE

This section is going to be shorter than the rest. Not because I'm going to skimp on any details, you should know me better than that by now, but because I've been threading information about Third Person Free Indirect Discourse throughout the other topics we've been discussing.

Hopefully you've been gleaning details of what Third Person Free Indirect Discourse in the previous pages, but let's put it all in one place and make it official.

Third Person Free Indirect Discourse is by far the most traditional way Speculative Fiction is written today. It's a hybrid, one that attempts to take advantages from the other Narrative types, while at the same time mitigating many of their disadvantages.

It's one-part Third Person Omniscient, and one-part Third Person Limited.

This means you have two Narrators. A disembodied third-party Omniscient Narrator, and at least one Focal Character who you can slip into as deeply as you wish, all the way down to treating them exactly as you would a Character Narrator inside a Third Person Limited story.

This Shifting ability is not defined. It's a sliding scale more than anything else. In other words, in some stories you'll find the writer uses the third-party Omniscient Narrator for the vast majority of their book, and the Character Narrator is only dipped into occasionally. In other books, you'll notice that the writer uses the third-party Omniscient Narrator very rarely, and the vast majority of the book stays within the confines of the Limited Character Narrator.

I can't give you any advice here as to which way works better. It's specific to the author and the story they're telling. This is part of what people refer to as the Author's Voice, or their Writing Style. This is something you're gonna have to figure out on your own. Like how sometimes I write "going to" and other times I use "gonna". That's my decision, not yours. My voice. You're either gonna appreciate it, or you're not going to.

And therein lies the rub.

Let me take a side trip here for a second. There's one thing all writers struggle with regardless of which Narrative they write in—one that you need to get over or this industry will grind you up and spit you out, a broken husk of a person. This is a truth that's ever-present to all writers in all genres.

Reading is subjective.

Because of this, nothing you write will please everyone.

I've been blessed in my career in the fact that my fans really like how I write. The first works I published came out of the gate averaging a 4 out of 5-star rating. What I write today tends to stay in the 4.5 to 4.9 out of 5-star range.

However, understand what that means.

It means that when 50 people read something I've written, 45 people feel it was worth their time reading it. But five... five felt it was a big ole steaming pile of meh.

It's the same story for all 50 people. So why didn't it resonate with the five?

Because it's subjective.

The problem is, all writers want 100% of the people who read their work to love it. But that'll never, ever, ever, ever, *ever* happen. There will always be people out there who don't appreciate what you do.

Worse, there's not a damn thing you can do about it.

Well, that's a lie. There's one. You can get over it.

And each of us must get over it in our own way. For me, here's the trick I use. When I get a bad review, it breaks my heart. It crushes my soul. It hurts like hell. It convinces me that I'm a worthless piece of crap who is just a poser, and not a real writer at all.

However, to bring things into perspective, and crawl out of the pit of despair the bad review has dropped me into, I hit Amazon. I've already stated my favorite author today is Brandon Sanderson.

Specifically, my favorite book of all time is *Mystborn*. That book resonated with me on all levels. The writing. The characters. The plot. The world. It was the first book of Brandon's I read, and it had a huge impact on me as a reader.

That being said, *Mystborn* has some scathing 1-star reviews. Like, horrifying vicious. Now, overall (as of the writing of this) it's running a 4.6 out of 5 stars with 1,503 reviews on the version I looked up just now. By far more people agree with me about this books merits. Still, others don't.

And it's those 1-star reviews I read.

I read all of Brandon's 1-star reviews because it reminds me that reading is subjective. I mean, as far as I'm concerned, all the people who give *Mystborn* a 1-star review are morons. That book's awesome. But it's awesome to *me*. I force myself to realize that as far as those 1-star reviewers are concerned, I'm the moron here. Shocking, I know. But to *them*, *Mystborn* sucked. The rub is, both of us are correct.

It's like Schrödinger's cat. *Mystborn* it both an amazing book, and a terrible one. It all comes down to perspective. The reader's perspective.

Worse for me, since out of all writers today, more reviewers compare me to how Brandon writes than any other, it means the people who hate his work are bound to hate mine as well.

C'est la vie.

So why did I go down this path? To drive home that since there aren't any hard-and-fast rules for writing Third Person Free Indirect Discourse, you're on your own. Where you fall on the sliding scale between your third-party Narrator and your Character Narrators will be your decision, and your decision alone.

This is the reason I began this book with my rant about it taking one-million words of writing before you'll become proficient enough at this craft to write anything worth selling.

Part of that time will be spent in figuring out which Narrative works for the types of stories you tell, and then practicing how to utilize that Narrative to tell those stories effectively.

Time. Effort.

To me, that's the hardest thing about Third Person Free Indirect Discourse. This Narrative is totally reliant on the writer's ability, the writer's talent, to use it effectively to tell stories.

For you to gain the skills you need, it's going to take you time and effort. Along the way, some people are going to enjoy what you're doing, others will not. What you can't afford to do is let criticism get to you.

As I always say, 100% of all writers who quit writing never become New York Times Bestselling Authors. It's the only statistic in this industry that's guaranteed.

So, while I can't help you decide how Omniscient or Limited you should be when writing in Third Person Free Indirect Discourse, I can tell you that you must never lose faith in yourself as you attempt to figure this out.

Ugg… did I really just write something in a positive way? Sorry. Not sure where all that touchy-feely crap came from. I'll try to not let it happen again.

But seriously, you're on your own.

Still, as with the rest of these topics, I can give you some guidance.

First, understanding this is the only Narrative type that has two different types of Narrators is a very important step. The ability to be Omniscient when the story needs it, and when to be Limited is amazing. It gives you tons of flexibility and control over your story.

As I've already said, however, I find that having an Observer Narrator for your third-party Narrator tends to work best. Making your third-party Narrator invisible means the reader can focus more on your Character Narrators.

Second, if you are going to write in Third Person Free Indirect Discourse, reread this book, and think about what I say for all the other Narratives—First Person, Third Person Omniscient, and Third Person Limited. But reread it while you look for things you want to steal, because that's what this Narrative does. Steals the best of what those other Narratives have to offer.

I've also discussed how you want to stick to just one Character Narrator per chapter/scene. No Head Hopping!!!

As with all Third Person Narratives, Information Dumps can become an issue quickly. Stay ever-vigilant against them, writing tightly by including only the details you feel are needed to ensure the reader can "see" what you want them to "see".

Be wary of Author Intrusion, it's still a huge problem within Third Person Free Indirect Discourse.

As with all Narrative, Filtering is still *public enemy number one.*

Basically, remember that everything I've written in this book from page one can and does apply to Third Person Free Indirect Discourse because Third Person Free Indirect Discourse can pull from all of it.

It's simply up to you to figure out how to meld it all together to create your Author Voice.

One final topic before we sail into the boring waters of grammar. I want to talk about…

Breaking the Rules

I decided to write this book using finite terms like, "you must", or "you can only", etc. I didn't want to be wishy-washy during my instructions.

Now, however, I want to go back over all that we've discussed with a blanket statement.

Creative Fiction is about breaking rules.

Breaking rules is how the masters became the masters. They pushed the boundaries and took chances.

The fact is though, you can't break a rule you don't fully understand. (Well, you can, but if you don't understand the rule to start with then there's no way you will break them without pissing off your readers.) So, yes, I talked about all these topics with the slant of, "do it my way or you suck". But trust me, everything I said was bull crap. (Ha! Bet you wished you'd known that before you read the entire book, huh?) ☺

No. I kid. All the information in this book is important. But none of it is rigid. Breaking rules is difficult. However, it can be done, and done effectively, but only with Time and Effort.

With enough Time and Effort, you can break every rule I stated here and create some pretty amazing tales.

Patrick Rothfuss' *The Name of the Wind* is a wonderful example of breaking the rules successfully. In this book, he uses both Third Person *AND* First Person Narratives. Something the *rules* state you can't do. And yet he did it. And his book is awesome.

Not that this is easy. It's definitely not something just anyone can pull off. *cough* Abraham Lincoln Vampire Hunger *cough*

Damn! I have no idea why that keeps happening. Perhaps I should see a doctor once we finish this discussion.

Anyway… as I was saying, breaking rules is difficult. But break them you must! Um? Perhaps I shouldn't use the word *must* in a chapter where I'm telling you that nothing is a must. Break them you *might*? No, that's not appropriate for this either. Break them if you want, I don't give a crap. Nailed it!

Seriously. It's called *Creative* writing. Sure, you need to learn the rules, understanding them at a very deep level. But that's only so that, at the end of the day, you can break those rules and not piss off your readers. Be careful, but be creative.

And that, my fine feathered friend, brings us to the end of our little adventure. All that's left to do is…

Stick a Fork in It

I know, right? A lot to take in. Hopefully it wasn't too painful to get through.

Look. I know it was. This was a lot. More than should be in one book. In the end, all you need to keep in mind is: this is a journey. A long, never ending journey that's more of a life's quest than something that has a destination at its end.

If you're not in a writer's critique group, join one. You can't grow as a writer unless you are both being critiqued and critiquing others.

Write every week. I don't care what your quota goal is, so long as you have one. 500 words a week. 1,000. Whatever. But force yourself to write every week.

Remember, one-million words. Time. Effort. If you don't write every week, you'll never develop the skills you need to do this professionally. Or, forget doing this professionally. If you don't write every week you'll never develop the skills to create something anyone will want to read period.

And last, know that I'm here for you, waiting inside the pages of this book to lend you a helping hand. Put me on your shelf for a while and go write. Edit. Spend a month or more seeking out other ways to learn the craft of writing. When you're ready to dig back into all this craziness, come see me. I'll be here. I won't say anything new, I mean, come on, "I'm" words in a book not the real Drake! The real Drake has been retired fifteen years and living like a king in Patagonia.

But the reality is, if you've grown as a writer, you'll interpret the things I say in new and exciting ways. Things you missed through this read will pop for you, opening your eyes to new and exciting ways to write creatively. And that's a magic like no other.

And now...

It's Your Turn

This is not a feel-good ending where I say something pathetic like, "Well! Now you have all the information you need, so go out and be a New York Times Best Seller!"

You should know me better than that by now.

No, I mean the title of this section literally – It's your turn.

If you learned anything from this book, if any of the words of wisdom I've poured onto the pages of this tome, ideas generated from nearly thirty-years of studying the craft of writing, have helped you become a better writer, then I ask that you now do something for me.

First, go to Amazon.com and write a review for this book. You needn't have purchased this book from Amazon to write a review on it, all you need is an Amazon account, which I know you have. Log in, put this book title in the search bar, and write a review for me.

Don't assume your fellow readers will write me a review – they won't. I've sold thousands of my last creative writing book, and yet there are only 32 reviews as of this writing.

Don't assume I have enough reviews for this book – I don't. 32 reviews aren't enough.

Reviews are the way to help me continue doing what I do. If I helped you at all, please return the favor.

Second, please share this book on your social media. You are a writer (Why else would you have suffered through this book?), so I know you're on some type of Social Media platform – Facebook, Twitter, Instagram, whatever. I also know that some of your friends on Social Media are writers themselves. Don't you think this book would be helpful for them as well? Again, if I've helped you out, please take the five minutes to throw me a bone here.

In closing, I want you to know I've thoroughly enjoyed our time together through this adventure. Your occasional interruptions this time, while still annoying, were productive as well. Once again, all in all, you weren't a terrible companion. As a reader, I'll give you a better grade than I did last time, and say you earned a solid A.

Oh, and... The End

"For a writer, there's *literally* no better feeling in the world than writing those two final, magical words."

Maxwell Alexander Drake